classroom management

*To my beautiful and brilliant wife Susan and
our inspirational children William, Bridget, Nicholas,
Amelia and Charlie. They have been the best
teachers of love and forgiveness who continue to amaze me
with their resourcefulness and resilience.*

Tim McDonald
classroom management
engaging students in learning

OXFORD
UNIVERSITY PRESS
AUSTRALIA & NEW ZEALAND

OXFORD
UNIVERSITY PRESS
AUSTRALIA & NEW ZEALAND

253 Normanby Road, South Melbourne, Victoria 3205, Australia

Oxford University Press is a department of the University of Oxford.
It furthers the University's objective of excellence in research,
scholarship, and education by publishing worldwide in

Oxford New York

Auckland Cape Town Dar es Salaam Hong Kong Karachi
Kuala Lumpur Madrid Melbourne Mexico City Nairobi
New Delhi Shanghai Taipei Toronto

With offices in

Argentina Austria Brazil Chile Czech Republic France Greece
Guatemala Hungary Italy Japan Poland Portugal Singapore
South Korea Switzerland Thailand Turkey Ukraine Vietnam

OXFORD is a trademark of Oxford University Press
in the UK and in certain other countries

National Library of Australia Cataloguing-in-Publication data

McDonald, Tim.
Classroom management: engaging students in learning / Tim McDonald.

ISBN 9780195564648 (pbk)

Includes index.
Bibliography.

Classroom management.
Teaching.
Learning.

371.1024

Edited by Kate McGregor
Text design by Mason Design
Typeset by Mason Design
Proofread and indexed by Puddingburn Publishing Services
Printed in Hong Kong by Sheck Wah Tong Printing Press Ltd

Contents

List of Figures

List of Tables

Preface

Student misbehaviour becomes a problem when students fail to engage in the academic program, challenge the authority of teachers, disrupt the order of the school and threaten the well-being of other students. Student misbehaviour is a problem for in-service teachers and an issue for teacher educators who want to learn how best to prepare pre-service teachers for the complex demands of the classroom and school life. There is little argument that student behaviour is linked to success at school. Schools are under increasing pressure to lift standards or levels of achievement while, at the same time, principals are reporting growing numbers of students who are difficult to teach. The Positive Learning Framework described in this text addresses these issues of student behaviour and academic achievement in a model that promotes quality learning environments. The first phase of the Positive Learning Framework starts outside the classroom, looking at the level of teacher awareness and skills and strategies to prevent student indiscipline. The second phase identifies the centrality of instruction in classroom management and focuses on lesson design and instructional techniques. The third phase of the framework explores the skills used to re-engage students in learning following indiscipline and to strategies to use when de-escalating conflict or working with students who continually exhibit challenging behaviour. A strength of this model is the capacity to work with these high-end behaviours with a view to re-engaging students in meaningful learning.

This book offers in-service and pre-service teachers a practical framework for creating quality learning environments in which all children thrive. The Positive Learning Framework gives university educators of classroom management a model of delivery, supported by an instructor's manual with tutorials and lectures resources, to use with pre-service teachers in developing classroom management skills and strategies.

The Positive Learning Framework builds on the theoretical foundations of universal needs as described in the 'Circle of Courage' (developed by Larry Brendtro, Martin Brokenleg, and Steve Van Bockern 2002). The Circle of Courage identifies four universal growth needs: belonging, mastery, independence and generosity. The Circle of Courage identifies the vital signs for positive health and growth. The Positive Learning Framework developed in this text offers a new lens through which to view students, behaviour and instruction. The application of this model is unique and builds upon the emerging findings in resilience research, restorative practices and the science of positive youth development.

Effective classroom management is more than quick-fix strategies or a bag of tricks. It is a purposeful philosophical, ethical and theoretical code of conduct. This book encourages pre-service and in-service teachers to reflect on the assumptions they hold about students, the role of the teacher, the purpose of discipline, how children learn, and the level of control given to students. To assist you in this journey there are critical reflection activities in each chapter. These reflections are challenging and, at times, may make you feel uncomfortable. This feeling of not knowing the answer or not having the correct response while reading this book will be a much milder discomfort than when not knowing an answer while twenty-five sets of students' eyes watch you for a response. Prevention and preparation are always the preferred option.

Your personal plan of how you connect, instruct and work with young children and youth is crucial to effective teaching. Effective teachers are reflective and have a capacity to establish and maintain safe learning environments that enable students to flourish academically as well as socio-emotionally. Quality learning environments meet the needs of the students and value their contribution.

One of the most important aims in developing you as an effective classroom manager is to help you develop a range of skills, a language of discipline and confidence to deal with the typical behaviours that face practising teachers. This aim cannot be achieved by simply presenting a range of theoretical classroom management models, as this approach does not prepare in-service or future teachers for dealing with misbehaviour effectively. If all we have is theory, then we will find working with student indiscipline difficult as our foundation will be brittle. In-service and pre-service teachers need the opportunity to develop a range of practical management skills, a working language of discipline and a plan for effective teaching. This can be developed by practising handling misbehaviour and practising procedures that are a common part of classroom life, whether at university or within a professional-development setting. These skills are best acquired through active participation in typical classroom situations in a safe and structured context. In this text, there are practice activities along the way. These activities will assist you to develop the necessary skills to engage students in meaningful learning.

Youth with emotional and behavioural problems are often discarded by families, friends and educational systems. Educational systems struggle to deal with students who openly defy authority, display antisocial behaviour and for whom school is meaningless. Schools and society often pay lip service to the needs of young people. This text will examine the strengths troubled youth bring to the school system. We will use research-based strategies from resilience research, positive youth development and strength-based approaches to help troubled youth. This text will be interactive and involves activities for practising skills in working with all students including challenging children and youth.

Often, when classroom management is taught as part of pre-service education courses it is set within a theoretical framework of models and approaches (and often it is not taught explicitly for an extended amount of time but rather it is relegated to a few lectures or left to be embedded in content units). Students study a text that has a range of models and theories presented. Student presentations are done, as part of their assessment, on particular models in the text. This text will make use of the theoretical approaches in order to develop a range of practical skills to help in-service teachers and pre-service education students learn how to engage their future students in learning. The Positive Learning Framework will help pre-service and in-service teachers develop a language of discipline needed to deal with student misbehaviour effectively and provide practical skills to show how to integrate instruction and classroom management.

Engaging students in meaningful learning that is important is a key theme to this book. In engaging students in meaningful learning, we need to develop our abilities to respond to young people's growth needs, sometimes in situations we find uncomfortable, as well as encouraging young people to grow in their abilities to respond to life in a positive way. This capacity to work with children in a positive way takes time, knowledge, experience and reflection.

We have aimed this text at teachers (pre-service and in-service) and teacher assistants, all of whom are working in a school setting. Some of the content and resources drawn upon in developing the Positive Learning Framework apply to people working with children, young people or youth outside of a school setting. This is evident in phase 1 of the framework in self-preparedness to work with youth as well as phase three in de-escalating conflict. Phase two involving instruction is less relevant outside the classroom, although successful youth programs need a high degree of organisation and planning. At times we will refer to children, young people or youth; however, these references can be read as applying to all students. This text is built upon the wisdom and experiences gained from working with many students and teachers. Throughout the text I refer to 'we' when discussing conclusions gained from this collaboration.

Acknowledgments

I would like to acknowledge the many students and teachers who have enriched my understanding of effective teaching and the power of positive relationships as a teacher. I have been privileged to have worked with some extremely talented teachers and had the opportunity to learn from many students, especially those who challenged my authority and role as a teacher.

This text is a reflection of the many discussions with teachers, university colleagues and university students on how to best educate pre-service teachers in classroom management. We haven't got it right but we are still talking, reflecting and challenging each other on possible ways forward. I would especially like to thank Jane Hawdon, Sheona Motroni, Melissa Shepherd, Rebecca Walker, Paul Fitzpatrick, Helen Egeberg and Christina Gray, who have significantly contributed to this text through our work with pre-service teachers.

Working with teachers in schools as part of professional learning programs I have delivered has been a source of inspiration as well as a reality check of the robust nature of my material. Your feedback has been invaluable.

I have found the work and person of Dr Larry Brendtro inspiring. This text is a result of his positive view of youth and belief that there can be no disposable children in our society. His positive view of challenging youth is amazing, as are his presentations and training. Larry provides a model to aspire to in delivering a genuine message of hope for all vulnerable youth. I have appreciated Larry's support, mentoring and friendship—thank you, Larry—and just as important is Larry's wife, Janna Brendtro.

Finally I would like to thank the many pre-service teachers who have engaged in a learning journey in classroom management and instruction that I have been a part of. Thank you for your honesty, vulnerability, talents and resilience in developing skills and a language of discipline in the endeavour of engaging students in meaningful learning.

I hope that future and current teachers benefit from this text.

The author and the publisher wish to thank the following copyright holders for reproduction of their material: Allen & Unwin, for the figure on p. 93, taken from L. Porter, *Student Behaviour*, Allen & Unwin, Sydney, 2000, www.allenandunwin.com; Circle of Courage, for the table on p. 8, adapted from Bredtro & du Toit, *Response Ability Pathways Training Manual*, 2005, and for the trademark on p. 7, used with permission from Circle of Courage Inc, www.circleofcourageinstitute.org; Circle of Courage—Starr Commonwealth, for the figure on p. 64, taken from Brendtro, Mitchell & McCall, *Deep Braining Learning: Pathways to Potential with Challenging Youth*, 2009, used with permission from Circle of Courage—Starr Commonwealth Ltd, www.circleofcourageinstitute.org; Copyright Clearance Center and Oxford University Press Australia, for the figure on p. 69, taken from Bowes (ed.), *Children, Families and Communities* (3rd edn), Oxford University Press Australia, 2008, adapted from Santrock, Brown & Benchmark, *Adolescence*, Dubuque, IA, 1996; PBIS Center, for the figure on p. 198, reproduced by permission of the PBIS Center, www.pbis.org.

Every effort has been made to trace the original source of copyright material contained in this book. The publisher will be pleased to hear from copyright holders to rectify any errors or omissions.

A Positive Learning Framework for Classroom Management

Learner outcomes

After reading this chapter, you should be able to:

- understand the foundations of the Positive Learning Framework
- describe the need for a positive focus on student behaviour
- begin to explore a developmental or needs-based framework in working with students
- explain the need for beginning teachers to articulate assumptions and beliefs in teaching
- appreciate the role of environment in influencing behaviour and meeting individual needs
- briefly explain the key concepts and research underpinning a strength-based approach.

Key terms

Attachment

Autonomy

Classroom management

Competence

Psychological needs

Quality teaching

Resilience

Self-esteem

Socio-emotional development

Strength-based approach

Developing a Positive Learning Framework

In Australia, classroom management and student engagement are significant issues for teachers, school leaders, system administrators and the public. They heavily affect community perception, teacher efficacy and wellbeing, and the standards of achievement of students including misbehaving students. As a practising or beginning teacher, I am sure student behaviour is of prime concern for you and will continue to be as you progress through your teaching career. The outcome of working through this text is for you to develop an approach that will enable you to develop a working language of discipline and to respond to student behaviour in a positive and effective manner to preserve the dignity of the young person.

Students come to school with a great diversity of backgrounds, interests and capabilities. Meeting their needs and engaging them in meaningful learning requires care and skill. One of the first tasks of teaching is to develop an orderly learning environment so that students can engage in meaningful activities that support their learning. Teachers who are able to engage students in this learning are those who have a management plan that begins before the students arrive. An orderly learning environment exists because teachers have clear ideas of the type of classroom they want and acceptable student behaviours that assist learning. Once the class begins, effective teachers work very hard to create this quality learning environment. This book outlines a framework that includes skills and strategies to support you to create a quality learning environment.

This chapter introduces you to the Positive Learning Framework (PLF) for classroom management. We also introduce you to the key constructs that underpin this framework from a strength-based model of working with students in a school setting. The framework is based on current resilience, self-worth, neurological research and positive psychology, which highlight the strengths that students have and how, as educators, we can draw upon these strengths in assisting all children to grow.

The benefits of a strength-based model for education are that it builds upon the personal competencies associated with healthy development each individual has. A strength-based approach identifies the resourcefulness and resilience that exists in all students. In focussing on the positive this approach helps teachers reframe how they see students and to view behaviour from a different perspective as well as to recognise the incredible resilience of students, especially those facing immense challenges in their lives. Recent psychological research has focused on deficit, disorder and damage, and the study of what makes life worth living has receded into the background. Positive psychology (www.ppc.sas.upenn.edu.htm) offers a revival of early youth pioneers who saw the positive in all young people. Martin Seligman is a world leader in the 'positive psychology' movement and was the president of the American Psychological Association and a leader in optimism research. Positive psychology is the 'study of the conditions and processes that contribute to the flourishing or optimal functioning of people, groups and institutions' (Gable and Haidt, 2005). For educators this is a good place from which to view behaviour as it enables motivations and needs to be addressed, rather than focusing on a deficit mentality, which views the child or family as at fault and does not recognise the environment or processes of interaction between student and teacher.

The three phases of the Positive Learning Framework

The PLF offers a continuum of teacher behaviours from pre-class planning, to in-class teaching incorporating how to respond to student behaviour. Often teacher education courses focus on isolated approaches to curriculum, instruction or management. It is left up to the pre-service teacher to put this all together to form a whole package of 'teaching'. The very nature or structure of these courses assists in atomising teaching skills and concepts. In developing a personal approach to teaching, teaching students are required to integrate information from numerous sources, some of which may be at odds with each other and they all may claim to have the answer! The Positive Learning Framework, on page x, offers a thorough evidenced-based synthesis of current knowledge in effective classroom management and instruction. The three phases of the framework begin with preparing to teach, then move to actual classroom teaching and finally to correcting student discipline in order to encourage learning. Incorporated into the approach are the practical skills and strategies used by teachers to prevent and respond to student indiscipline. Applying the PLF across a school assists in developing consistent quality learning environments throughout the school. The three phases are outlined in brief below, and the rest of the text will explain each section in detail.

Effective teaching and prevention of student indiscipline are key ingredients to successful student engagement in learning. The first phase begins with preparation before the class begins. One crucial ingredient in this prevention and preparation phase is how we not only prepare the learning environment but how we as teachers prepare ourselves for the type of learning and classroom we are developing. How do I, as the teacher, prepare for the elements listed in this phase? I need to think about these elements before they happen! This is all before I start planning the lesson and how I will teach it.

Positive Learning Framework: three-phase model

Prevention: self awareness and management plan	Prevention: lesson design	Corrective actions
At the start of the year and before each class • self awareness • proactive thinking—indiscipline will happen at some stage • caring and welcoming classroom • classroom layout and resources • high and specific expectations • rules, routines and procedures	*Beginning* • whole-class attention (C2S) • clear outcomes conveyed to students • motivation 'hook for learning'—set induction • advanced organiser • recall prior learning • level of student engagement	*Low-level responses (minimal/no disruption to lesson flow)* • use of dignity (privacy/politeness/tone of voice) • minimal language (use succinct messages, an assertive tone with eye contact, avoid 'why' questions, redirect to lesson) • proximity • name and thanks • look/eye contact • non-verbal communication/gestures/signals • redirection • defer to private catch up later • clear desists • tactical ignoring
During lessons • connecting • C2S • managing student movement • 'with-it-ness'	*Middle* • teaching/learning strategy—active student involvement • collaborative learning strategies	*Moderate-level responses* • circle-time, conferencing • identifying motivation • identifying the 'game' • empathetic statements • offering escape routes

• acknowledgment of appropriate behaviour • opportunities for autonomy and responsibility	• group work • student movement for resources • questioning and responding to student answers • promoting student success	• offering choices giving student responsibility for actions
	Ending/closure • check for understanding against outcome • evaluation expectations • lesson summary • link learning to outside of classroom • next lesson—what we will be doing next lesson is …	*Escalating/crisis response* • awareness of escalation phase • de-escalation/defusing strategies • crisis-response strategies
		Restorative responses • skills for connecting, clarifying and restoring relationships

Alongside your personal and professional preparation before class, you need to plan how you will teach. The lesson design phase of this model is deliberately simple and distils the main elements of a lesson. In a lesson, you need to get the students settled, get their attention, identify the lesson outcome/objective, engage them in meaningful and important learning, identify what they have learnt and link to future learning.

The third phase of the Positive Learning Framework identifies the skills and strategies that teachers use to maintain students' attention in learning, as well as re-engaging those who have gone off-task. The majority of student indiscipline is low level (Scottish Executive, 2006), but some students will increase the intensity or frequency of their misbehaviour and need different levels of teacher intervention or correction to bring them back to learning. These moderate-level strategies are included here, as well as teacher skills and strategies for power struggles with students or for behaviour that is escalating to 'peak' or explosive levels.

The PLF offers a continuum of teacher behaviours from pre-class planning, to in-class teaching incorporating how to respond to student behaviour. The chapters that follow explore the various elements of the framework in more detail. Importantly, specific classroom management skills are identified in the 'practice activity' in each chapter. In this chapter, we have outlined the skill of Cue to Start (C2S), which is an alerting skill, helping you get student attention to start a lesson or for whole-class instruction. The practice activity identifies the step included in a C2S and sets out some low-level teacher responses to student indiscipline. For more complex skills, some later sections are dedicated to exploring how to de-escalate student conflict with the view that you will develop not only a language of discipline but skills and strategies that will engage motivated as well as reluctant learners in meaningful learning.

Critical reflection

My ideal classroom

Before we progress too far into the text, let us explore what you think is your ideal classroom. Your management plan developed throughout the text reflects the classroom you want to develop. Using a Y-chart write down what your ideal class would *look* like, *sound* like and *feel* like. If you are stuck, think of a class that you have experienced that has been creative and had engaging content and teaching that you loved being a part of.

Figure 1.1 A Y-chart

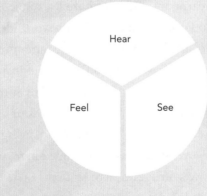

Meeting student needs

Underpinning the Positive Learning Framework is an attitude: 'How do I use these skills and strategies, which will enable me to develop environments where all students feel they **belong** and can trust others? Where they get tangible experience of **mastery** so they know they have talent? Where they have opportunities to be responsible and have power and **independence**? And where they feel worthwhile in their contributions and presence so that they see a purpose in showing **generosity**?' By learning to use our skills effectively, we will develop quality learning environments characterised by positive teacher–student relationships.

The PLF is built on the 'Circle of Courage'. The Circle of Courage model is grounded in positive psychology and has been developed by Larry Brendtro, Martin Brokenleg, and Steve Van Bockern (2002). The Circle of Courage identifies four universal growth needs. It identifies the 'vital signs' for positive health and growth. All children need opportunities to experience belonging, mastery, independence and generosity, as shown in Figure 1.2 below.

Figure 1.2 The Circle of Courage

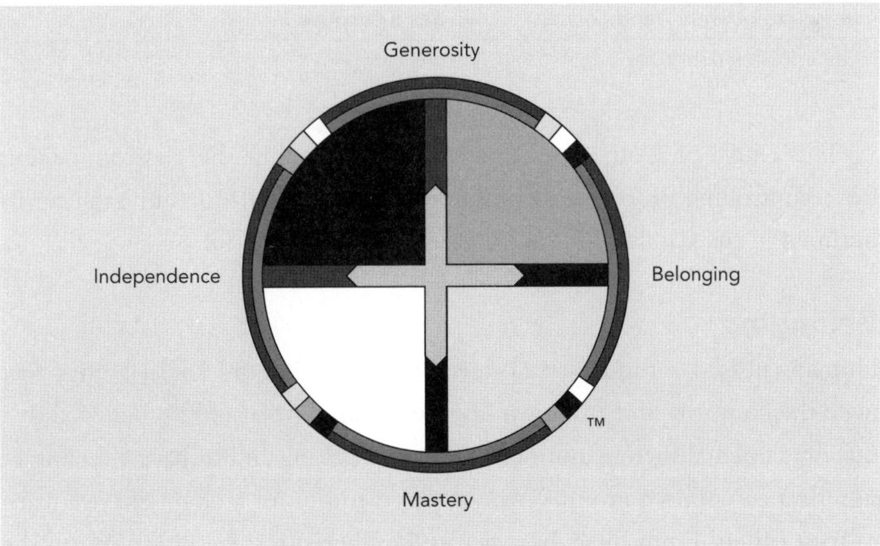

Source: Brendtro, Brokenleg & Van Bockern, 2002

This Positive Learning Framework is supported by research on resilience and self-worth and esteem by Stanley Coopersmith as well as epidemiological research conducted in Australia by Fiona Stanley, Sue Richardson and Margot Prior (2005).

Table 1.1 Universal needs

Resilience research	The Circle of Courage	Self-worth research	Stanley, Richardson and Prior (2005, p. 19)
Attachment Motivation to affiliate and form social bonds	*Belonging* Opportunity to establish trusting connections	*Significance* The individual believes, 'I am appreciated'.	*Belonging*
Achievement Motivation to work hard and attain excellence	*Mastery* Opportunity to solve problems and meet goals	*Competence* The individual believes, 'I can solve problems'.	*Competence*
Autonomy Motivation to manage self and exert influence	*Independence* Opportunity to build self control and responsibility	*Power* The individual believes, 'I set my life pathway'.	*Independence*
Altruism Motivation to help and be of service to others	*Generosity* Opportunity to show respect and concern	*Virtue* The individual believes, 'My life has a purpose'.	*Connectedness to the broader social environment*

Source: adapted from Brendtro & du Toit, 2005

The Circle of Courage enables educators to shift the classroom focus from controlling problems to building strengths. The four universal needs outlined in the Circle of Courage are simple yet powerful.

Belonging

Humans possess a fundamental need to belong. We are social beings that need the company and attention of others. Alfred Adler (1927) believed that our fundamental socio-emotional need is to belong and to have a feeling of significance within a group. With the opportunity for attachment, we learn to trust others. From birth, humans are hardwired to read emotions on the faces of others. In indigenous cultures, being treated as kin helps to develop powerful bonds that bring people into relationships of respect. Students want to belong in our classrooms. Students are looking for relationships in the classroom. Students want to trust their teacher. For educators, the task is to create an environment where all students feel they belong and are wanted and trusted in the learning environment.

Mastery

A big motivator in all humans is to feel they have achieved something and to be seen as competent. All of us want to be recognised as being good at something. Young learners can achieve a great deal of new knowledge, but their learning only becomes significant or crystallised with the support of adults or more skilful peers (Brendtro and du Toit, 2005). Given the opportunity to achieve, a student learns that they have talent. Mastery is more than mere intelligence as tested in standardised tests. Often the testing regime in a school only confirms to students how dumb they think they are. Instead, children need opportunities to develop problem-solving abilities and demonstrate their level of creativity and talent. As educators, we need to structure our learning environments so that all our students receive recognition, can develop competence and have the chance to realise that they have talent.

Independence

All young people want to control their lives and influence events in their world. Resilience research helps us to identify how resilient youth have the confidence to make life better even in adverse conditions. Even if life is difficult, these young people believe that they can make it better. With the opportunity for autonomy, the young person learns that they have power. Anyone who has worked with adolescents will attest to observing how the emerging adult exhibits a heightened desire for autonomy. Adolescents risk take and push the limits of adult control. It is as if rule breaking becomes a trial run at independence. Interestingly, youths seek autonomy while teachers and adults seek control. For some educators, it can be confronting to establish roles or positions of responsibility that assist the student in developing autonomy. In reality, as we will discuss later, it is relatively simple and, in practice, increases the power of the teacher with the students.

Generosity

When young people feel they belong to a community, they have the potential to be exposed to the feedback that they are valued and esteemed. In working with others, we are more likely to see that our life has a purpose or, at least, that some of our efforts are appreciated. In helping others, young people discover they have the power to influence their world in a positive way. With the opportunity to practise altruism, a young person learns, 'my life has purpose'. Schools have realised the power of working for others to improve moral development and to develop a sense of purpose through structured community service or service learning programs. In the classroom, cooperative learning opportunities also assist in providing opportunities to collaborate with other students, share opinions and attempt to see the world from other perspectives.

The Circle of Courage is rooted in universal human needs. Belonging, mastery, independence and generosity are vital elements of positive growth. A young person who grows up in a supportive environment will attach to positive and caring adults who support the child to achieve, gain independence and contribute to the community around them. For teachers, the Circle of Courage offers a foundation from which to view children and underpins a Positive Learning Framework that enables them to structure a safe and accountable learning environment.

Case study

Applying the universal needs

A number of writers have researched and identified the major needs that influence student behaviour. In this chapter, we have referred to the Circle of Courage's four universal needs as a basis for working with students. Other prominent theorists include Alfred Adler (1930), Rudolf Dreikurs (1957), William Glasser (1990), Stanley Coopersmith (1967), and Alfie Kohn (1993). (A description of the major theorists is provided in Table 7.1 on page 241.)

Read the following scenarios and identify the universal need that the student has to develop.

Scenario 1

Ahmed is in upper primary at the local school. He is a shy boy who craves friendship with peers. He is easily misled and would do almost anything to get other students to like him and involve him in their games. He has just been sent to the office for turning the tap on in the classroom that is used for Art and Science. The water has flowed over the sink and the floor is flooded. Ahmed did this because his friends told him to do it. Sitting in the office, he feels very guilty and not happy about himself because he doesn't have friends. He is the only one at the office as the others left just as the teacher arrived.

This student needs to develop _____

_____ .

(Hint: NOT belonging).

Scenario 2

Mikayla is a teenage bully. She intimidates students she perceives as weaker than her. Mikayla is in the Principal's office for hitting another student because she thought she heard him say something about her to another student. She doesn't recall what was said but it sounded as if he was saying something about her. Mikayla interprets the other student's behaviour as a lack of respect. Respect for Mikayla means power. She believes that no one messes with her, if they do she responds with aggression and no remorse. Mikayla usually gets what she wants when she wants it and is not afraid to step over others to get things. She is very self-centred, and does not feel guilty as she thinks the other student deserved it.

This student needs to develop _____

_____ .

Scenario 3

Chantelle is in primary school and has no friends and terrible self-esteem. Nobody wants to play with her or include her in any activities outside of class. Chantelle is lonely at school and does not know how to make friends. When teachers or other students show Chantelle some attention or kindness she believes they want to be her friend so she hugs them or clings to them around the school grounds. This puts students off and they pull away or say things to get her to leave them alone, which makes Chantelle cry.

This student needs to develop _____

_____ .

(Hint: yes, she needs to belong, but she will not belong until she works on another need first).

Scenario 4

Mark is an Indigenous student in a predominantly white school. He is extremely conscious of how people look at him and greet him. Mark has been watching which teachers smile and welcome him and he has only found two who do this all year. He conveys an image of toughness and is wary of adults. Mark's brother is in prison and people are scared of his family. He does not trust adults or other students for fear they will 'stab him in the back'.

This student needs to develop _____

_____ .

Adapted from the *Response Ability Pathways (RAP) Manual for Training 1.5*, Brendtro and du Toit (2005).

Critical reflection

Reflecting on my universal needs

Being an effective teacher means being a life-long learner. In working through this text, you will acquire skills and strategies to develop a quality learning environment. However, the 'glue' that will bind these individual skills together into a potent force is your capacity to understand your personal beliefs about teaching, student learning and discipline. Classroom management is more than the individual skills and strategies of 'getting kids to work and behave'. Developing this reflective capacity is another component in developing as an effective teacher.

Thinking back to your family or school days, who were the people that assisted you in developing as a valued individual? Can you identify examples when this happened and how you felt?

List some examples from your life where someone assisted you to have:

- belonging—you felt you counted, were valued and you could trust
- mastery—you believed you had talent
- independence—you believed you had power and responsibility
- generosity—your life had a purpose and direction.

Why use a Positive Learning Framework?

There are many models with which to approach student behaviour and learning. You only need to pick up a text on classroom management to see the plethora of theories available. The strength of the Positive Learning Framework, based on the Circle of Courage, is that it:

1 is simple to understand and implement
2 is focussed on prevention and instruction to develop quality learning environments
3 includes strategies for dealing with challenging behaviour and vulnerable students
4 can be applied to a whole-school setting.

The PLF encompasses the assumptions that underpin the majority of models of classroom management currently available. (Table 7.1 on page 241 outlines the major theorists and the assumptions that underpin their theories.) These sit under the banner of psycho-educational approaches and we will explore this theory base in Chapter 2. These models are based on Alfred Adler's work in Germany (1930s), before he moved to the USA. Psycho-educational theories are concerned with the private logic or beliefs that students have of themselves that will influence how they solve their problems or behave to meet their social needs. This approach enables teachers to view the needs (Circle of Courage) of the student and understand the motivations for behaviour that take into account the link between the student's beliefs, thinking and emotions. Brendtro and du Toit (2005) use a triangle (Figure 1.3) to illustrate this point in their Response Ability Pathways training. The triangle is similar to an iceberg that is protruding above the waterline. The exposed part is the behaviour that is visible to the teacher and peers. Often teachers and schools respond to the behaviour and do not pay attention to the huge iceberg below the surface, which is the student's thinking and emotions that contribute to the behaviour. The PLF incorporates the abilities of teachers to respond to the 'inside' student and not just react to the 'outside' behaviour.

Figure 1.3 The influence of thinking and emotions on behaviour

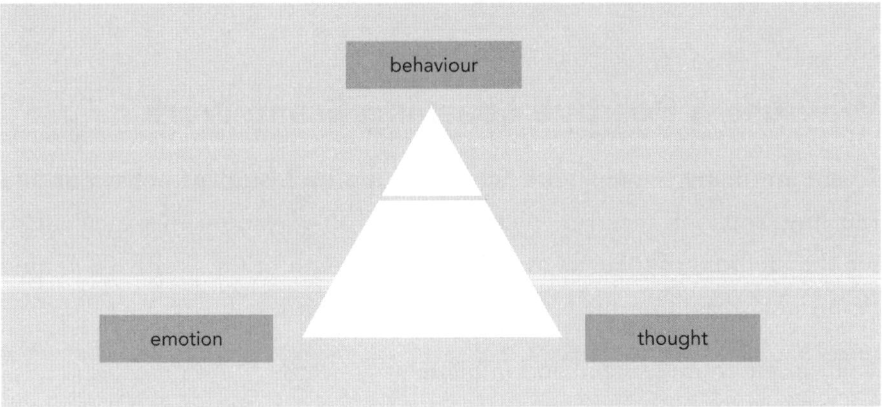

Source: Brendtro & du Toit, 2005

Experiences with the Positive Learning Framework

The PLF has been developed around the Circle of Courage based on my experience in mainstream primary and secondary education, my work with students excluded from school, my time as a teacher educator at university, and through being involved with in-service teachers in professional learning programs in schools. I am like many teachers who graduated from university or teachers college and did not know my style or plan on which I was going to base my teaching. All I knew was that I was hoping to teach well and that I would definitely start out very strict because I feared that I would not be able to control the students. I had in my mind a picture of a good teacher as one that was very strict with unobtainable academic expectations and set lots of busy work so that the students knew that in my class it was about work and no 'mucking around'. In my teacher training, I was not given the opportunity to challenge this thinking nor to think about what sort of teacher I wanted to be and on what basis I made this decision. I had no plan for managing my learning environment nor did I have any insight into how I had developed the beliefs or assumptions on which I was basing my teaching. As you read this text, you have the opportunity to plan how to engage students in learning and can answer questions aimed at helping you reflect on your beliefs and assumptions about students, learning and the role of teachers and schools.

In my teaching journey, I was exposed to a range of the mainstream theorists such as Canter's Assertive Discipline approach, Gordon's Teacher Effectiveness Training, and Glasser's Reality Therapy (see Table 7.1 on page 241 for a brief description of these and other theorists), as well as an amalgam (numerous days spent in school-based professional development) of people espousing quick-fix approaches to student behaviour. I remember one of the sessions offered to staff was from a presenter who advertised the session to the theme song of Bob the Builder, spruiking that if you came to his session with a problem he could fix it: 'Can we fix it? Yes we can'. The assumption was that all I needed to 'fix' my students or classroom was to go to a half-day course. Instinctively teachers know that student behaviour and learning are very complex and they cannot be fixed in a few hours. As a teacher, my expertise is in teaching, learning and engaging students—not in fixing them. In practice, I should not attempt to fix them. We will explore this urge to fix students in later chapters. Yet student misbehaviour can be difficult to deal with and teachers often look for solutions in an attempt to control the disruptive students so that the rest of the class can learn and to make teaching easier. The PLF offers pre-service and in-service teachers a framework in which to engage students in meaningful learning and develop respectful, caring classrooms.

It wasn't until I had the chance to work with students who were referred to an alternative education program that I was made to reflect on an approach that was positive, understood children and was not 'faddish' or based on pop psychology but rather had a solid evidence base to support it. More importantly for busy teachers, the Circle of Courage was simple to understand. I could easily use the four universal needs in my classroom in a way that was practical and resulted in significant learning engagement, even for the students who had a history of failure, resentment to schools or those that hated teachers.

I also found that the four universal needs provided me with a language to speak with other teachers that was not negative and did not dwell on the deficits of the students but was more about how to assist students to re-engage in learning. The learning focus was paramount for me. I am neither a psychologist nor a social worker but am concerned about how to facilitate learning for the students I have in my class. I knew that I couldn't fix vulnerable students (this is the job of other professionals such as psychologists) but I could engage them in learning for the time I had them. The labels others had for students were not important to me.

The conversations with other staff were natural when speaking about how to make classrooms welcoming environments, places where we can connect with students and develop relationships over the year (belonging). It is possible to share teaching strategies and assessment structures that assist all students to gain some achievement (mastery) and to create opportunities in the classroom where students can develop responsibility, autonomy and insight into feelings and emotions (independence). In addition, we can create opportunities within the class or school where children can have a sense of purpose, care for others, develop empathy and have a sense of being a productive person within the school and broader community (generosity). Nothing in the language used or concepts employed in these conversations are alien, or alienating, to teachers. The Circle of Courage underpins the PLF and offers a positive lens through which to view working with students and engaging them in learning. In the chapters that follow, the text will explore the PLF through establishing positive learning environments, preventing student misbehaviour, correcting student behaviour and providing thorough instruction.

Critical reflection

What do effective teachers do to create quality learning environments?

Ineffective teachers

Think back to your school years and remember a teacher you thought was ineffective, one that you would not want to spend another day with. Picture the room and the other students. What did this teacher do as students or students misbehaved in his or her class? Write down ten things they said and did. If you are with other members of your class or workplace share your responses.

Effective teachers

Think back to your school years and remember a teacher you thought was effective, one that you would want to spend another year with, a teacher that you would walk across broken glass to get to his or her class.

What did this teacher do when someone misbehaved in his or her class? Write down ten things they said and did. If you are with other members of your class or workplace share your responses.

1   For which of these teachers was it easier to think of things they said and did?
2   Can you explain why this is the case?
3   All classes have students who misbehave in them, so what was different about the effective teacher?
4   Can you identify techniques that the effective teacher did to enhance learning in the class by preventing and correcting misbehaviour?

As you begin this text and, possibly, your teaching journey, this exercise gives a clear direction of development. No one wants to start a course and be ineffective or be a teacher that students remember as ineffective. The task is to incorporate the effective teacher behaviours into your teaching and to lessen the frequency of ineffective behaviours.

The need for classroom management and instructional knowledge in teacher education

It is only recently that classroom management has been viewed as a distinct body of knowledge (Evertson and Weinstein, 2006). Classroom management was often seen as something gained from experience and there was little classroom management knowledge available to teachers and students in universities. As a result, teachers had to rely on intuition or popular myths such as, 'don't smile until Easter'! Research on the amount of time given over to classroom management in universities also highlights the lack of education on the fundamentals that underpin effective classroom management (Farkas and Johns, 1997).

Often, university lecturers and tutors saw the benefit of teaching classroom management, however, little time was given over to teaching it. This might have been because educators could not come to a consensus on what needed to be included in a course on classroom management. This indecision is also reflected currently in the range of styles and content in texts on classroom management. Most texts on the market are compilations of other people's theories and do not offer a coherent, simple model or framework that incorporates skills and strategies for engaging students in learning. If my experience is common, a course offered on classroom management at university often consists of a range of different models and the students are expected to select a model that best suits them. These courses 'fail to provide students with a comprehensive, coherent study of the basic principles and skills of classroom management' (Evertson and Weinstein, 2006, p.4). The PLF presented in this text is aimed at addressing this imbalance.

Another factor that contributes to the absence of classroom-management education in teacher education courses is that the term 'classroom management' is often associated with authoritarian teacher behaviours, which are coercive or punitive. This is seen to be in opposition to education in curriculum and instruction that promotes problem solving, independence, negotiation, active participation, and personal accountability. From this perspective, classroom management is more what a teacher does to the students to achieve compliance and less to do with positive learning environments built on positive student/teacher relationships.

I would also suspect that the lack of identity or place that classroom management education had in teacher education courses is because early research into student behaviour was undertaken by distinct fields of inquiry such as psychology, sociology, anthropology or special education. This is evident in the range of journals that publish articles on student behaviour. Little had been done under a unified banner of classroom management. This discipline-based inquiry could probably have contributed to the thinking that classroom management was more about a 'bag of tricks' than a field of inquiry that includes evidenced-based principles, concepts and knowledge. Teacher educators would come across information from a range of sources and pick strategies and skills on an ad hoc basis rather than see them as part of a whole field.

The structure of teacher education courses in universities may also assist in classroom-management education going under the radar. In discipline-based structures it is hard to see where classroom management 'fits'. Often it is relegated to a few lectures in an educational psychology class or in a curriculum methods unit. Rarely is it offered as a distinct unit and one that incorporates skills and strategies rather than theoretical models. If it is embedded into subject-specific units it is more often than not relegated to the end of the course, behind more important material or content that that the lecturer is more knowledgeable about and more comfortable teaching.

Classroom management is also one of those subjects that nearly all teacher educators (and classroom teachers) feel they 'know' because they already have teaching experience. This is similar to some parents' belief that they know schools, learning and teaching because they have been to school. If a unit is offered on learning environments or guiding behaviour that has a classroom management component it can be difficult to staff—as staff will naturally align themselves with an area like maths, literacy and language, social sciences, sciences, educational psychology or child development. It could be that whoever has time left over or needs to pick up some hours will be given the 'classroom management' unit. One way to view how inappropriate this is, is to use the example of literacy teaching. Would a person who speaks English and has read a book, but has done no further study or reading in language or literacy be qualified to teach literacy and language to early childhood and primary pre-service teachers? The answer would be a loud NO! Similarly, we should not let an unqualified person teach classroom management. We need experienced practitioners who have done further learning in this area, who have demonstrated a positive outlook on student behaviour and who have credibility in the field.

Defining classroom management in the Positive Learning Framework

This brief overview highlights the need for a PLF in teacher education. There are a range of education interest groups who all espouse their own term or meaning to classroom management, which reflects their approach to learning environments and student learning (special education, early childhood, primary secondary, alternative education programs). The Positive Learning Framework attempts broaden the understanding of the term classroom management and, at the same time, assist in clarifying it. Drawing on the field of positive psychology, resilience research, positive youth development work and the recent classroom management research, this book's approach is that: *classroom management involves teacher actions and instructional techniques to create a learning environment that facilitates and supports active engagement in both academic and socio-emotional learning.* This definition incorporates a number of tasks:

1   connecting and developing caring relationships with students with high and explicit expectations
2   organising and structuring instruction that facilitates deep learning, in an environment clearly focussed on meaningful learning that is important to students
3   assisting students to clarify challenges and problems and respond to their needs
4   promoting abilities for internal self-regulation and positive social skills, and
5   developing strength-based interventions for vulnerable students with challenging behaviours.

The first task above only confirms what indigenous cultures have known for centuries: that relationships, a sense of belonging and connectedness are crucial for healthy development. The Circle of Courage encapsulates these needs as vital elements that help children to flourish. In the following chapters, we will discuss the centrality of relationships in engaging students in learning in more depth. The importance of relationships in the Circle of Courage is obvious, as Pinata states:

> In analysis of classroom management, child–teacher relationships are a key unit of analysis. A focus on relationships rather than discrete behaviors, or interpreting such behavior in light of their meaning for relationships, is an important conceptual advance in the classroom literature, and may be particularly important for teacher training (Evertson and Weinstein, 2006, p.704).

As an introduction, it is obvious that classroom management is a complex issue and consists of far more than establishing and imposing rules, rewards and behavioural incentives to control behaviour.

Practice activity

Let us start practicing some of the techniques identified in the Reflection activity above. Effective teachers respond to off-task behaviour with minimal or no disruption to lesson flow and student learning (refer to Kounin for more information on this). In reality, they are using very skilled techniques to keep students engaged. Some of these skills and techniques include the following (we will build on the number of skills as we progress through the text).

Connecting	To be discussed in Chapter 2.
Cue to Start (C2S)	What you say and do to begin a lesson or to gain whole-class attention.
Proximity	Moving toward or standing next to students.
Look/eye contact	The look has gradations, from 'hello' to 'stop that behaviour', which you will need to practice: 'I know you are listening when you are looking at me'.
Name, pause, thanks	In this sequence, student name, pause while looking at them and then say thank you when they give you their attention.
Non-verbal gestures	Hand up to stop or be silent, finger over lips for quiet, tap head to signal 'hat off', big smile or thumbs up signal for well done and so on.

Before we start practising these skills, write down individually what you think you will use or have used as your C2S. Share this with peers or study partners, give feedback and amend if needed. Your C2S should be short, succinct and said with a confident assertive tone.

The 'flow' of a C2S goes something like this. The teacher:

- stands in the centre of the room (proximity)
- says their short verbal statement such as 'Good morning/afternoon everyone, can I have your attention please.' During the lesson it may be 'Good work people, can I have your pens down and eyes to me please.' (See early years examples below.)
- the teacher pauses, makes eye contact with the entire class (scan the group)
- says the name for any student not ready, pauses, and thanks them when they give their attention
- finishes their C2S with 'Thank you' (always complete instructions with politeness)
- begins teacher instruction.

This example is more for middle primary to secondary. This will differ if teachers and schools use the universal signal for silence (you raise your arm and hold it in the air while students raise their hands and stop talking, then when everyone has their hand up and is quiet, you begin). Early years may use clapping or signing as a C2S.

Practise starting a class (link up with peers or do in a tutorial)

Practise an effective C2S incorporating the other skills of proximity, look/eye contact, name, pause, thanks and non-verbal gestures. Have someone be the 'teacher' and leave the room. His or her task is to begin teaching something (it doesn't matter what as long as they can sustain it for five minutes or so). If it is early on in a teacher education course 'teachers' could be forewarned and have a mini lesson prepared as part of their subject area or curriculum class. Assign 'misbehaviours' to class members. The misbehaviours are low level and no matter what the teacher says and does, the behaviour must stop. We will escalate student behaviour later in the text.

Suggested behaviours:

- two students talking when the teacher starts the class
- one student looking out the window
- one student rummaging through their bag for a pen
- one student fiddling or tapping their pen.

Make the activity age specific according to the group of students you will be teaching. Begin! This activity should not go on for more than five minutes. Try to space out the behaviours. Offer feedback to the teacher on how they performed, the words spoken, tone, non-verbals and ability to continue teaching. This activity is about maintaining the flow of the lesson and engaging students in meaningful learning.

C2S in the early years

Gaining students' attention for whole-class instruction or as students move (transition) from one activity to another is crucial for an orderly room. Some examples of how to do this include:

1   Used when getting students to move to the mat or the floor (sung to the tune of 'If you're happy and you know it')

Teacher	'Put your bottom on the floor on the floor'
Students	Clap twice
Teacher	'Put your bottom on the floor on the floor'
Students	Clap twice
Teacher	'Put your bottom on the floor not the ceiling or the door, put your bottom on the floor on the floor'
Students	Clap twice

2   Used to get class attention at start of seated work or a written activity

Teacher	'1, 2, 3, 4'
Students	'Are your feet on the floor?'
Teacher	'5, 6, 7, 8'
Students	'Chair in, back straight'
Teacher	'9, 10, 11, 12'
Students (holding up pencils)	'Show me how your pencil's held'

3   When students are moving from one activity to another and when students are involved in different activity centres around the room with considerable noise. Teacher claps in a sequence and the students need to follow the sequence, stop talking and look at the teacher for instructions.

Assumptions and beliefs in this text

The theory and research evidence that underpins the Positive Learning Framework are encompassed in the Circle of Courage and the universal needs. The tasks emanating from our definition of classroom management also highlight beliefs about teaching and student behaviour. However, to assist you in the task of identifying what your approach or philosophy is to teaching, we will articulate early on and transparently the assumptions that underpin this text. This text is based on the following assumptions of school, children and teachers.

• All youth have positive potential, even those who exhibit challenging behaviour, and there are no 'disposable' children.
• Problems of children and youth are not the sole domain of impoverished communities but exist in all communities and, therefore, it is a community's responsibility to work on these problems.
• Children need concerned adults who respond to their needs if they are to succeed in the face of risk.
• The goal of classroom management is to promote quality learning environments that foster self-discipline and personal responsibility.

- Most behaviour problems can be avoided if teachers use good preventative strategies and recognise that the way they think about management strongly influences what they do.
- How teachers manage positive learning environments will vary across different classrooms, ages, and ability levels of students.
- Classroom management and instructional techniques are inseparable.
- Becoming an effective teacher requires professional and personal knowledge, reflection, continued optimism and time.

The content and reflections, as well as the activities, in this text will reflect these assumptions. The key for you is to determine the assumptions that underpin your teaching. The critical reflection below is aimed at supporting the reflection process and assisting you to develop the philosophy section of your management plan. In relation to Teacher Education courses and the publishing of guiding principles it is worth while having a look at the six principles that underlie the Teachers for Tomorrow's Schools Teacher Education Program at Mills College in the USA. The program's six principles present a practical vision for teacher education that emphasises social justice. The six principles are outlined in their text, which is referenced in the Further Reading section at the end of this chapter.

Critical reflection

Thinking about your classroom management plan

1 Examining core beliefs and assumptions
  Write a brief statement on what you believe about:
  - human nature
  - role of schools
  - role of teachers
  - how students grow
  - how students learn
  - the importance of teacher control vs. student autonomy
  - to what degree children are self-managing, or controlled by the environment
  - to what degree motives affect student behaviour.

2 Does my classroom practice reflect my core beliefs?
Take one of your statements above (e.g. on human nature) and try to identify the principles that underlie this belief. What are the theories of human nature and human development that appeal to you? Identify and list specific ways that your classroom practice reflects this belief.

Case study

Teacher assumptions and beliefs about learning

Miss Tonellini, Mr Roper and Mrs Gowland worked together as middle primary teachers in a suburban school. Although they worked together and shared some classes, they had very different styles of teaching and, in reality, as a team they were nearly dysfunctional. Read the brief description of these teachers and answer the questions that follow.

Miss Tonellini is a recent graduate who is a strict disciplinarian and expects that students should obey every rule or teacher instruction. She has set her classroom up in single rows and often gives her class work that frustrates them or fails to capture their attention or interest. When students misbehave she often uses sarcasm or ridicule to control them. When the Assistant Principal walks by the room, he is impressed with how quiet the class is.

Mr Roper has set his class up on a competition basis. His teaching methods rely heavily on competition with active (physical) games woven into the class. The competition extends to students earning token money for winning. Students are allowed to 'spend' their money on a Friday at the shop he has set up on his desk. Students can buy games, comics or toys. When students misbehave, he will deduct money from their account that he has displayed on the wall.

Mrs Gowland uses teaching techniques that rely on students working in groups and collaborating with each other to solve problems. The class is colourful with student work hanging from the ceiling and on the walls. Mrs Gowland has worked hard at providing a classroom environment where the students feel safe and have the confidence to risk a wrong answer or opinion in the group work. During work time, Mrs Gowland is always walking around encouraging students and bringing students who are off-task back on task before they misbehave. When students do misbehave, she attempts to re-engage them quickly, quietly and in private.

1   What do you think the assumptions and beliefs were for each of the teachers regarding:
    a   student learning?
    b   role of the teacher?
    c   cause of misbehaviour?
    d   instructional activities that are engaging?
    e   potential for the students to be self-managing?
    f   aim or outcome of discipline?
    Answer for each teacher.
2   Which one of the teachers or elements of their approach most closely aligns with some of your early thoughts on teaching?
3   What approaches or teacher behaviours do you like least and why?

Developing my classroom management plan

Effective teachers have a plan that is developed out of knowledge, experience, professional learning, reflection and time. The development of quality learning environments does not just happen. Quality learning environments are developed because of purposeful construction by the teacher based on a plan that includes their philosophy of education, support from current theorists, teacher strategies and skills.

The need for supportive and caring relationships will depend on the teacher and his or her beliefs as to the necessity or prominence in the teaching-learning process. This will depend on your assumptions and beliefs about teaching, students, behaviour and the role of schools. These assumptions need to be addressed because 'as we think, so we act'. As pre-service or in-service teachers, we need to be aware of our thinking and reactions to student behaviour. One of the outcomes of this text is that you will develop a plan of how you are going to teach and work with students in a positive way. In order to do this, you need to be aware of your starting point and what you bring to the teaching profession.

The management plan you are encouraged to develop as you read this text consists of three parts—philosophy, theory and practice. Your philosophy has to do with how you view the nature of students. In your opinion, do they have a will and the capacity to be self-regulating or do they primarily respond to needs, satisfying stimuli in their immediate environment. How do you understand how students learn and why they behave the way they do? When you correct student behaviour, what is your intention or intended outcome? Is it compliance or obedience, or more long-term development of the student's capacity to make better choices? How you teach and speak with students should be a reflection of your philosophy of education. The theory section is for you to support your educational philosophy with reference to what seminal writers have said over the years about student behaviour, learning and strategies for correcting misbehaviour. The combination of the philosophy and selected elements from supportive theory's guides teachers in responding authentically to the complexity of the classroom. In practice, your classroom is a reflection of your philosophy. A key to translating your philosophy to practice is a sound understanding of your beliefs and assumptions on student learning, behaviour and your role as a teacher. The broad outline of your plan is set out in Table 1.2 below.

Table 1.2 My management plan

Philosophy	My beliefs and assumptions on: • the nature of children • how children learn • causes of behaviour • outcome and intention of discipline interventions • degree of control or coercion that is desirable • potential for students to be self-managing • role of the teacher • place of instruction.
Theory	In relation to your philosophy: • what broad grouping of theories best suits you (laissez-faire, interventionist, leadership and so on—refer to Table 7.1 on page 241) • key elements of existing CM theories support your philosophy.
Practice	What does your philosophy look like in the classroom? • practical steps you will use that reflect your philosophy (rules, code of conduct, responsibility rosters, class motto, seating plan, student work, procedures and routines, classroom layout and so on.)

Summary

Classroom management is a complex and multifaceted issue confronting all teachers, in-service and pre-service, in every classroom around the world. The Positive Learning Framework addresses the issue of student behaviour and academic achievement in a model that promotes quality learning environments.

The first phase of the Positive Learning Framework starts outside the classroom with teacher awareness and the skills and strategies to prevent student indiscipline. The second phase of the model identifies the centrality of instruction in classroom management and focuses on lesson design and instructional techniques. The third phase explores the skills used to re-engage students in learning following indiscipline through to strategies to use when de-escalating conflict or working with students who continually exhibit challenging behaviour. A strength of this model is the capacity to work with these high-end behaviours with a view to re-engaging them in meaningful learning.

Effective classroom management is more than quick-fix strategies or a bag of tricks. It is a purposeful philosophical, ethical and theoretical code of conduct. In this chapter, we addressed how the Positive Learning Framework provides a basis for teachers to develop a management plan that assists them to develop quality learning environments that are welcoming and caring.

In the next chapter, we explore not only the importance of connecting with students as a preventative strategy but also the first step in developing relationships with students as the central element of effective teaching.

FURTHER READING

Benard, B. 2004, *Resiliency: What we have Learned*, WestEd, San Francisco.

Brendtro, L. and Shahbazian, M. 2004, *Troubled Children and Youth: Turning Problems into Opportunities*, Research Press, Illinois.

Brendtro, L., Brokenleg, M., & Van Bockern, S. (2002). *Reclaiming Youth at Risk: Our Hope for the Future*, rev. edn. National Education Service, Bloomington, IN.

Dewey, J. 1933, *How we Think*, D.C. Heath, Boston.

Edwards, C. 2008, *Classroom Discipline and Management*, 5th edn, John Wiley & Sons, Queensland.

Freiberg, J. 1999, *Beyond Behaviourism: Changing the Classroom Management Paradigm*, Allyn & Bacon, Boston.

Kroll, L., et al. 2005, *Teaching as Principled Practice: Managing Complexity for Social Justice*, Sage Publications, Thousand Oaks.

WEBSITES

www.reclaiming.com

Website for Reclaiming Youth International, the home of the Circle of Courage and Response Ability Pathways training.

www.ppc.sas.upenn.edu

Positive psychology resources from the Positive Psychology Centre based at the University of Pennsylvania.

www.search-institute.org

The Search Institute researched young people and came up with forty developmental assets associated with healthy personal development.

www.alfiekohn.org

Alfie Kohn's website has articles that critique approaches to classroom management. This is a good site to be aware of as you begin to reflect on your assumptions and outcomes of education.

Connecting
with Students

Quality classrooms where students 'belong'

Effective teachers have the capacity to make students feel welcome in class. Students tell us repeatedly that the teachers they like best are the ones who they can have a relationship with and that this relationship occurs in an environment that creates success. This chapter will explore how effective teachers welcome and connect with students to make them feel they belong (as outlined in the Circle of Courage descriptions introduced in Chapter 1) and are wanted in their class. We will also explore the causes of student misbehaviour and why some students distrust teachers. In developing your classroom management plan, you will need to address why students behave in the way they do. In addressing the stress that some students find themselves in, we will highlight the need for us to have a positive lens in which to view students as well as the effective teacher skills and strategies that enable us to connect with all students. The skills and strategies we will be exploring are outlined in the Positive Learning Framework in the first prevention phase as outlined below.

Positive Learning Framework

Prevention: self awareness and management plan

At the start of the year and before each class
- self awareness
- proactive thinking—indiscipline will happen at some stage
- caring and welcoming classroom
- classroom layout and resources
- rules, routines and procedures
- high and specific expectations.

Much of current youth culture encourages students to disconnect from other humans and retreat into depersonalised cyber worlds. Schools and classrooms need to be places of human interaction where students feel welcomed and accepted. It is important that teachers connect with students in order to make them feel that they belong.

Students thrive in welcoming and caring learning environments where they feel safe and supported. In developing an understanding of what a welcoming classroom looks, sounds and feels like, start with reflecting on your life experience.

- What is it that other people do that makes you feel welcome?
- How do you welcome your friends? What do you do to make your space special for that friend?
- When you are at the shops or a restaurant, what characteristics do these places have that are welcoming? What makes you want to return?
- When you make a mistake, what kind of feedback do you find helpful?
- What is it that people giving feedback say that is supportive or helpful for you?
- In your school or work environment, who are the people that make you feel competent? What is it that they do that makes you feel this way?

- What are some of the things that you could do or say that would assist you in relating to your students?

Your answers to these questions give you a head start in working positively with children and young people. What makes you feel welcome, competent and valued can be incorporated into your teacher behaviours so that you can develop a sense of belonging in your classroom. In professional development sessions with teachers, we use these questions to look at how teachers currently connect with or welcome students into their class. In some sessions, it is frightening to hear the silence when teachers are asked who makes them feel competent in the school. If we do not feel supported, welcomed or that we belong in our role as teachers it would be interesting to ask the students how they viewed the teachers or school climate. One of our greatest strategies in working with students is how we model values and behaviours.

The questions above highlight that we already have ideas and strategies in relating to children and youth. We already have existing ideas about making quality learning environments from our own life experience. We can use our experiences in working positively with students rather than leaving them at the university door because we think we need complicated 'edu speak'. Students will connect with a person when the experience is human and trustworthy far more than with a theoretician. As you go through this book, we hope you will develop a repertoire of strategies that suit your personality and begin to increase your capacity to deliver these skills. It is up to all of us to make our classrooms havens of encouragement where the students experience care along with a relevant curriculum in a world that often offers a more depersonalised existence.

Case study

How would you welcome these students?

It is term 3 and you have been appointed the new teacher for the rest of the year. The teacher who has taught this class for the first two terms has left on maternity leave. The teacher that left was not popular with the students as according to the students she was 'too strict' and 'wouldn't let us do anything'. You will be the sixth teacher this class has had in the last two and a half years. The class has a predominance of boys and their achievement level on national literacy and numeracy testing is below the national benchmark for their age. The change of teachers over the years has made the class wary of teacher relationships.

1   What would you do to connect with this class and individual students?
2   How would you go about making the class a welcoming environment?
3   On the first day, what would you say and do with the class that sends a clear message that you are a teacher to be trusted and that the students count in this class?

The need for connections

Positive relationships with students are the precursor to success in the classroom. This is also the case in mental health therapy where positive relationships are the precondition to effective intervention. In reviewing effective therapeutic interventions, Hubble (1999) found that relationships were twice as important to the patient getting better than the type of intervention used. This is good news for teachers; despite the year level or learning area we teach, it is our relationships with students that are important. In order to develop positive relationships with students we need to connect with them.

As you have experienced in your life, relationships take time to develop. As a teacher, you will develop some wonderful relationships with your students during the year and over the course of your career. But you will not have developed deep relationships by the end of the first day. However, a skilled teacher will have connected with their class and with individual students in the first couple of minutes of the lesson.

As a teacher, you will not be able to develop relationships with all your students to same depth or degree. Particularly in large schools, it is not possible. However, brief encounters with students provide powerful teaching moments for developing connections. Connections are what Larry Brendtro (2003) calls 'positive emotional bonds'. When you meet people for the first time, your brain is scanning the other person for cues that tell you they are friendly or a threat. Students will do this with their teachers, thinking, 'is this teacher a threat or not?' This scanning and reading of people happens automatically by the emotional part of our brain (the limbic brain) more so than the logical part (the prefrontal cortex, which gradually develops into the executive functioning part of the brain responsible for reasoning and managing emotions). Experts in non-verbal communication identify that two thirds of the meaning we ascribe to social interaction comes from non-verbal emotional cues like facial expression, tone of voice and gestures (Burgoon, Buller and Woodall, 1996).

As teachers we cannot rely on saying 'you can trust me' if our tone, gestures and facial expressions are saying 'you can't trust me'. We can't pretend to be trustworthy; we need to be skilled at connecting with all students, especially the students who don't want to know.

Practice activity

Failing and succeeding connections

1a Pair up with a peer, someone from your study group or a family member. Have one of you begin to tell the other something you are passionate about. The other person should look very uninterested during the conversation. Do this for 30 seconds and then discuss how the person speaking felt.

1b Now switch speaking roles. The listener this time keeps interrupting with questions or a comment every sentence or two. Do this for thirty seconds and then discuss how the person speaking felt.

2   Think back to a teacher who you really connected with at school. What did they say and do that helped you to connect with them? What about the teacher who you did not have as a classroom teacher but when you met you 'clicked' straight away——what was it about that person that assisted you to click with them? Think about the non-verbals cues that were present. Was this the same person you identified in Chapter 1 as the 'effective teacher'? Why do think this was?

Making our classrooms welcoming

Connecting with students assists teachers to establish quality learning environments that are safe and give the students a sense of belonging. Teachers who appear to have natural ability to connect with students meet the students' need to belong. When connecting with students we are building trust with them so that we can build an environment where the number one socio-emotional need to belong is met (Brendtro, Brokenleg and Van Bockern, 2002). In working with young people, Brendtro and du Toit in their Response Ability Pathway training (2005) identify that building a sense of belonging requires trust. Effective teachers are aware that these concepts are crucial in connecting with students in classroom and schools.

In developing trust, teachers should not just tell students to trust them. Rather the trust has to be experienced. We need to feel comfortable with students and the students cannot fear us as teachers. As humans, we cannot trust people we fear. This is an interesting point when contrasted with the old advice of 'don't smile until Easter'. It is very hard to get the students' trust back once they have felt coerced or dominated for the first ten weeks of the school year.

When a student trusts a teacher it does not just come from a feeling but is based on a set of specific behaviours that work together to inform the student that this person is safe and they are secure. Haim Ginott knew the power of communication in his text *Teacher and Child* (1972). Ginott's 'Congruent Communication' outlines a process of teacher communication to assist the teacher to build a 'climate' that is conducive to learning in the classroom. Ginott knew the power that the teacher has in developing positive or negative classrooms. Ginott identified this power in his oft-quoted philosophy:

> I have come to a frightening conclusion. I am the decisive element in the classroom. It is my personal approach that creates the climate. It is my daily mood that makes the weather. As a teacher, I posses tremendous power to make a child's life miserable or joyous. I can be a tool of torture or an instrument of inspiration. I can humiliate or humor, hurt or heal. In all situations, it is my response that decides whether a crisis will be escalated or de-escalated, and a child humanized or de-humanized.

Students will be defensive and will not trust a teacher if they experience behaviours that convey the message that the teacher finds them unappealing. Students will shy away from a teacher who they believe is deceptive or not genuine; who they feel needs to dominate them with little regard for equality or who they feel doesn't respect them. Students want you, as the teacher, to be interested in them and what they are doing. A quick way to squash developing trust is to be disinterested or not involved with the students. Students who feel they can't trust a teacher because of the behaviours they have experienced will mask their real emotions and be vigilant of your actions as the school year progresses.

Student voices captured in research continually highlight that 'good' teachers care about them and are there for them personally and academically (McDonald, 2001; Osterman, 2000; Pomeroy, 1999). Ethnographic research by Valenzuela (1999) highlights that for vulnerable students, being cared for was a precondition for caring about school. A personal connection with a teacher can help the student develop a connection to the school community. For some vulnerable students, this could be one of the few positive connections or relationships they have encountered in their lives to date. Ginott was right about the power we have as teachers!

Students will often say that a particular teacher 'really understands me'. When students say this, they are often commenting on how the teacher has the capacity to respond with empathy to their needs. Responding with empathy is about teachers' ability to see the world from the students' point of view, as well as being able to feel the emotions of others. Developing care with students requires giving students periods of undivided attention. These periods of undivided attention also enable us to speak to students in a manner that conveys our care and trust. The capacity to care for others may be non-existent or underdeveloped in some students. Our teacher attentiveness to students is crucial to help students develop the capacity to care. Noddings (2002) explains that to care involves being in a relationship with another person in a special kind of attentiveness.

Students will connect with those who they believe are there to assist or empower them. Empowering students means building upon the strengths the student has rather than concentrating on what is wrong with them. Teachers who build upon young people's strengths do so through positive thinking, positive behaviour and positive feelings. Research from the University of Michigan (cited in Brendtro and Shahbazian, 2004) shows that delinquent youth saw permissive adults as weak and adults who were dictatorial as hostile or uncaring. The teachers who succeeded with these youth had clear, as well as high, expectations and a strong concern for the young person. We will come back to his point in Chapter 4 when we are looking at the research about effective rules and routines for increasing academic learning.

Teachers who empower young people have a belief in the potential for greatness in every student. Larry Brendtro and Leslie du Toit (2005) in their *Response Ability Pathways* training manual quote Karl Wilker, who was an advocate for building on the strengths of young people in Berlin after the First World War when he wrote:

> What we want to achieve in our work with young people is to find and strengthen the positive and healthy elements, no matter how deeply they are hidden. We enthusiastically believe in the existence of those elements, even in the seemingly worst of our adolescents.

Connecting with diverse groups

The classrooms that we will be working in are not culture-free. They are rich social settings filled with students and teachers who bring with them a wealth of ideas, values, beliefs and behaviours. It is common for teachers to believe that others share their values and cultural norms. In Australia, most schools follow the values, norms and behaviour patterns of white, middle-class European cultures. The difficulty is that the values of student population may not match the values and norms of the school. When this happens, conflict and alienation from schooling may occur. When these differences in values and customs occur, it is a challenge for the teacher to make sure that all students feel valued and belong in the class. As teachers, we need to be aware of this challenge and able to confront it so that students can thrive in a diverse classroom. For these students to belong we need to connect with them.

When teachers and students hold different values, customs and norms of behaviour, the potential for misunderstanding and conflict are greatly increased. When students feel that there are cultural differences there can be a lack of cultural synchronisation in the class and school. The term synchronisation is appropriate here as it refers to being out of step with each other. Connecting, or developing a relationship, is difficult to do when you and the student are out of step with each other. This cultural disharmony can be viewed as a contributing factor in the disproportionate representations of Indigenous students in suspension and exclusion data. What is important for beginning teachers is reflecting on how we view different cultural groups, where we ascribe the cause of misbehaviour and how we view behaviour from different cultural groups.

One of the challenges for teachers to avoid stereotyping cultural groups, as this does not take into account individual differences and possible changes in groups over time. The universal needs identified in Chapter 1 provide a solid basis for working across cultural groups. They provide a solid foundation on which to work with all people and they have been acknowledged across numerous cultural and Indigenous groups. These needs are not culturally specific. Charles (2007) highlights some general suggestions for working with students from culturally diverse backgrounds. He suggests that teachers should:

- learn students' value systems: what they consider important and how they relate to adults, teachers and each other
- show genuine acceptance for the student and their families—develop a sense of belonging
- work with the students to achieve success and let them know that they will help them achieve this
- look at the way discipline is used in the home and in their culture
- adapt teaching styles to include students' out-of-school experiences and family lifestyles
- involve family in their child's progress and work together to benefit the child
- survey students on their interests, cultural background, languages spoken, significant events, achievements, traditions, history, holidays, and likes and dislikes; and use this information to connect with students.

It is important for teachers to have a working knowledge of all students' backgrounds. Knowledge of students from different cultural backgrounds assists teachers in their cross-cultural conversations and capacity to make these students feel welcomed and develop a sense of belonging.

The classrooms and schools we work in will never be culturally neutral or value-free as they are situated within a particular cultural context. The more we can synchronise the culture of the teacher and the culture of the student, the more we can involve diverse groups in learning and develop positive relationships with them.

Connecting with students who experience difficulty with learning

The general guidelines discussed in this chapter on making our classes welcoming and connecting with students applies equally to students who experience difficulty with learning and those who may have additional needs. The universal needs are also relevant for students who have trouble with learning. The skills and strategies outlined in this text are effective in preventing, responding positively and problem-solving behavioural challenges with all students. Students who experience difficulty with learning or who have neurological problems, such as autism, exhibit the same behaviours as other students, however, they may exhibit these at a higher degree of intensity or in a more unpredictable pattern. It is important that teachers working in inclusive classrooms have knowledge of strategies that are helpful in working with students who do have additional needs and ensuring they have success in their learning. These strategies will also be helpful for other students, who may not have difficulties with learning or a 'special needs' diagnosis, but who also struggle to regulate or control their behaviour.

In developing your management plan, it is worthwhile highlighting the skills and strategies covered in this text that you believe you could use with students with additional needs. Levin and Nolan (2007, p. 260–261) highlight this approach and suggest a number of guidelines that are intended to increase appropriate behaviour. These guidelines assume that instruction has already been modified and they suggest teachers:

- develop a sense of belonging
- accept parents have a better understanding of their child's behaviour
- use the expertise of other professionals and specialists
- help the student problem-solve – 'be a student of the student's behaviour'
- recognise effort and positive behaviour
- build on students' strengths
- make the classroom safe with predictable routine
- have appropriate high expectations
- work on social skills that students haven't mastered as yet
- teach and develop self-management skills.

The points mentioned above are supportive of a quality learning environment that is safe and accommodates all students. Students who experience difficulty with learning are vulnerable and can be alienated by classroom practices. They will need understanding from the teacher to enable them to feel that they belong, have talent, have power and that their life has a rich purpose. These guidelines and the universal needs can assist us in working with all students and can help us to be sensitive to those students for whom schooling is not necessarily a place of academic achievement.

Critical reflection

Connecting with a diverse student population

Connecting with students is a skill that can be developed with experience and practice. One of the challenges in working with a wide range of students is connecting with people we find 'unattractive', or overcoming a lack of appeal.

Although potentially difficult to address, it is worth reflecting on particular people or traits that you find unappealing. If we are not aware of our personal perceptions, or we give in to them, then we will struggle to connect with our students. In our classroom practice, we will reject particular students with little understanding as to why.

Connecting with only certain students in schools is not really an option. At times, we need to separate our personal beliefs, morals and judgments to feel compassion for students we may find personally unattractive. Ask yourself the following questions.

1   Who are the students that you struggle to connect with?
2   What student behaviours do you find offensive or confronting?
3   What student attitudes do you find difficult to understand?
4   Are there groups of students that you feel you have no affinity with? What is it about these groups that you do not like?
5   Are there physical attributes of students that you find confronting or try to avoid?
6   Are there racial groups that you fear or, through a lack of cultural knowledge, you purposely try to avoid?
7   Are you aware of any preconceived ideas you have of set behaviours that types of students or groups have? What are they?
8   How do you think these beliefs or assumptions will affect your teaching? How will you know if they have an influence?

How teachers connect with students

Teachers connect with students when they demonstrate trust, respect and have empathy for the needs of students. The capacity to view students through a positive lens is critical but there are discrete teacher behaviours, strategies and activities that we can do to develop these connections with students.

From an early age, humans scan our surroundings to see who is coming into our world. Once we see a person, we make a decision as to whether this person is friendly or a threat. Over millions of years, we have developed elaborate systems for deciding whether to avoid or approach. When students meet you in the classroom for the first time they will be assessing you to see if you are someone to avoid or approach. We do this with the part of our brain called the amygdala, which is in charge of security screening. The amygdala scans a person's eyes, face and non-verbal demeanour. Within an instant, the brain has made a decision as to whether this person is a friend or foe. This information is also processed by our higher-reasoning brain, which scans its database of experiences to see whether this new information matches a profile of a safe or unsafe person. The amygdala is a powerful sentry for us and raises the alarm about something that is changing or stressful. For example, when you hear a loud noise or explosion your amygdala automatically sends you into a startle reflex: your heart is pounding and your body is getting ready to run or fight, before your higher brain has worked out that the noise is only a car backfiring. We can see this reaction in the film showed of the bombing at the Atlanta Olympics. People in the stands ducked when they heard the noise as an automatic reaction—without knowing what to do in the event of a bomb! In small children, we can see the amygdala at work when a child sees an unhappy or fearful face from another person. The child begins to be unhappy or fearful themselves. The non-verbal cues are powerful conveyers of meaning and emotion.

Obviously, as teachers we want to reassure our students that we are non-threatening. Let us explore some strategies that we can use to develop personal connections with students.

Smile and acknowledge students. Students want to feel wanted and that they count in your classroom. A smile and acknowledgment of their presence or efforts engenders a feeling of importance because: 'I have been noticed by the teacher'. It costs nothing to do and the payback can be enormous. Use this smile and acknowledgment of students when you are walking to class, on lunch duty or moving around the school. It is amazing how students will respond and see you as one of the 'good' teachers even if you don't teach them. We are naturally drawn to people who appear friendly—our brain will determine in a split second for us if the person is friend or foe.

Greet students as they come to class. Being at the door as students arrive is a professional responsibility but it is also a wonderful opportunity to greet students. Meeting students at the door also helps in 'taking the temperature' of the class to see how settled or unsettled they are for your lesson. If something has happened at break time, it gives you the chance to re-think your lesson so that you can maximise learning. It could be that there has been some bullying at lunch or students were wrongly accused of something in the lesson before and the group is on edge. With this knowledge, it is possible to defuse the emotion as part of your lesson introduction rather than be highjacked by the group's feeling as you begin teaching. The power of the greeting is enhanced when we use the students' names with eye contact.

In a professional learning session I was leading in a school, one of the teachers shared his rule that he had to greet every student as he or she entered the classroom. The other staff members were amazed at this rule and wanted to know more from this teacher. The teacher then went on to explain the benefits of meeting every student as they entered his classroom: getting to know every student, picking up early if someone was not having a good day, and encouraging a general atmosphere of friendliness that created a positive class with students willing to get involved in learning. The other staff were clearly interested in this connecting strategy. In the next session the following week, numbers of staff shared how they had tried welcoming everyone before class and how it had made a big difference to the feel of the class and the level of engagement in learning. It did not cost much for the teacher but the pay-offs were well worth it.

Another benefit of greeting students as they come to your class is that it gives you the chance to **acknowledge the return of a student who missed the last lesson**. It is important that our students feel that they are noticed. Often students who are alienated or disengaged at school feel unnoticed. Being noticed and having your presence appreciated is powerful.

Recognising the student who was away also gives you the chance to give them work they missed or reassurance that you will help them catch up if needed.

'Thank you' or **'I appreciate the way you ...'** notes. All of us like our efforts recognised and appreciated. Students in your class are no different. This is another easy, simple and quick strategy for developing connections with students. The notes can be designed by a student or you can make up an outline of a note that can be photocopied and have copies of this in your desk or in your teacher's chronicle/work pad. When a student does something that you believe warrants acknowledgment you simply fill it out and hand it to the student. An important aspect to this strategy is to fold the note in half and give it to the students during the normal flow of the lesson with verbal thanks rather than putting it in an envelope or sending it home. As you walk away, watch the student read it and beam with pride. In a secondary setting, this is usually one note that does make it home! These simple thank you notes allow us to thank the student who always does the right things in the class but hardly ever gets feedback on doing the expected.

Be human. Students appreciate teachers who are human. Research with students who were excluded from school highlights that when they enter into an alternative education program what they value is the fact that the teachers are human, an experience that they believe they never had in mainstream school (McDonald, 2001). Students like to know that you are 'normal' and have a life outside of school. Share a little of your story with them. Teachers who are good at this weave their life outside of school into the classroom in a positive and often instructive way. You can discuss a sport you play or follow or what you do for birthday celebrations or special days such as Mother's/Father's Day. If the students are curious and respectful of the information then a positive connection has occurred. However, you do need to balance this sharing of your story. It is not meant to be therapeutic for you or overly burdensome for the students! When this strategy is done well, the sharing of the story becomes part of the normal activity of the class throughout the year and is a great way to make talking about yourself natural and acceptable in the class.

Do an activity together. One way to connect with students who resist teacher relationships is to do an activity together out of class time. This could be a community service initiative or a social justice activity like 'Clean Up Australia Day', removing graffiti or planting trees on Arbor Day. The possibilities are endless. One activity that I have done with a lower secondary class is to decorate our classroom. As a class, this involved planning the theme and type of decorations, organising materials and giving up time after school or on the weekend to complete the project. What transpired was that, often, the students who said they didn't like school were the ones who turned up on the weekend and worked hard for the class. This gave me a great opportunity to connect with these students in an informal, non-evaluative manner which was different from some interactions in class. With a few of these students, our relationship then blossomed during class time. This supports Valenzula's findings cited earlier: students, perceiving that someone cared enough to give up their time, became more engaged in classroom activities. Another strategy is to go and see your students perform in a play or musical, dance or sporting activities that they are involved in outside of school time.

Importantly, a structured group or teacher activity does not guarantee connection, as we understand the concept. Connections happen when teachers trust students, respect them and speak with them in ways that respond to their needs. Our brains will make a judgment very quickly as to whether to trust or not. Students will pick up signs of any threat, dislike or disinterest from our part. We can't fake liking students.

Critical reflection

How do students try to connect with you?

1 When you are out in a school or teaching how do the students try to connect with you?
2 How do you try to connect with people that you meet, study or work with?
3 Do you have preferred strategies or approaches that you use repeatedly?
4 Have you had an experience where you tried to connect with someone and they ignored or rejected your attempt? What did you feel like and what action did you take?

Problems of disconnection

As discussed in Chapter 1, Fiona Stanley, Australian of the Year in 2003 and an internationally renowned child development expert, identifies four universal needs for child development. For children to thrive they need to feel that they belong and that they are competent, independent and connected to the broader social environment. Students will flourish in social contexts that nurture their physical, emotional and intellectual needs. Young people who are flourishing are usually characterised by a sense of connectedness to school and other groups, such as clubs, churches or cultural groups, and usually have a sense of how to relate to others respectfully. Urie Bronfenbrenner, a world leader on human development, highlights that all children need at least one adult who cares for them throughout their lives. Many children in our schools today lack even this semblance of human nurturance.

The process of disconnection from peers, teachers and schools is complex. Many factors may contribute to a student disconnecting from school life or being resistant to a positive student–teacher relationship. In this area of student behaviour, there are competing paradigms (mental health, justice and health) that aim to shed light on the reasons or causes behind student behaviour. In the next chapter, we will explore the frameworks most commonly used to view students' behaviour in more detail. In this chapter we have been looking at how teachers can connect with students by developing the positive relationships that are central to effective teaching and positive social and academic outcomes. However, one way to explore how a student is disconnected is to understand the child's ecology, which involves family, community, school and peers. Psychiatrist Edward Hallowell believes that students' disconnection from people and school often signals a deficiency in human connections. We are experiencing an increase in the number of students who are discouraged and disconnected in schools (Hallowell, 1999).

Families in stress

The nature and size of Australian families has changed over the past twenty years. Stanley, Richardson and Prior believe that these changes 'have been profound and potentially damaging to children and youth' (2005, p. 11). One way to assess the impact that lack of financial resources, reduction in opportunities for attachment and poor parenting styles has on student disconnection from schooling is to assess the impact these changes have on the stress levels of students. Lazarus and Folkman (1984) state that the starting point for all problems is stress, which signals some challenge or difficulty. An understanding of stress is helpful in interpreting students' acting out behaviour as prolonged states of stress or periods of intense stress result in what Brendtro and du Toit (2005) term 'pain-based' behaviour. Many children in our classrooms exhibit pain-based behaviour.

There are hundreds of factors that cause families stress. Some of these can be external, such as racism and poverty. Many pressures come from the lack of extended family, poor access to caring relatives, divorce, solo parenting and lack of out-of-home care arrangements. The most pertinent stressors are the ones that are unique to the child's family. These can include punishing work schedules, parent illness, family conflict, substance abuse, very low income or dependence on social welfare, absent or unloving mothers and fathers, poor nutrition and inadequate housing. Irrespective of the cause, stress factors affect parenting and interfere with the development of healthy parent–child relationships.

We have all been in pain at some stage in our lives. We have experienced pain and have witnessed the pain in others. When we are in this pain, it is difficult to see the world from another's perspective. Parents who are stressed or consumed by their own problems may not see the issues their son or daughter has, nor have the ability to empathise with them. Minor conflicts are often conflated to major conflicts. Problems that arise from normal growing up and human interaction are portrayed as intentional defiance. When in this state of stress, parents often resort to discipline strategies they encountered growing up, which involved punishment and threats and were based on power. All reason, logic and affection are abandoned. This process is similar in the classroom where teachers are confronted with a situation in which they feel threatened or unsure how to respond and they resort back to methods and strategies used on them by teachers who employed punitive and demeaning tactics.

Families have a pivotal role in a child's early development. Nurturing environments are safe and involve positive relationships with others. Children look to adults for safety and security. If a parent or caregiver is a source of danger, the child has nowhere to go in seeking protection. Brendtro and

Shahbazian cite Glantz and Pearce (1989, p.78) who state that, 'the family that should be safe is dangerous. The outside world which should be approached warily is safer than home. Children in this predicament may experience nothing as safe'. We have learnt so much in recent times from resiliency research. All students have the potential to adapt resiliently to a variety of environments. However, nothing in students' resilient genetic code equips them to withstand violence and abuse from adults. When the threat is in the home it can be even more endangering. Students who are adult-wary are in our classrooms and provide a challenge for teachers to connect with, but we need to engage them in meaningful learning despite their levels of stress.

Parenting style is important for early socialisation and academic outcomes. Research by Baumrind (1991) and Chao (1994) found these variations in parenting style and outcomes across social, cultural and ethnic groups. Research in this area has highlighted that children who exhibited more self-control, success in social relationships and were more self-reliant (characteristics that are highly prized and rewarded in our current schooling structure) were exposed to an 'authoritative' parenting style. In contrast, students who were less competent tended to have parents who used a more 'authoritarian' or 'permissive' style of parenting. Baumrind's research involved preschool students. Follow-up research by Pratt, Green, MacVicar and Bountrogianni (1992) involved fifth-grade students with similar findings. Studies using older children also supported Baumrind's findings.

The three main elements to authoritative parenting include setting reasonable demands and high expectations that are age specific, being sensitive to the child's learning needs and developmental level and allowing sufficient opportunity for the child to develop autonomy. These findings highlight the centrality of the universal needs in the Circle of Courage but also reinforce three of the five tasks incorporated into our definition of classroom management:

1 connecting and developing caring relationships with students and having high and explicit expectations of them
2 organising and structuring instruction that facilitates deep learning in an environment clearly focussed on learning that is meaningful and important to students
3 promoting internal abilities for self-regulation and positive social skills.

Most parents want to be good parents. No one sets out to be a poor parent or one that is unloving but there are barriers that can get in the way of good parenting. I suspect that many parents feel undervalued. Society needs to place a higher value on parenting, which would translate into active support and education that is funded as well as accessible to all. Parents are doing an amazing social service in raising the next generation. They should be recognised for this work and supported in creative work and community-based childcare arrangements. These custodians of tomorrows' leaders should have access to continued or further education through funded initiatives sensitive to abilities and childcare arrangements. Finally, as a community, we need to shift away from an outlook that devalues the efforts and work of parents to a positive outlook that recognises the effort and contribution parents give to the community in their role as parents.

As a teacher we cannot fix students' family situations. This does not diminish the anguish we may feel about a particular student and his or her situation. What we can do is listen to their story and assist them in developing their ability to respond positively to stress or conflict. In this way, we are contributing to their development of resilience and capacity to deal with stress. Students will want to tell their story to trusted adults. We would hope that, as teachers, we are among the trusted adults that students relate to in developing their independence.

Stress in school

Being connected to their school assists in the positive development of students. Schools and teachers offer students under stress a place where they can experience success, a sense of belonging and respect. These are important platforms for increasing favourable life outcomes. A school culture that promotes positive youth incorporates respect and discipline that is fair, consistent and explicit. Students at this kind of school attend even though they are held accountable for learning and participating in lessons. Positive schools can be oases of security, caring and relevance for children in stress.

Many of the conflicts that a student has originate outside of the school community. However, schools can increase students' stress levels through a negative school culture. A negative school atmosphere views students as adversaries rather than partners in the learning journey. Discipline is inconsistent and unfair. Students are controlled through coercion, which results in a sense of powerlessness, which can in turn lead to rebellion. For students who are already in a state of stress, this usually ends up in suspension or exclusion. In these schools, students feel alienated and disconnected. Teacher behaviours can increase students' alienation through poor instruction that is not relevant to real life. These schools, where the ambience created in the classroom is depersonalised, punitive and with poor instruction, cannot possibly meet the needs of students to have success, a sense that they belong, and growth in autonomy.

The Circle of Courage offers a good whole-school framework for assessing a positive or negative climate. Does the school foster belonging, mastery, independence and generosity? These points offer a quick and easy survey to students and parents on how they view the school. Importantly, staff need to be involved in determining how the school and leadership of the school fosters belonging, mastery, independence and generosity in the staff. I have used this approach with schools as a way to map out a professional learning program that is responsive to staff needs. At times, it is confronting to identify how the school encourages teaches to be independent, to develop a healthy self-efficacy and what independence looks like in the school. Often in school marketing material they will highlight how welcoming or community oriented the school is for students. It can be useful to have a conversation about how the school structures opportunities for staff to belong and develop a sense of being competent and valued in the school. What is it that the school does that makes staff feel welcomed and respected?

Schools are still one of the safest places in our community. There are a few recent examples in the United States, such as Columbine High School, where stressed students who experienced sustained disrespect acted out of their pain. These students had experienced social exclusion by their peers. Our most basic socio-emotional need is to belong. To be excluded triggers feelings of rejection and shame. These students were overwhelmed by the stress in their life. Importantly for peers and teachers, stressed students seeking revenge for perceived social exclusion often express their pain in a variety of ways. Often their thinking is captured in art or poetry. Sometimes peers knew of the brewing trouble but failed to share this insight with others. As a learning community, we need to be sensitive to the thinking and feelings of our class members. In Australian schools, violence is a rare but shocking and destructive occurence; it has no place in our schools.

Peers can have a positive influence on healthy growth. Positive relationships with peers can help students overcome previous destructive relationships with adults or other students. Students will operate in groups in school, which can foster prosocial behaviours but, equally, can initiate students into antisocial behaviour. In the adolescent years, groups are significant and provide students with a ready-made 'identity'. In schools, these groups are usually centred on a common interest or ability like sport (jocks), surfing (dudes), drug-taking (druggies), lack of social skills or status (loners), or intelligent (nerds). These groups are very influential in developing values and norms of behaviour. Negative peer cultures see anti-social behaviour as the norm and members will act out these behaviours in defiance of adult norms in front of their peer group. Close friendships are made within the group, with the group providing a sense of belonging and support. Students who have an anti-authority outlook will search out other like-minded students. These negative peer groups develop early in primary school.

As mentioned earlier, the best protective factor we can provide students who feel under stress at school is to make them welcome and to give them a sense of belonging to the class and school. We demonstrate our belief in students' worth in how we discipline them, speak to them and empathise with them when they are vulnerable or in pain. We will cover some of the skills needed to do this effectively as we progress through the book.

Reframing negative behaviour labels

Think of a challenging student you have taught while on school placement. Think of what they did in the lesson to disrupt it or how they refused to do work and encouraged others to join their rebellion. Try to remember how you felt about him or her at this time. Maybe it was a student who openly challenged you and your authority. Their behaviour and non-verbals shouted out, 'you can't make me'.

Working with a peer, divide a piece of paper in half with a column down the middle of the page and answer the following questions:

1 Write ten negative labels for this student. Be as honest as possible.
2 On the other side of the page, write ten positive labels for this student. Compare them and discuss with your partner.

3 Do these redeeming qualities change your mind about this student? In the situation you remembered, could you see his or her behaviour from a positive viewpoint? What helps or hinders you in seeing this student in a positive way?

4 Which set of labels would be easier to talk about in the staffroom? Why do you think this is?

5 Knowing the student, what do you think was the motivation for their behaviour? Which need do you think was most unmet?

A positive, strength-based approach enables us to see students who challenge us in a different way.

Adapted from the *Response Ability Pathways (RAP) Manual for Training 1.5*, Brendtro and du Toit (2005).

Alone in communities

Recent neuroscience highlights the need for children to experience secure and loving attachments where they learn to trust others, such as mothers, fathers, siblings, relatives and other trusted carers. As mentioned earlier, Australian families are changing to smaller, nuclear structures that lessen the opportunity for children to attach to important others. Children and youth who are poorly connected to adults often act out because they feel alone. As a community, we need to support these students. As Brendtro and Shahbazian (2004) rightly identify, 'whereas other special needs children are targets of telethons, these children become the target of attack' (p.18).

As a community, we have a vested interest to invest in our social capital—children. Developing students who are responsible and civic-minded can only assist future generations. It is not possible to develop individual responsibility with students if schools and communities operate out of a 'zero tolerance' mentality. As a community, we need to support children with troubled pasts in employment and further education. It is not helpful if employers do not hire students with a history of drug use or criminal behaviour. It is not helpful to troubled youth if courts lock up juveniles 'to protect the community' instead of developing internal abilities for positive development and assisting them with external supports across the community. In practice, we need to put the value of children at the centre of our communities. Stanley, Richardson and Prior (2005) identify the kind of child-centred society that they are advocating:

'we have to improve Australia as a nurturing environment for children. We trust that you understand that to nurture children is not only good for our future as a competent, developed nation, but is an inherently good and just thing to do. As Nelson Mandela said, "a society that is good for children is good for everyone" (p.161–162).

In the community that these authors envision there can be no 'disposable' students.

Case study

Establishing a quality learning environment

Read the following scenario and answer the questions that follow.

I was doing casual teaching for a number of years while my own children were growing up, and was looking for more permanent work. I was working in several schools when the principal from one of them asked me if I was interested in taking over a Year 5 class full-time in the new term. I was ecstatic, as I had worked in this school for few years; I knew the staff and felt comfortable working there. I was less excited about the Year 5 class as they were not an easy group to teach.

The class was very full with 31 students. The national testing data for the group at Year 3 was alarming; with most students not reaching set targets in either literacy or numeracy. It was culturally diverse and there had been incidences of name-calling and bullying. The classroom behaviour was poor with students walking around during seat work, calling out, talking out of turn, constant put-downs, climbing over desks and some students walking out of the classroom when they felt like it. The class was a 'nightmare' but I was determined to make a go of it.

The first day came and I was prepared to get along with the students and make the class a success. The day started off poorly with students being openly rude to me as their new teacher, most walked in and didn't acknowledge me or return my 'good morning', then proceeded to sit in the groups they wanted and ignored my seating arrangement. As the day progressed, I felt myself getting frustrated and angry to the point of shouting and asking one of the students to leave the room for talking. The problem was I picked on one of the better students as I thought the people that deserved to be asked to leave probably wouldn't whereas I knew this girl would, so I made an example of her! I felt terrible and, to make things worse, it made no difference to the noise or engagement levels of the class. As the day progressed, I felt totally disillusioned with my abilities, the students, education and the future. As I drove home I began to cry but was determined that I was going to make a difference and that these students deserved a fresh start.

1 How would you assist this teacher in establishing a quality learning environment?
2 What does she or he need to do to get the class 'back on track'?
3 Outline a step-by-step process that you would advise him or her for the next day—be specific and, if possible, identify the language to use. You may wish to use this activity as part of your management plan and identify strategies you may use to re-engage disengaged students.

This response is not meant to be a full intervention package but rather it is intended to get you to think about how you would respond to students who are disengaged from learning.

Critical reflection

The Developmental Audit (Brendtro & Shahbazian, 2004) is an assessment method used to scan a young person's ecology. The Developmental Audit is developed by Reclaiming Youth International and provides strength-based assessment rather than a deficit-oriented assessment. The Developmental Audit incorporates the private logic and goals of the young person.

1 Using the principles and ecology pro-forma of the Developmental Audit, develop an ecology profile of young person you know. Note that this is merely a description of the students and their interests and is not intended to be therapeutic. If you do not have access to a young person, speak with a peer. Do not do this on a school student you encounter while in a school, as it is unethical.

2   Working with a young person (or peer) you know fairly well, identify the positive connections the students has in his or her:
–   family (who is in the family, structure and history)
–   peers (friends, what they like doing)
–   school (level of ability, behaviour, teachers liked, favourite subjects, best elements of school)
–   community (activities, clubs, sports).

Figure 2.1 Principles and ecology pro-forma

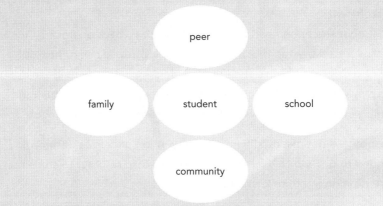

Write up your 'ecological scan' of this young person.
–   How is this picture different or similar to what you knew or thought of this young person before?
–   Identify this person's support networks and potential sources of stress in his or her life.
I am sure that, as you spoke, you also found out about their 'social history' or life story that went beyond the four areas above. This information will also assist you in understanding influences on their behaviour.
–   Write down five strengths that this young person possesses. In working with challenging youth, this should be the first thing discussed before you get onto any 'problems' they have caused.
This is a simple activity to help teachers understand the private logic or thinking behind young people's behaviour.
3   Picture a student you had on field placement or on teaching practice that you struggled to manage or connect with, or who was a known

student with behaviour problems that staff spoke about constantly. Imagine if you did a scan of his or her ecology. I can imagine a very different picture would emerge on which to base conversations and solutions. Can you identify five strengths this student had? If not, what is getting in the way?

Developing my classroom management plan

In this chapter, we have discussed the need to connect with students as a precursor to building positive relationships. We have also said that students should be 'welcome' in our classrooms and are given opportunities for success. We also looked at some of the causes of problem behaviour that can lead students to become disengaged with learning and disconnected from their peers and school. Below are some questions related to how these ideas may fit into your emerging plan.

1   Do you agree with establishing welcoming classrooms? To what lengths do we need to go to create these?
2   To what degree do we need to connect with students?
3   Is connecting and welcoming part of the role of the teacher?
4   In what ways has this chapter assisted you in developing an understanding of some of the causes of student behaviour?
5   If you were to develop a welcoming classroom where you connected with the students how would a parent know that this is the case when they walked into the room? What makes your class standout from others (the 'practice' section of the plan)?

Summary

Children need love and limits. To thrive, students need their physical, emotional and growth needs met by adults. Students tell us repeatedly that the teachers they like best are the ones who they can have a relationship with and that this relationship occurs in an environment that creates success. In this chapter, we explored how effective teachers welcome and connect with students to make them feel they belong and are wanted in their class. We also looked at the students who find trusting teachers difficult and how these disconnections are developed in the family, schools and in the peer group. Disconnected students are the responsibility of the whole community. These students require skilled adults to work in partnership with them to develop the internal strengths needed for prosocial behaviour and external supports across the community.

FURTHER READING

Hallowell, E. M. 1999, *Connect*, Simon & Schuster, New York.

Brendtro, L., Ness, A., and Mitchell, M. 2001, *No Disposable Kids*, Sopris West, Longmont, CO.

Curwin, R. and Mendler, A. 1988, *Discipline with Dignity*, Association for Supervision and Curriculum Development, Alexandria, VA.

Gibbs, J. 2006, *Reaching all by Creating Tribes: Learning Communities*, CenterSource Systems, Santa Rosa.

Mendler, A. 2001, *Connecting with Students*, Association for Supervision and Curriculum Development, Alexandria, VA.

Noddings, N. 2002, *Educating Moral People: A Caring Alternative to Character Education*, Teacher's College Press, New York.

Stanley, F., Richardson, S., Prior, M. 2005, *Children of the Lucky Country?: How Australian Society has Turned its Back on Children and Why Children Matter*, Pan Macmillan, Sydney.

Ward, C. and Craigen, J. 2004, *What's This Got to Do with Anything?*, Kagan Cooperative Learning, San Clemente.

WEBSITES

www.teachnet.com/how-to/manage

A comprehensive site that has management tips and other ideas on creating a caring classroom.

www.teachers.tv

This website is full of advice and film clips of teachers teaching. They have themes that are very helpful and their resources are excellent. Specific videos include:

www.teachers.tv/video/30035

How can secondary schools teach emotional skills to teenagers? This programme examines two schools' approaches to the subject and uncovers what their pupils think.

www.teachers.tv/video/25762

Jake, who left school at the age of 14 after being excluded from mainstream education, reflects on the complexities of a good working teacher–pupil relationship.

www.teachers.tv/video/2627

The message for class management is clear: interesting activities are vital, and apply the two Rs—rules and relationships.

www.ascd.org

The Association for Supervision and Curriculum Development is an educational leadership organisation dedicated to advancing best practices and policies for the success of each learner. At this site, you will find lots of links to some great organisations, publications and research.

www.eurekalert.org/pub_releases/2002-04/uom-cml040902.php

Schools that have classrooms where students get along with each other, pay attention, and hand in assignments on time could be a key to reducing teenagers' risk for violence, substance abuse, suicide, and pregnancy, according to new findings from the largest survey ever conducted with adolescents in the United States.

Frameworks to View Student Behaviour

Learner outcomes

After reading this chapter, you should be able to:

- identify a range of frameworks to view student behaviour
- explain the history and relevant research perspectives that have influenced our understanding of student behaviour
- understand that different perspectives have fundamental assumptions, which underpin different frameworks
- identify the theoretical and philosophical underpinnings to the Positive Learning Framework
- identify a preferred lens in which to view student behaviour that is supportive of your assumptions and beliefs about students, behaviour and learning
- recognise that there has been a shift in thinking and evidence about student behaviour that is responsive to student needs and set within safe and caring learning environments.

Key terms

Consilience

Evidence-based practice

Personal ecology

Positive psychology

Positive youth framework

Productive and unproductive behaviours

Resilience

Restorative approaches

Introduction

In looking at ways to understand student behaviour let us start with a quick question. As a pre-service or in-service teacher, what do you want from your job? Most will respond that they want 'satisfaction', 'a sense of accomplishment or purpose', 'happiness' or 'joy in knowing they are making a difference'. If you were to ask parents what they want most for their children they would typically reply 'happiness', 'competence', 'satisfaction', 'being a good citizen', 'confidence' and the like. In this case, both teachers and parents want well-being and positive outcomes.

If we were to ask parents or students what schools are about we would hear 'success', 'passing grades', 'discipline', 'conformity', 'numeracy', 'literacy' and so on. These two responses are very different. For the most part, schools have been about students achieving academic success as a prerequisite for the transition into post-school work. We are not against the development of literacy, numeracy and academic achievement. However, it is possible to combine the two elements and teach the skills of achievement as well as responding to students' needs, which builds upon the strengths and virtues of the students. The Positive Learning Framework incorporates both elements. In developing your personal management plan, you are required to support your position or assumptions with reference to theory. In assisting you with a process to identify which theory supports your preferred approach, this chapter will explore the theoretical underpinnings of the PLF and provide a positive lens in which to view student indiscipline.

The PLF views students positively and incorporates the potential for developing quality learning environments that are responsive to student needs and are built on trust and care. Theoretical lenses used to view student behaviour have shifted in recent years. The importance of this shift is not in the strategies in a particular program but the philosophical shift in teachers' thinking about the roles and place of the learner and the changing role of teachers in this learning partnership. This philosophical shift is possible when teachers and schools move beyond discipline to an instructional and person-centred approach with a socio-emotional emphasis that incorporates caring and trust, elements that are at the heart of teaching.

In this chapter, we will explore the changing frameworks to view student behaviour. In evaluating a framework or popular approaches to classroom management we need to go beyond discipline and incorporate knowledge of learning, effective teaching, brain development, social-emotional development and include the values that underpin our democratic society. From this inclusive vantage point, traditional territory wars between approaches (behaviourist vs. humanist) are irrelevant to the central task of developing quality learning environments where children flourish. What is crucial is developing a better match between the level of student–teacher interaction styles, the need for developing greater student autonomy and the redistribution of control as well as responsibility for learning from teachers to students. It is difficult to advocate developing student autonomy, active learners and self-responsibility when your approach to discipline is based on mindless compliance. This approach fails to develop students to be active citizens, problem solvers and life-long learners when they leave school. In this chapter, we are calling for more than cooperative or collaborative management strategies—moving to a real partnership of ideas and unity of knowledge that assists our students to be engaged in learning and to develop their capacity for greatness. For this unity of knowledge to happen, teachers need to be self-reflective and engage with theory.

Teachers need theory

One of the oft-recited mantras at professional learning sessions by presenters in classroom management is that 'teachers do not need theory'. This is often said in an attempt to connect the presenter with the group to demonstrate that he or she 'knows' teachers, that this session is 'real' and almost implies that what teachers learnt at university was useless 'so sit back and here comes the real stuff'. Theory and concepts are crucial to effective teaching. If pre-service and in-service teachers are merely taught practical tips then the capacity for the teacher to make decisions or problem solve when a new situation arises they will flounder and more than likely revert to how they were taught by a punitive teacher. The fallacy in this thinking is that experience alone is all that is needed to develop knowledge, which is not the case. Theory and concepts will sustain early career teachers when teaching in challenging environments or in isolated remote schools that demand a high degree of autonomy, ability to analyse and solve problems, and empathy, which are skills of resilience. As Kurt Lewin states 'Nothing is as practical as a good theory'.

The converse of Lewin's saying is true, as there is nothing as impractical as a flawed theory. Historical lenses used to view student behaviour have often been clouded by perspectives that present distorted images of human behaviour. Traditional behaviourist views in the 1950s saw people as passive individuals who responded to stimuli. The use of external reinforcements either weakened or strengthened these responses. The empirical evidence highlighted that the 'drives, tissue needs, instincts and conflicts from child-hood pushed each of us around' (Seligman and Csikszentmihalyi, 2000). Psychology's empirical focus shifted to fixing individual suffering. Young people were viewed within a disease model that aimed at fixing the damage —damaged childhoods, damaged brains or damaged habits. The study of disorder and damage dominated the view of human behaviour.

A decade later in the 1960s the 'third way' of looking at human behaviour emerged. Abraham Maslow and Carl Rogers heralded a new humanistic perspective to the entrenched behavioural (first way) and the clinical (psychoanalytic-second way) approaches. Humanistic psychology had imme-diate impact and promised enormous potential. Humanistic psychology differed from behaviourist views in that it did not have the empirical base or intellectual credibility. Its credibility has not been helped by the myriad of self-help books (crystal healing, reaching the inner child) developed under the humanistic psychology banner. It can be argued that Maslow and Rogers did not accentuate the centrality of the 'self' or 'self-centredness' as some pro-ponents of humanistic psychology suggest. Opponent views posit self-focus as detrimental to collective well-being. The latest writing of Maslow, discovered after his death, counters this claim. Maslow had added another need to his hierarchy that broadened his original needs framework. He termed it 'self-transcendence'—where humans seek to further a cause beyond self.

Schools also work within flawed theories that embrace policies of zero tolerance, which exclude and discard students. Often our neediest and most vulnerable students are discarded in more hostile environments (such as juvenile detention centres) that are not equipped to meet the needs of vulnerable youth. The emphasis on 'raising standards' in national standardised test scores through a sterile curriculum also fails to engage students in meaningful learning and promotes alienation from schooling.

Teachers need sound theory. When formal theories do not match the reality of schools and student behaviour, teachers will resort to what Heider, in 1958, referred to as 'naïve psychology' and operate out of folk theories of behaviour. This is where the capacity to reflect on and identify your assumptions is crucial. Without an organising framework or theory, it is possible that, as teachers, you will operate out of your unknown assumptions or beliefs, which when applied to students in a learning setting are primitive. For example, a teacher may observe a boy in Year 1 who constantly fidgets and distract others when doing group activities. The teacher, using naïve psychology, may view this distraction merely as annoying behaviour that is typical of boys—and especially this boy as his brother was the same. In reality, the student may be incredibly anxious about achieving and is interrupting others to check to see if he is getting things right. Another example may be a secondary teacher attributing the cause of a few students' non-engagement as a reflection on the attitudes of their parents to the importance of schoolwork. In fact, these students may be struggling with the content as they have reading abilities well below their peers and do not understand the work. A characteristic of ineffective teachers is that they continue to use ineffective strategies in the classroom. It is possible that these teachers lack a unifying theory and therefore continue looking for quick-fix solutions to the very complex issue of student behaviour.

As teachers, we need to disentangle ourselves from folk or pop psychology and narrow theories of student behaviour. What is required is a new approach that links together research, evidence-based practices, a positive view of youth and mutual respect. This new approach is an integration of knowledge, used by Enlightenment philosophers of science.

Case study

Without a theory we operate out of naïve psychology

Mr Thompson is a teacher at a secondary school that is classified as a 'hard to staff' school. He has been at the school for the past ten years. Over the ten years, many students have spoken to the Deputy over their treatment by Mr Thompson. Mr Thompson teaches Health and Physical Education and, in his eyes, disciplines students consistently and fairly. As a sportsman, Mr Thompson believes that everyone should be able to play sport and he does not tolerate students who don't participate in his sport class. His Thursday Year 10 class is his toughest and he doesn't look forward to it. It contains some special education students and students from the gifted and talented program. To compensate for the fact that he does not like the class, Mr Thompson tries to make it the most physically demanding of all his classes. Week after week, he is frustrated and he singles out the same students for not handling the ball properly or being 'bright but not sporty'. This is the only class where Mr Thompson allows a student not to participate. He lets Ronan sit on the sidelines, as Mr Thompson knows he comes from a poor family that cannot afford sports shoes.

1   What are some of the 'folk theories' Mr Thompson is using with his students?
2   Could you justify some of Mr Thompson's actions with reference to current literature?
3   Do you think that this class is a quality learning environment?
4   What would assist Mr Thompson to have a more involved class?

An integrated approach to viewing student behaviour

Philosophers from the Enlightenment, in the seventeenth and eighteenth centuries, believed that it was possible to unite knowledge from different disciplines. They thought this was possible, as they believed that a common body of inherent principles could help to explain human behaviour. William Whewell (1794–1866) termed this integration of knowledge *consilience*. William Whewell was an influential scientist of the nineteenth century who wrote on numerous subjects including geology, mineralogy, mechanics, astronomy, educational reform and theology. Whewell was interested in the connections between these different disciplines. Whewell was a wordsmith and invented the terms anode, cathode and ion for eminent scientist Michael Faraday. Whewell also invented the word 'scientist' at a request from the poet Coleridge in 1833.

Whewell believed that before new understandings in science became empirical truths they needed to be cross-checked with other 'truths' found in different disciplines so that there was a 'jumping together' of the evidence or, in other words, a consilience of findings. Whewell also used 'coherence' over time as a test for truth. In Whewell's view, the notion of consilience enabled the sciences to make generalisations that would advance the study of science. In relation to student behaviour, we need a framework that incorporates a number of perspectives that is inclusive of the student's genetics, development, brain, environment and school interplay.

The need for the re-emergence of consilience was made by Edward O. Wilson, a world famous biologist and Pulitzer Prize winner named by *Time* magazine as one of America's twenty-five most influential people of the twentieth century. Wilson contends that science has become too specific: broken down into ever smaller pieces of information. This atomisation of knowledge has meant we have lost Whewell's idea of unity—consilience. Consilience aims to link findings from different fields of inquiry to discover simpler universal principles. A 'simple framework' does not imply it is simplistic but rather it is clear and understandable. We have used the diagram of consilience taken from the book titled *Deep Brain Learning: Pathways to Potential with Challenging Youth* by Larry Brendtro, Martin Mitchell and Herman McCall (2009). The consilience figure they use (below) outlines how consilience is achieved by tapping ideas from different disciplines. The section in the middle that overlaps is where the ideas 'fall into place' and we are one step closer to the truth.

The human brain is constantly making connections between ideas. An example of this is when a student 'gets' what you are teaching them or illustrating—that 'A-ha' moment. It is as if the ideas or concepts being covered 'jump together'.

Figure 3.1 Consilience

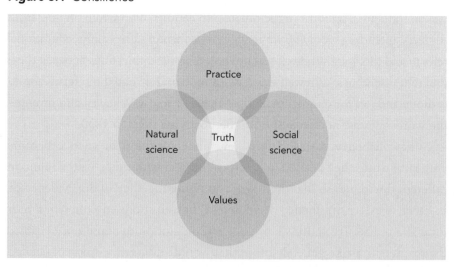

Source: Brendtro, Mitchell & McCall, 2009

Classrooms are complex environments that are characterised by a multi-dimensionality (Doyle, 1986) that other work environments do not possess. As teachers, we need all the knowledge we can collect to enable us to create quality learning environments that are caring and respectful. Using the consilience figure above, let us briefly explore the consilience in these four views about developing a quality learning environment.

- **Biological science** highlights that brains have inbuilt programs for attachment, which motivate students to seek out trusted and caring adults. We are beginning to learn that psychological well-being assists student to learn and think creatively.
- **Social science** reveals that students thrive in more democratic learning environments rather than those that are coercive or permissive. It also makes us aware of the strategies and skills needed for powerful instruction (we will explore cooperative learning as a democratic approach to instruction in Chapter 5).
- **Practical expertise**—from listening to students we know the power that caring and human relationships play in education. We have also learnt from pioneers in youth education who highlight the role of mutual respect in creating positive classrooms.
- **Values** of human dignity motivate us to create learning environments where all students and staff are psychologically and physically safe, where children thrive and where mutual respect is paramount.

'Evidence based' is a much abused term in education theory and policy. Some classroom management and professional development programs are advertised as being 'evidence based' when they may be devoid of any scientific rationale. Some of these programs promise solutions to very difficult problems and are attractive to teachers who are desperate to find solutions. Desperate teachers will hold onto these approaches even though there is no solid evidence they will work. What is required are research methods that are matched to the practical challenges of students in schools and classrooms.

Evidence-based practice (EBP) has a long history in medical research. Possibly the best definition, which has wide appeal, comes from the American Psychological Association (2006). The definition incorporates three elements in EBP:

Best research evidence obtained through intervention strategies, observation, different methodologies (qualitative, quantitative, ethnographic, naturalistic, and randomised controlled trials);

Clinical expertise involves clinical competencies including interpersonal expertise, knowledge of research, cultural awareness, and diagnostic judgements;

Person characteristics highlight the strengths, problems, level of support, values, culture, environmental context, personal preferences or world view.

The benefit of this definition is that it highlights that, as teachers, our knowledge of the individual is used in conjunction with expertise that comes from working with students as well as research from multiple sources. In this way, we can 'triangulate' evidence from a range of sources. In working with adolescents, the APA recommend that any intervention or 'treatment must be cross-discipline, culturally responsive and should reach all youths'. This approach reflects consilience.

In developing your management plan, it is important to view 'off-the shelf' programs that claim to 'fix' student behaviour and learning engagement critically. As you are becoming aware, this area is complex and one size does not fit all. The Positive Learning Framework encompasses a number of broad frameworks to view student behaviour that have rich and deep traditions. This is far more powerful than using the same approach to understand student behaviour because that is all we know. The concept of consilience provides an organisational capacity to bring together research, practice and values of mutual respect. As a concept, consilience urges us to incorporate more than our opinion, to 'think outside the square' and to develop a management plan that incorporates broad theoretical assumptions, reflects effective evidence-based practice and is authentic to your beliefs.

Case study

Consilience in the classroom

Ms Gordon thought outside the square when it came to engaging her students in meaningful learning. Ms Gordon always greeted her students every morning and made an effort to say something to every student that was 'special' just to them. It could be a comment from a conversation she had with them yesterday, a comment on their homework, or how they looked as they filed into class. She knew how important it was for them to know they were wanted and cared for.

Ms Gordon always planned her lessons very well and the students were clear as to what they were learning and what they should be learning next. She often asked other staff for ideas on how to teach certain topics or she brought in ideas she had picked up outside of the school. Ms Gordon ran the class with input from the students about how topics were taught, what activities could be included and what groups they worked in. The students loved the chance to contribute and to have their voice heard in this class. When conflict arose, Ms Gordon encouraged the students to solve the issue themselves using the conflict resolution process agreed to as a class in the first week. If students needed a trusted adult to talk to, Ms Gordon assisted as much as possible, and if that adult was the gardener or canteen person then that was how it went. Ms Gordon always referred to past educators or heroes she liked. If she came across a student who appeared vulnerable, she consulted others for assistance and she would contact parents or outside agencies in an attempt to help the student. At parent nights, she highlighted the evidence and rationale for any new practice or process. She was a popular teacher at the school.

Consilience is achieved by tapping ideas from different disciplines.

1   Referring to the different disciplines outlined in the consilience figure on page 64, highlight examples of consilience in the way that Ms Gordon taught and interacted with her students.

2   How does Ms Gordon's approach highlight the belief that all knowledge is related or, in other words, highlight consilience?

An ecological understanding of student behaviour

Urie Bronfenbrenner's bioecological model provides a powerful example of consilience in an approach to students in a school setting. Bronfenbrenner is among the world's best-known psychologists and has been publishing articles and books for over sixty years. Bronfenbrenner was based at Cornell University and is widely known as one of the world's leading scholars in developmental psychology and recognised for his interdisciplinary approach, enshrined in the human ecology model. Bronfenbrenner's model acknowledges that as humans we do not develop in isolation but in relation to our family, school, community and society. The interactions that occur among these environments are key to human development. Bronfenbrenner saw traditional psychological research as flawed, saying, 'much of developmental psychology, as it now exists, is *the science of the strange behaviour of children in strange situations with strange adults for the briefest possible periods of time*' (1979, p. 19). Thomas Weisner, in reviewing Bronfenbrenner's last book, comments that his bioecological model is among the most widely cited and frequently taught in human development.

Bronfenbrenner's model promoted the centrality of relationships. He saw trusting bonds with children as the most developmentally significant and called for the American government to provide policies that enabled families to spend more time together without distractions and stress. Time should be made available for both poor and rich, using provisions like better leave entitlements and childcare, so that all families could have more time together without work disruptions. As Bronfenbrenner said, 'a child needs the enduring, irrational involvement of one or more adults … in short, *somebody has to be crazy about that kid*' (2005, p. 262). Bronfenbrenner recognised that children thrive in ecologies with caring adults, teachers and communities who care and with positive peers. He proposed, in his 1970 book, that when comparing childhood in the then USSR with America a better index for child well-being within society is 'the concern of one generation for the next' (p. 216).

The child is at the centre of Bronfenbrenner's model (Figure 3.2). Around the child are settings in which he or she spends time, and his or her family, school, peers, and community. Central to this ecology is an individual who develops over time throughout the life course. This unique child inter-acts with the ever-changing and multilevel settings and the number and quality of the interactions between the settings have important implications for development. Surrounding these immediate settings are broader circles of influence such as economic, cultural, and political forces. Bronfenbrenner termed the closest environments, for example family, school, peers and community, as a child's microsystem. The interaction or connection between these groups is the mesosystem. Beyond this is are the broader circles of influence called the exosystem and in the outer circle of influence are the cultural values, national customs and societal forces that make up the macrosystem.

Figure 3.2 Bronfenbrenner's social ecology model

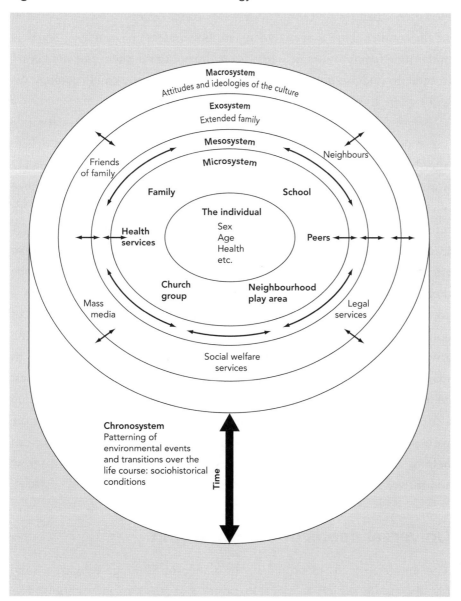

Source: Bowes & Grace, 2009, p. 9

The importance of Bronfenbrenner's model is that in the classroom we can begin to recognise the potent influence we can have on students. The immediate micro-ecologies of family, school, peers and community have the potential for greater influence than the broader circles. The classroom or school can offset destructive interactions that may occur in the community or at home by addressing the young person's needs. Ideally, the micro-ecologies all work together in harmony to develop positive behaviours and deep values. However, when the micro-ecology sends contradictory messages, children are in conflict. This is seen when families undermine teachers, teachers undermine family values or when peers disrupt the influence of the family. In order to understand the child, we need to explore the child's ecology. We will explore this more in Chapter 6.

Bronfenbrenner's view of human development is helpful in understanding student behaviour. He was dismissive of the nature vs. nurture debate since both biology and culture affects behaviour and brain development. He was more interested in psychology focussing on the strengths and resilience of children. Human behaviour is reciprocal and not a linear process. A parent interacts and influences a child but a child also influences the parent. A teacher influences students' behaviour and a student's behaviour has an effect on a teacher's behaviour. Children select their peer group, influence them, and are influenced by them. Working with children is a reciprocal arrangement. Bronfenbrenner's bioecological approach is an example of consilience as it is breaking down barriers between disciplines and providing a way forward that enables administrators, teachers, parents and students to work together for positive youth development. Student behaviour is best addressed by a consilience of perspectives. This strength-based partnership assists in establishing resilient and responsible youth. In the next section, we will explore the role of resilience in the PLF approach and how we can help to create environments that address students' needs so they can grow and thrive.

Universal needs in the classroom

The universal needs identified in the Circle of Courage provide a solid foundation on which to develop positive classrooms and schools. The Circle of Courage is grounded in positive psychology and in its simplicity brings together the findings from resilience research and positive youth development. The concise nature of the Circle of Courage makes it read more like a resilience code because it translates strength-based research into a simple and understandable format. The Circle of Courage as a resilience code describes the four universal human growth needs. We have introduced the theoretical underpinnings of the Circle of Courage in Chapter 1, so this next section will highlight the application of the universal needs in a school and classroom context.

The development of positive learning environments is made more potent when these environments are consistently developed across the whole school. A school-wide approach is preferred to inconsistent approaches to teaching, behaviour, expectations, values and respect. A term that we have been using in this text around student behaviour and universal needs that includes the whole school but also broadens the definition to include the community is 'positive youth development'. The term includes the individual, peers, parents, teachers, school and opens up the ecology to include the community in which the school is set. Let us explore what is involved in 'positive youth development'.

Positive youth development focuses on creating an environment, such as a school where students can fulfil their potential and be actively involved and who are integral partners in this development. These positive environments cannot be willed into being. They are purposely constructed, as are quality learning environments. They take planning, knowledge and effort by teachers, administrators and parents. These environments are characterised by a continuum of opportunities for student participation as well as the broader community being actively engaged. Positive youth environments view the potential of young people and build upon their assets and strengths. It is not about only prevention or categorising youth according to their deficits.

There is any number of whole-school approaches available. However, few 'packaged' whole-school approaches incorporate the broader community and actively seek to support students in positive development both in the classroom and around the school. One of the positive approaches that does incorporate this level of support and views students as leaders as well as active partners is Jerome Freiberg's Consistency Management and Cooperative Discipline (CMCD, 1999). We will explore further this approach and another whole-school program in Chapter 6. The point is that within a positive youth framework there needs to be a number of supports or essential elements that assist students to thrive and reach their potential. The four universal needs in the Circle of Courage highlight the four needs for positive growth. The move or shift to a whole school positive youth development approach has little to do with policy and programs. The need for some schools is to 'fundamentally alter relationships, beliefs, and power opportunities to focus on human capacities and gifts rather than on challenges and problems' (Bernard, 2004, p. 4).

If we go back to Kurt Lewin's quote, 'Nothing is as practical as a good theory', let us see how this theoretical knowledge and research woven into the Circle of Courage can assist in building the strengths of resilience by providing opportunities for belonging, mastery, independence and generosity. The following table sets out a practical application to develop resilience and quality learning environments.

Table 3.1 Belonging: opportunity for attachments

Key components	In practice (what the teacher says and does)	Research
A caring relationship with a trusted adult	• caring and responsive • connecting strategies (Ch. 2) • humour • shares personal stories • shows interest in student lives • empathetic • school-wide climate of respect • notices when a child is away and welcomes back	Young people possess a need to belong. Children need caring and trusted adults in their lives. Children need adults who respond to their needs. As Bronfenbrenner says, *somebody has to be crazy about that kid*. Caring relationships conveys loving trust, care and fundamental positive regard. We need to create a climate of belonging in our schools. In this climate, teachers and students work together for 'mastery'. Attachment is a pre-requisite for learning from adults.

Safe learning environment	<ul><li>high expectations</li><li>positive youth-centred messages—you can do it, persevere</li><li>peaceful conflict resolution</li><li>develop leadership opportunities</li><li>focus on problem solving</li><li>student voice is heard</li><li>mutual respect</li></ul>	At the centre of caring relationships are high expectations, which are clear, positive and motivate students to succeed. In the learning environment, students need to feel safe and know that they can access your support. Students want clear limits and love. Students need opportunities to develop personal responsibility, where they can risk a wrong answer and still save face.
Community learning environment	<ul><li>group cohesion and identity</li><li>social engagement</li><li>ownership for behaviour and learning</li><li>cooperative strategies</li><li>acceptance of others</li></ul>	Indigenous child-rearing practices realised the need for the 'village to raise the child'. Seeing others as part of 'our' group helps to forge strong and respectful relationships.

Table 3.2 Mastery: opportunity for achievement

Engaged in learning	<ul><li>creative teaching</li><li>age and ability appropriate</li><li>relevant content connected to life outside of school</li><li>develop curiosity</li><li>attuned to student interests</li><li>problem solving and students making decisions</li></ul>	Effective teachers have the ability to take mandated curriculum and make it interesting to students. The instruction is varied. In the classroom, students need the opportunity to develop problem solving ability, realise they have talent and to be creative.
Developing competence	<ul><li>active construction of knowledge</li><li>striving for personal attainment</li><li>opportunities for success</li><li>opportunities to teach</li><li>developing responsibility</li><li>model and think aloud</li><li>make mistakes and discuss</li><li>authentic tasks (connected to issues in students lives)</li><li>opportunities for small group tasks</li></ul>	Students need to know they have talent. Students thrive when the work is just challenging enough so that they can master new skills, which assist them to handle future challenges. Personal improvement is more important than social comparison. The best person to be compared with is you.

High expectations	• individualised expectations and goal setting • belief that the student can achieve • provide a safe and predictable environment • positive teacher talk affirming worth and ability	High expectations convey a message that the teacher has a belief that the student has the capacity to achieve and be all he or she can be—'she believed in me when I didn't' 'Turnaround' teachers tap into an interest in the student and build upon this strength and help the student to see themselves as resilient.

Table 3.3 Independence: developing autonomy

Active member of the community	• opportunities for student voice • mutual respect and trust • modelling peaceful resolution to conflict • active citizenship	Students need to experience that their lives have influence and that they have power (internal locus of control). In developing personal resilience, students need to experience that they can make things better.
A sense of responsibility	• opportunities for self control • ability to make decisions without coercion • roles within the class • involved in rule creation and input into classroom processes • opportunities for reflection	In developing responsibility students gain autonomy. Inviting students to be a part of the 'climate' of the class or to assist in solving a peer or class dilemma signals a belief and respect for the students' ability to act responsibly. The biggest shift could be in assisting teachers to believe in the capacity of students and let go of control-oriented thinking and to see students as a valuable resource.

Table 3.4 Generosity: developing altruism

Developing empathy	• opportunities to care for others—class or school • treated with respect • sense of importance—you have something to offer this class/school • developing class values • peaceful conflict resolution strategies • part of the taught curriculum —social skills, emotional education	Students are more likely to develop empathy when a part of supportive community. In working with others and fulfilling roles within the class, they will discover they are valued and have worth. Working with others assists in developing the capacity to see other people's perspectives, thoughts and feelings.

Opportunity for service	• working in partnership with others—your opinion counts • solving community or real life problems • work on a charity as a class	One way that students can find meaning in their life is to commit to a problem beyond themselves. In looking beyond ourselves, we can learn concern for others, which will assist students to grow in moral development.

Bonnie Benard (2004) offers a succinct summary of the need for whole of school structures to assist all children to thrive.

What resilience research offers is a well documented support for an educational approach based on meeting young people's basic psychological needs—for belonging and affiliation, a sense of competence and meaning, feeling of autonomy, and safety (p. 68).

In this section, we have presented a useful theory for viewing student behaviour and a structure to assist in developing positive outcomes for resilient students. The useful theory of the universal needs draws from a wide theoretical base and from a range of disciplines. The theoretical framework presented here is broad, varied and contemporary and is incorporated throughout the Positive Learning Framework. In taking a consilience of perspectives the framework draws upon the fields of positive psychology, resilience research, neuroscience, social biology, sociology, positive youth development and teacher pedagogy. One of the tasks of your learning journey is to identify elements of theories that support your beliefs and assumptions. To assist in this journey the next section will look at some of the alternative paradigms for the study of classroom management and then highlight some emergent perspectives on classroom management.

Why students behave as they do—developing your own answer

Before we go into the history of classroom-management research and writing, let us take time to address your management plan. As we are aware, the nature of classrooms is complex (Weinstein, 1996; Doyle, 1987) and the response to this complexity requires management responses that are evidence based and have their foundations in research. Effective teachers have a well-planned approach to student indiscipline that is respectful and flows authentically from their beliefs and values about students and learning. We need to understand our own personal values and reflect on our opinions of child development, how students learn and the degree of autonomy and choice you think students need. As Edward's states 'an educational philosophy first and foremost includes explanations regarding how children learn and why they behave as they do' (2008, p. 25).

Critical reflection

1   When you were on field placement or on school-based practicum, what, in your opinion, was the predominant view or understanding of student behaviour from the teachers there?
2   What are the teacher behaviours or actions that assist you in forming your opinion?
3   Do you see any 'theories' or frameworks as more helpful in managing student behaviour and engaging students in learning?
4   When misbehaviour occurs, what is it that the teacher says and does in response to the student or behaviour? Be very specific in noting the teacher's actions and words.

Changing vantage points from which to view student behaviour

Early conceptions of classroom management

The theoretical underpinnings outlined above include broad concepts and understandings on which to build a positive plan. However, what is presented is a consilience of perspectives that draws from a wide range of research paradigms. We believe this consilience offers an opportunity to select the most appropriate and potent approaches to engaging students in quality learning environments that are caring and respectful. However, the research literature on classroom management is often written up in distinct paradigms that are mutually exclusive. Particular approaches espouse set philosophical principles and often imply that this approach is superior to others. This dichotomy is part of the natural progression of finding new insights gleaned from research, as well as on shifts in practice informing us about student thinking and behaviour. The following section is presented as a history of research in classroom management, and shows how particular viewpoints held sway at particular periods. Finally, this section looks at the philosophical shift in approaches to classroom management.

The vantage points from which to view student behaviour have evolved over the last century and have had a significant impact on the understanding of behaviour and practical approaches to students. It is important to look at what lessons we can learn from the past when attempting to develop a broader understanding of student behaviour and when exploring a greater repertoire of skills and strategies to work positively with all students. The changing understanding of student misbehaviour has reflected the vantage point (research, theoretical knowledge, advances in neuroscience) from which student behaviour has been viewed. Key lessons can be found in the different theoretical points of observation that have informed working with students in school. This research also sheds light on what evidence is available to support current approaches to classroom management and instruction, as well as providing a bigger picture to locate approaches. For beginning teachers, we need to have a position on causes of misbehaviour, as this understanding will influence how we respond to students who misbehave.

Systematic research or empirical studies into classroom management began in earnest in the 1950s. Before this, writings on classroom management were mainly confined to author's opinions or common sense and few of the works included citations to previous research. Rather, they cited other authors or textbooks. A good example of these early writings was the works of William Chandler Bagley (1907). Bagley wrote his treatise based on his observations of good teachers, textbooks on classroom management, his personal experience and psychological principles. Although possibly more a text of his instinct on what makes a good teacher than empirical research, his observations are very relevant today. He viewed school as a preparation for citizenship after students leave and, therefore, management interventions needed to look to the long term and not just for short-term gains. Bagley thought that teacher interventions that were punitive or that raised anxiety were unnecessary, as were overly competitive strategies that might lead students to be selfish or antisocial in their behaviour.

Other notable texts written in the early parts of the twentieth century included a text by Breed (1933). Breed attributed the absence of books dedicated to classroom management to new understandings emerging from the classroom which were centred on the classroom level (curriculum and instruction) or school level (administration). Classroom management, he suggested, fell between these topics. Breed's book exemplified this with chapters on testing, grading and curriculum issues. Even the title highlighted the disparity: *Classroom Organisation and Management*. Most of the generic research in this early part of the century supported conclusions that positive environments that acknowledged students were preferred to negative, punishment-oriented classrooms and that a more authoritative teaching style that promoted student input and self-regulation was preferred to authoritarian or more permissive styles.

At the turn of the last century, Britain established its first child study laboratory. This laboratory was devoted to psychology; however, it also contained an education section where students and teachers received a systematic course in child study (Bridgeland, 1971). Previously, the founder of this laboratory, Sully, had written about childhood deviance in *Studies in Childhood* (1895). These two events gave rise to the psychological study of childhood deviance or 'maladjustment'. Up until this point children had been classified in medical terms as 'idiot', imbecile' or 'fatuous' (Bridgeland 1971, p. 46). The underlying belief was that the children's 'maladaptive' behaviour was a result of their physiological defect.

Sully, however, proposed that these children were not defective and that change was possible. Sully believed that, 'the normal child is one who is in adequate adjustment with his environment; the so-called abnormal child is, in the vast majority of cases, merely a maladjusted child, not a child suffering gross pathological defect' (Bridgeland 1971, p. 50). He suggested that through environmental manipulation, moral conduct and emotional problems were amenable to change. This belief significantly influenced the way people began to approach maladjusted children.

Sully's understanding of maladjustment was supported by the Christian moral tradition that had directed early workers like Mary Carpenter in her work with juvenile delinquents. She believed that there was a need to redress the balance of discipline and child-centred care in juvenile institutions.

Carpenter set up a number of schools where corporal punishment was banned and the discipline was carried out through 'the master's own firmness, order and kindness' (Bridgeland 1971, cited in Cooper 1999, p. 16). As far back as 1851, Mary Carpenter was campaigning for approaches which 'touched the inner spirit' of the child (Cole et al, 1998, p. 8).

Behavioural view

Britain's early venture into understanding the behaviour of children was followed in America in the 1950s. In America, two different groups begin to look into classrooms in a more systematic way to address specific aspects of managing a class. The first group were the behaviourists, who drew from a rich knowledge base built on a history of experimental studies. The behaviourists were exploring emerging principles and concepts in classroom management and began to develop new techniques to apply to the classroom. The second group were ecological researchers who developed strategies for classroom use by documenting variations in student behaviour in different settings and then in response to differences in teacher behaviour. Let us briefly explore the contribution these groups made to developing a more psychological vantage point to view student misbehaviour.

Behavioural research blossomed in the second half of the twentieth century as it applied its rich empirical foundations to socially relevant problems with children in clinical settings and then in a classroom setting. In particular, the research used the key elements of positive reinforcement, the operant view that behaviour is influenced by its consequences and that shaping behaviour is contingent on extinction and punishment. This field of study led to the development of Applied Behaviour Analysis (Baer, Wolf, and Risley, 1968; Kazdin, 1978).

> 'Applied Behaviour Analysis' refers to the systematic efforts to change socially important behaviours in positive ways through the application of behavioural principles, with strict reliance in the frequent, repeated assessment of observable and dependent variables (Landrum and Kauffman, cited in Evertson and Weinstein, 2006, p. 53).

The development of Applied Behaviour Analysis enabled the systematic study of behaviour in classrooms. Initial studies were limited to shaping low-level behaviours, such as students continually talking or getting out of their seat, through schedules of reinforcement. Early research identified that generalising or transferring laboratory techniques to the classroom needed altering. Alterations were needed because, unlike animals, humans had language—so it was possible to offer verbal prompts and reinforcers rather than just waiting for the desired behaviours to appear and then reinforce them. What developed was the 'Rules, Ignore and Praise' (RIP) sequence of behaviourist management.

The second learning for behavioural researchers was that the behavioural reinforcements needed to sustain appropriate behaviour were impossible to enforce with the number of students in the class. Behaviourists developed the reinforcement of a group of behaviours (such as achievement on tests, participation in class, and completion of work) rather than just discrete behaviours. Behaviourists developed a range of refinements that were more appropriate to the classroom—individual or group points rather than giving out and collecting up tokens; options to select the type of reinforcement from a range of options to avoid reinforcement saturation. Behavioural research was faithful to its empirical base; however, it did expand the application beyond the laboratory to suit the classroom. An example of this is the principle 'extinction through ignoring'. It is potentially dangerous to ignore some behaviours as well as the reality of these behaviours affecting the other students. Ignoring students is still a strategy we can use, but it has faded from being a key behavioural technique.

Critical reflection

> Quick fix behaviour management programs have short lives because they seek to bleach the complexity from the colourful life of classrooms....simply put, my argument revolves around the belief that discipline is much more than the imposition of someone else's order (Roger Slee, cited in Freiberg, J. (1999) *Beyond Behaviourism: Changing the Classroom Management Paradigm.* Allyn and Bacon: Boston, p. 38).

Roger Slee argues for a particular approach to classroom management and is critical of other more teacher-centred approaches.

1 Working with a peer, discuss Slee's statement and your level of agreement.

2 What do you think Slee is implying by stating that discipline is more than the imposition of someone else's order?

3 In relation to your management plan, develop a stance on classroom management and defend this stance with reference to literature and the research evidence outlined above.

THE RISE OF BEHAVIOURISM IN THE UNITED KINGDOM

As a result of the Underwood Report in 1955 a shift in thinking towards the behavioural approach began in Britain; however, it was not until the 1970s that the education system moved more to a behavioural approach. The 1970s witnessed a gradual rejection of the pioneers' humanistic approach with their belief in meeting the educational needs of the child. This new educational perspective was partly in response to the increase in day school provision for maladjusted students and the change in thinking about the approach to maladjustment. The belief that these new educational settings could make a difference and be accessible to the maladjusted child was influenced by the school of behavioural psychology. This new approach gave importance to the educational psychologist who now possessed knowledge and skills that could help teachers improve their classroom management without attending lengthy courses in psychotherapy (Cooper, 1999b). This meant that there was now a means of intervention that could potentially take place in the classroom. The ascendancy of the educational psychologist and behavioural approaches to classroom management in Britain heralded a new educational perspective. By the 1980s, the 'behavioural model' had become central to the theory and practice of dealing with behaviour problems in children. The Elton Report (1989) was commissioned in response to teacher concerns about safety and the increase in disruptive student behaviour. The report had 136 recommendations and highlighted the growing influence of behavioural psychology in approaches to classroom management.

Although behavioural approaches to classroom management have a long history and involvement in empirical studies, some commentators think that behaviourists do not know as much as they report (Gallagher, 2004) and that the empirical data does not provide teachers with much direction. Within teacher education institutions, the inclusion of behaviourist approaches or the study of behaviourist principles is hotly debated. Often the inclusion of a behavioural approach is dependent on the lecturer and her or his background in teaching. Special educators (skilled in Applied Behaviour Analysis and frequent readers of functional assessment reports) are more likely to include and focus heavily on behavioural approaches compared with regular classroom teachers. The debate is often polarised between those that support the principles to guide and nurture classroom practices and opponents of this approach, who view the principles as being developed on animals in a laboratory and think they are employed in an unsympathetic clinical manner, which should be avoided when teaching children. This dichotomy highlights a shift in thinking about methods of engaging students in meaningful learning towards something more than a unidimensional system of rewards and punishments, obedience and control. It is this unidimensional view that is linked to behaviourist approaches, and whether right or not, that is where people accept or reject behaviourist thinking.

Placemat activity: what is classroom management?

How is your management plan developing? So far, we have had the chance to reflect on our beliefs or assumptions to student learning, behaviour and the level of control we are comfortable with, which is a good start. As you read the resilience research and the theory behind the Positive Learning Framework, we need to begin to identify the key characteristics of a definition or description of classroom management. One way to do this is for you to explore the key characteristics in classroom management and compare your ideas with other students or friends.

This activity can be done by yourself, however, in keeping with the idea of developing a range of strategies to use with students, we have set out a cooperative learning strategy as an example of how you can involve all students in a way that is safe and that makes them accountable for contributing to the class. It is called a placemat activity.

Placemat

The placemat is drawn on a large sheet of paper. The page is divided so that each group member (groups of four are ideal) has a section to write in with a square or circle in the middle to record the group response. Students are given an issue, topic or question to consider and they begin the process by considering their responses and ideas. Responses are recorded in their section of the placemat. Students share their perspectives and a team response is recorded in the middle of the sheet. Possible follow-up activities could include class members walking around the classroom, considering the responses given by different groups and how these vary from their own responses.

Figure 3.3 A placemat template

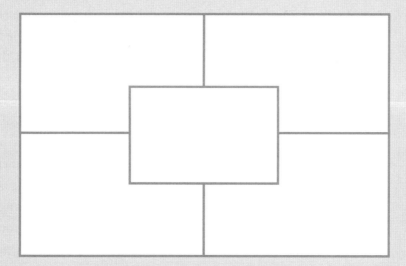

1   Have a go at drawing up a placemat.
2   In your space on the placemat write down:
    a   What does classroom management mean to you?
    b   What does classroom management look like, feel like and sound like in your class?
    Allow yourself or your group of friends five minutes to complete this task.
3   Once everyone has explained what is in their section, the group will need to write down the common elements in the middle box. Allow two minutes each for feedback and five minutes for noting what you have in common.
4   From this activity, begin to write a short definition of classroom management that reflects your main ideas and emerging philosophy. Keep this definition so that it can be re-worked and developed as you read the text and develop your management plan.

Ecological viewpoints

The origins of the ecological perspective in classroom management are nestled in the broader field of research that focussed on classroom organisation and management. Urie Bronfenbrenner (1989) proposed this interdisciplinary perspective of child development in his seminal work *The Ecology of Human Development*. Bronfenbrenner acknowledged that humans do not develop in isolation but in relation to their family, home, school, community and society. Research in the 1970s in America used Bronfenbrenner's concept of the ecology or *habitat* in a 'context with distinct characteristic purposes, dimensions, features, and processes that have consequences for the occupants in that setting' (Doyle 1986). From an ecological perspective, the classroom is an environment where students are grouped into a class with one teacher for the purposes of learning. The characteristics of the individuals, the physical setting, and the dimensions of the classroom (Doyle, 1986) all combine to create demands and pressures on everyone in the classroom. The demands of thirty students in a room with one teacher highlight the tasks of classroom management, where the teacher will engage all students in meaningful learning for the duration of their time together. Student behaviour is context specific.

A foundation stone of the ecological approach to human behaviour is the notion that the origins and purpose of human behaviour interact. Bronfenbrenner's (1979) work on human development has significantly furthered the ways in which the ecological approach can be used. Bronfenbrenner (1979) uses an ecological orientation to view behaviour and development. He states that 'what matters for behaviour and development is the environment as it is *perceived* rather than as it may exist in "objective" reality'. Bronfenbrenner believed that children and adults acted differently in the laboratory than they did in the actual settings of life. As a result, these differences are significant as they 'illuminate the various meanings of these types of settings to the participants, as partly a function of their social background and experience.'(Bronfenbrenner, 1979, p. 5). An ecological approach encourages seeking out a broader understanding of the behaviour than just from one narrow context.

As mentioned as part of our consilience of perspectives, Bronfenbrenner (2004) developed his ecology of human development further in his last textbook. The text *Making Human Beings Human* is the culmination of

Bronfenbrenner's work. In this book, Bronfenbrenner extends his model to highlight the potential humans possess for positive development. In the book's introduction he states, 'To a greater extent than any other species human beings create the environments that shape the course of human development … their actions influence the multiple physical and cultural tiers of the ecology that shapes them, and this agency makes humans—for better or for worse—active producers of their development'. As participants in creating positive environments, we recognise that students need communities (home, school, peer, broader communities) that nurture their physical, emotional and intellectual needs. Bronfenbrenner believed that the absolute minimum dosage of connection for each child was at least one adult who is crazy about him or her.

Process–outcome and school effectiveness research view

The next phase in our research understanding of classroom management was different in nature and intent from previous behavioural and ecological studies. Process–outcome (teacher effects) studies were more interested in the effects of teacher behaviours on student outcomes and not psychologically oriented per se. Process–outcome (teacher effects) studies began in the 1960s and continued in the 1980s and are gaining favour again with the spotlight on teacher and school accountability as well as on raising student achievement standards. Process–outcome research explored the relationship between teacher behaviours and interaction patterns, and their subsequent outcomes, such as achievement. Several of these studies built upon and extended the earlier study by Kounin (Anderson, Evertson and Brophy, 1979: Brophy and Evertson, 1976).

Anderson, Evertson and Brophy, (1979) identified clusters of behaviours that effective teachers displayed in their Third Grade study. Brophy (cited in Evertson and Weinstein, 2006, p. 30) lists the following findings:

- conveying purposefulness
- teaching students appropriate conduct
- maintaining student attention.

These effective classroom managers clearly established expectations for student behaviour. Similarly, Evertson and Emmer (1982) in their Junior High study found similar teacher behaviours. Brophy (cited in Evertson and

Weinstein, 2006, p. 31–2) notes that effective teachers in the Junior High School study had the following characteristics:

- instructing student in rules and procedures
- monitoring student compliance with rules
- communicating information
- organising instruction.

This research has had a significant impact on teacher education as it identified discrete behaviours that pre-service teachers can learn and practice while in schools. However, it is important to note that the predominant approach to classroom management was the behavioural paradigm. Students were managed by consequences or rewards and punished if needed. Although we will explore these discrete behaviours in Chapter 4, the classroom has moved on from a teacher-directed classroom to a more student-centred classroom since this research was conducted.

A number of influential theorists began to develop approaches to the classroom in the 1960s that had their origins in clinical practice or psychiatry outside of classroom rather than empirical studies. These theorists focussed more on the interpersonal aspect of education and student socialisation. They did not produce marketable packaged programs. Early pioneers in this area were Fritz Redl and William Wattenberg (refer to Table 7.1 on 241 for more information). Their work with delinquent youth provided them with a positive framework from which to view youth. They believed that young people need support in showing self-control and reality appraisal. Reality appraisal refers to students' ability to see the consequences of their behaviour on the broader community, which assists them to overcome, in the moment, frustrations with situational assistance. For teachers, the lasting contribution of Redl and Wattenberg is their explanation of 'group dynamics' or 'group life in the classroom'. They believed that students assume roles in groups and behave in that role, which is different from individual behaviour.

In their book, *Children Who Hate* Redl and Wattenberg (1951) explored the distorted private logic of youth in conflict. They describe in detail their thinking errors. Subsequent research by Dodge (1993) and work by psychologist John Gibbs and colleagues (Gibbs, Potter and Goldstein, 1995) also highlighted patterns of thinking errors of youth in conflict. Redl had enormous experience in working with troubled youth and was a campaigner for their better treatment. Brendtro and Shahbazian (2004) quote Redl as describing America as an 'underdeveloped country' in the way that the citizens of the country profess their love of children but practice neglect of children and youth in conflict. In 1957, Redl and Wineman wrote *The Aggressive Child*. In this text, they outlined how teachers and frontline workers with youth need skills that are proven, practical and can be used in the real world in the young person's 'life space'. This model was refined by William Morse and Nicholas Long and then subsequently renamed *Life Space Crisis Intervention* by Long, Wood and Fescer (1991).

In the late 1950s and 1960s, Rudolph Dreikurs produced his theory of Democratic Teaching and Management. Dreikurs developed this approach based on the seminal work of Alfred Adler (1927, 1930). Dreikurs proposed to teachers that students behave out of 'mistaken goals' as a way of compensating for feelings of inferiority, or lacking a sense of belonging to the classroom, which triggers behaviour designed to get attention, gain power, exact revenge or gain sympathy through displays of inferiority. Dreikurs also emphasised that teachers should allow students to experience natural consequences to their behaviour or, in certain situations, impose consequences that are logically related to the behaviour. Bommarito (1977) suggested that Dreikurs' lack of clarity around consequences means they are no better than punishments in a behavioural approach. Alfie Kohn (1993) has also referred to Dreikurs logical consequences as 'thin veiled threats' and 'punishment light'. Dreikurs viewed the school as a site to nurture young people and to develop social interest in assisting students feel they belong, feel valued and develop positive self-worth (Pryor and Tollerud, 1999). This need affirmation was best done in a 'democratic' classroom that was characterised by 'encouragement' rather than praise. In relation to our research story, there has been practically no research on the effectiveness of Dreikur's or Adler's approach, however Hartwell (1975) reported increased student behaviour after professional learning in Dreikur's methods.

In the 1970s, Rogerian person-centred psychology was the basis for Teacher Effectiveness Training (TET) developed by Gordon (1974). TET was a program that trained teachers in a range of approaches to handle student misbehaviour. Importantly it looked at who owned the problem in an effort to work towards a no-lose agreement with students. Problem ownership attempts to help students develop responsibility for changing their behaviour. TET included a set of skills that the teacher could use to increase their listening capacity and their ability to defuse situations through empathic understanding and the use of 'I-messages'. (I messages are three-part messages that are intended to help students understand how their behaviour affects others in the room. A number of studies have used elements of TET in their research. Gordon's concept of problem ownership was incorporated into research in how teachers perceive and cope with difficult behaviour (Brophy, 1996; Brophy and McCaslin, 1992). Two studies used 'I statements' with disruptive students and found that the behaviour was influenced positively (Carducci, 1976, Peterson et al, 1979).

At the time, Gordon was developing TET, William Glasser was making some influential contributions to classroom management and school management. Glasser's earlier work was on Reality Therapy (1965) and Control Theory (1986). However, his Choice Theory (1997) has the most currency with classroom teachers. Glasser's work can be seen to build upon Adler's earlier work as it believes all humans have needs for survival, to belong, for power, for freedom and for fun. The task of educators is to meet these needs in the classroom and students will then choose appropriate behaviour. Glasser maintained that in a 'Quality School' (1993) it is possible to meet these needs.

Approaches to classroom management that are derived from clinical psychology or psychiatry are more difficult to quantify. Work done by Redl, Morse, Dreikurs, and Gordon, and elements of Glasser's work do not have the rich empirical history that behavioural approaches have. Behavioural approaches are concerned with observable behaviour, which is different to students' private logic, emotions and beliefs. This is not to say that there is no evidence of the veracity or application to the classroom of the psychological approach. On the contrary, as we have seen in Chapters 1 and 2, we have an emerging body of evidence to support these approaches in the classroom and at a whole-school approach.

A major shift from intervention to prevention

Often the approaches to student learning are grounded in the last century's thinking, which linked effective teaching with obedience and emphasised compliance over student creativity and self-direction. As we have mentioned in earlier sections, classroom management is more than external controls and relying on rewards or punishment; it is about developing self-regulated, responsible students who are in a learning partnership with the teacher. The research story above reflects this major shift from intervention to prevention. Freiberg and LaPointe, cited in Evertson and Weinstein (2006) highlight how current approaches to classroom management and student behaviour have 'emerged from decades of behaviourism to instructional and person-centred approaches to classroom management' (Rogers and Freiberg, 1994; Good and Brophy, 2003). The importance of this shift is not in the strategies included in a particular program but the philosophical shift in teachers' thinking about the roles and place of the learner and the changing role of teachers in this learning partnership.

Weinstein reviews the shift in paradigms in Freiberg's (1999) text *Beyond Behaviourism: Changing the Classroom Management Paradigm*. Weinstein described the emerging themes in the shift as:

a   from management as a bag of tricks to management as decision making that necessitates ongoing professional development, expertise in knowledge, practice and introspection

b   from an emphasis on obedience and compliance to procedures that advance self-direction

c   from an emphasis on rules to the socio-emotional relationship that includes trust and caring

d   from management that is teacher-directed work (busy work) to an active student-centred learning environment.

The shift in thinking and evidence about student misbehaviour and approaches in classroom management does not disregard lessons learned from previous knowledge or vantage points. Instead, what we are seeing is a new era that is different from earlier years. The Positive Learning Framework, built on the Circle of Courage, was created in response to this new era. The PLF identifies an approach that views students positively and believes in the development of quality learning environments that are responsive to student needs, caring and where meaningful learning occurs. This approach is challenging for some teachers and schools and explains why we have stated, as one of our guiding principles to this book, that to make this shift will require *professional knowledge, reflection, continued optimism and time.*

Education frameworks to view student behaviour

The rhetoric in most countries is for public education systems to raise the achievement levels of all students. The ideas of 'no child left behind' and 'success for all' assumes that when children start school they will experience success and any individual differences will be minimised as the students progress through schooling. Research identifies that this is not the case: students who do well will get better and the ones that are struggling will get worse. Initial disadvantage is compounded over time in a phenomenon known as the Matthew effect. The focus on a national curriculum and the introduction of standardised testing with the publishing of league tables of school performance will increase the pressure on schools and teachers to raise the academic achievement of students so that they are above the national benchmarks.

There is no single way to lessen the achievement gap or for public education systems to strengthen their schools. Most studies of student academic progress are only a snapshot of a single year. Many studies do not take into account the student's classroom behaviour. It is conceivable that students fall behind their peers because of their classroom behaviour. If this is the case then appropriate interventions that focus on moderating that behaviour might improve their performance and indeed set them on a successful academic trajectory.

Most of our current understanding of student misbehaviour emanates from a mental health paradigm. This research is distinctive in nature as it usually focuses on children and adolescents with severe behavioural problems. This research aims to improve the diagnosis of the problem to help improve the clinical intervention provided by psychologists and psychiatrists. From a research point of view or public health perspective, schools are attractive as they offer large populations of students for study. Teachers are usually not partners in this process but rather used as data collectors, as educational issues are seldom directly addressed in this work. While teachers do have children in their classes with mental health issues, their responsibility serves a different purpose; their job is to teach a prescribed curriculum.

From an educational perspective, student behaviour is problematic when it impedes classroom teaching and academic performance; whether the behaviour meets the definitional criteria for mental health disorders is of lesser consequence. This is not to ignore the substantial numbers of students with diagnosable disorders who attend schools and it does not lessen the fact that students with challenging behaviours demand an inordinate amount of time and resources and can threaten the safety of others and interrupt learning. However, there are many students in our classrooms that have not been clinically diagnosed with a mental health disorder, and yet they behave in ways that that impede their academic progress. For these students, the mental health and medical research is largely irrelevant. While students who act out their frustration are likely to be disengaged, students who quietly opt out of activities may be just as disengaged, despite not showing it outwardly. Hence, the meaning of 'behaviour problem' depends very much on the perspective adopted.

Teachers attend to student behaviour that restricts learning, which is not of interest to mental health experts. Motivating and engaging a class of students in learning is a constant challenge to teachers. One single student can throw a lesson into disarray—other students are then distracted and time for learning is lost. However, passive, unthreatening behaviour can also impede learning because successful understanding of concepts and skills often takes concentration and persistent effort. An educational view needs to build an understanding, and distinction between, productive behaviours (those that enable learning) and unproductive behaviours (those that impede learning).

The Pipeline Project is a recent longitudinal study in Western Australia (Angus, McDonald, Ormond, Rybarczyk, Taylor and Winterton, 2009) entitled 'Trajectories of Classroom Behaviour and Academic Progress: A Study of Engagement with Learning'. It attempts to develop an educational view of behaviour and academic achievement. The Pipeline Project aimed to investigate whether students who behave unproductively or perform poorly on academic tests tend to recover or whether they slide inexorably into the tail 'pipeline' of low-performing, troublesome students. The project also sought to describe the kinds of student behaviour that were impeding the students' academic progress. These were referred to as unproductive behaviours.

The idea of describing behaviours as productive or unproductive is a departure from the conventional practice of classifying child and adolescent behaviour. These constructs bring together two concepts that traditionally have been kept separate, namely behaviour exhibited in classrooms and academic performance. The research asked teachers to make judgments about whether the students exhibited particular forms of behaviour and whether the behaviour was affecting their academic performance. In this respect, the Pipeline Project broke new ground. This is helpful for us to get a picture of student behaviour as well a language to use that focuses our interventions on re-engaging students in a bid to enhance their academic progress.

Models of classroom management

One way to bring together the broad discussion of frameworks is to see how current models are grouped according to assumptions and theories that align themselves with these broader frameworks (Table 7.1 on page 241 provides an overview of current theorists). Out of these broad philosophies, particular theorists have developed models of classroom management that are aligned to the core assumptions in each framework. A process that categorises these models using student autonomy or the theoretical basis to the model is very helpful. Several authors have tried to categorise these broad approaches and align current theories to particular approaches. Edwards (2008) has grouped the theories into three categories:

- management theories
- nondirective intervention theories
- leadership theories.

Management theories present students' growth and development as consequences of external control. Students are blank slates that are written on by their environment. In this category, changing students' behaviours is a matter of changing the environmental conditions so that they elicit desired responses. Theorists include Skinner (Behaviour Modification), Jones (Jones model) and Canter (Assertive Discipline).

Non-directive intervention theories are at the opposite end of the child autonomy continuum from management theories. In this category, children have the capacity for self-regulation and self-actualisation. Coercive control interventions are unnecessary for children to reach their potential, as they will naturally learn and become more self-directed as they grow. Theorists include Thomas Gordon (Teacher Effectiveness Training).

Leadership theories are a mixture of the two previous theories, in that children grow through a process of interaction of both internal and external influences. Children grow from a constant interplay between themselves and their social world. Theorists include Glasser (Choice theory) and Dreikurs (Logical Consequences).

Louise Porter (2000) categorised the models of classroom management based on a 'Power Continuum' of student autonomy. At one end of the continuum, the teacher had all the power and the student had none, while at the other end the teacher had little power while the students had most. Porter then placed theories of student behaviour along the continuum according to their level of student autonomy. In Figure 3.4 we have taken the theorists outlined in Table 7.1 (page 241) and placed them along Porter's continuum.

Figure 3.4 Porter's continuum

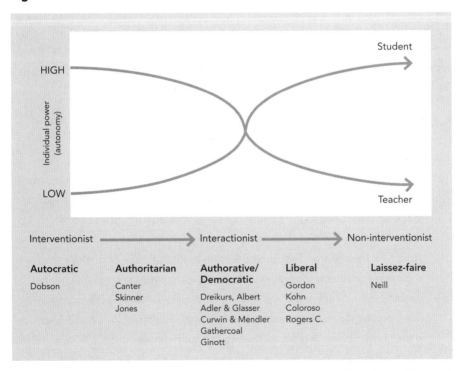

Source: adapted from Porter, 2000, p. 11

Porter has given us a quick summary of the models and their origins in broader frameworks. We can also see how Edwards and Porter are supportive of each other as to where they have placed models along the continuum.

As you become aware of your philosophical assumptions and beliefs in your classroom management plan, you can use the Porter continuum to guide your reading on likeminded theories in a range of models.

This chapter did not set out to give you a comprehensive summary of the main classroom management theorists currently on the market. It is preferable for you to pursue ideas and approaches that appeal to you from the natural history of classroom management described above rather than read a collection of theorists that do not appear to match your beliefs and philosophy. The Critical Reflection questions at the conclusion of Chapter 1 and the Critical Reflections in this chapter will assist you in clarifying how you view students and their behaviour in a classroom setting.

Case study

The extract is an email from a pre-service teacher in their final year of teacher education. They are out in school on their final placement. The school is in the country and the pre-service teacher is finding the going tough.

My first week at school was hand over and I was lucky in the sense the previous teacher was still there to guide and help me, she has been moved into a specialist role within the school. The first day I walked into the classroom there where children climbing on desks and running around the room yelling when it was time to work at their desks. In no uncertain terms, my children are 'feral'. The behaviour is not only in my classroom but also in the whole school and is a challenge daily. I am now into the second week of having my own class full time, by myself. The first week I was very strict with the children and came down on them like a ton of bricks. I am still having problems though with their behaviour and am constantly trying new things and seeking advice from other teachers. Nothing is working at the moment. As much as I keep smiling things are coming to a head. Last week I broke down in tears and wanted to come home.

Do you have any strategies on managing the behaviour within my class? I have tried all that I know and it is driving me insane. I had a really bad week last week as the students bounce off the walls. I have tried using sport to tire them out but that doesn't work either. I am open to any suggestions you may have.

As a behaviour management consultant, develop a response that is helpful to him or her. What would you suggest to the teacher so that he or she can gain control of the class and learning can begin?

Once you have developed a plan, try to identify the following elements in your response:

1 What are the guiding assumptions about the nature of young people and development of student responsibility included in your response?
2 Can you identify where you have articulated:
    a   a vision for working with youth within a learning environment?
    b   the essential components for effective instruction?
    c   elements of a safe and accountable learning environment?
3 Can you identify the paradigms from which your response is built or what research perspectives are obvious in your response? Are they consistent with your beliefs and values?

Developing my classroom management plan

In this chapter, we have explored a range of ways to view student behaviour and how, in particular periods of history, certain viewpoints have held more sway than others. In reflecting on your philosophy section of your management plan, consider the following questions.

1 How do you view student behaviour—is it needs-based, environmental, genetic, socio-cultural, ecological?
2 Where do you position the 'problem' of behaviour? Is it within the child, all external or a combination of both?
3 When you discipline a child, what do you want as the long-term outcome?
4 To what extent can the school/teacher change a student's behaviour?
5 Looking at Porter's continuum, where would you position yourself? Can you support where you are in your assumptions?
6 Which theorists outlined in Table 7.1 (page 241) support your assumptions? Can you identify the parts or elements of their theory that support your approach?

Summary

The natural history of research and program development in classroom management reflects a major shift from intervention to prevention. Current approaches to classroom management and student behaviour have 'emerged from decades of behaviourism to instructional and person-centred approaches to classroom management' (Rogers and Freiberg, 1994; Good and Brophy, 2003). The importance of this shift is not in the strategies included in a particular program but the philosophical movement in teachers' thinking about the roles and place of the learner and the changing role of teachers in this learning partnership. The shift in thinking is reflected in an approach to develop an educational framework of student behaviour that focuses on behaviours that are productive or unproductive in academic achievement.

All classroom management programs are built upon a set of assumptions or approaches that will align themselves to different philosophical orientations. In analysing forty current programs available to schools from different philosophical orientations, Freiberg (2006) identifies three common themes and two sub-themes. The three common themes are moving beyond discipline to an instructional and person-centred approach; school connectedness, where more students are invited and involved in activities across the school; and socio-emotional emphasis, which is just as important as academic achievement and caring and trust, and which is at the heart of teaching. The two sub-themes are positive school and classroom climates—classroom and instructional management in a safe school is vital.

This shift in thinking and evidence about student misbehaviour and approaches in classroom management does not disregard lessons learned from previous knowledge or vantage points. Instead, we are seeing a new era. The Positive Learning Framework, built on the Circle of Courage, is a response to this new era. The PLF identifies an approach similar to the themes in effective programs identified by Freiberg that views students positively and believes in the development of quality learning environments that are responsive to student needs and are built on care and trust. The PLF also builds on evidence-based research on effective classroom practices to engage students in learning. We will explore these practices, and how to apply them in the classroom, in the next chapter.

FURTHER READING

Bronfenbrenner, U. 2004, *Making Human Beings Human: Bioecological Perspectives on Human Development*, Sage Publications, Thousand Oaks, CA.

Edwards, C. & Watts, V. 2004, *Classroom Discipline and Management: An Australasian Perspective*, John Wiley & Sons, Milton, Qld.

Levin, J. & Nolan, J. 2007, *Principles of Classroom Management: A Professional Decision-Making Model*, 5th edn, Allyn & Bacon, Boston.

Jones, V. & Jones, L. 2007, *Comprehensive Classroom Management: Creating Communities of Support and Solving Problems*, Pearson, Boston.

Glasser, W. 2005, *Every Student can Succeed*, William Glasser, Inc., Chatsworth, CA.

Kohn, A. 2001, *Beyond Discipline: From Compliance to Community*, Merrill/Prentice, Upper Saddle River, NJ.

Manning L. K. & Bucher, K. T. 2007, *Classroom Management: Models, Applications, and Cases*, 2nd edn, Pearson Educational, New Jersey.

Pryor, D. B. & Tollerud, T. R. 1999, 'Applications in Adlerian Principles in School Settings', *Professional School Counselling*, 2(4), pp. 299–304.

Sackett D. L. 1996, et al. 'Evidence Based Medicine: What it is and What it isn't', *British Medical Journal*, 312, pp. 71–72.

Seligman, M. 2007, *The Optimistic Child*, Mariner Books, New York.

Tremblay, R., Hartup, W. & Archer, J. 2005, *Developmental Origins of Aggression*, Guilford Press, New York.

WEBSITES

www.ted.com/talks/martin_seligman_on_the_state_of_psychology.html
    Martin Seligman talks about psychology, what makes us happy, and positive interventions and skills of happiness.

www.minniscomms.com.au/educationtoday/articles.php?articleid=148
    In 2008, Geelong Grammar introduced Martin Seligman's Positive Education program—this article gives an overview of the program and its implementation.

www.mindmatters.edu.au
    MindMatters is a national mental health initiative for secondary schools. MindMatters is a resource and professional development program supporting Australian secondary schools in promoting and protecting the mental health, social and emotional wellbeing of all the members of school communities.

www.wested.org/cs/we/view/u/339
    Bonnie Benard's website, with resources, training and professional development in the field of prevention and resilience/youth development theory and policy.

http://resilnet.uiuc.edu/library.html

The ResilienceNet Virtual Library is a collection of publications related to the resilience of children and families in the face of adversity.

www.health.gov.au/internet/main/publishing.nsf/Content/70DA14F816CC7A8F CA25728800104564/$File/young.pdf

Link to the report on the Mental Health of Young People in Australia – the child and adolescent component of the National Survey of Health and Well-being conducted in 2000

http://nceph.anu.edu.au/Staff_Students/staff_pages/eckersley_publications.htm

Publications by Richard Eckersley a visiting fellow at the National Centre for Epidemiology and Population Health at the Australian National University.

www.scotland.gov.uk/Resource/Doc/149771/0039878.pdf

The Scottish Executive has committed to instituting 'regular major surveys of teachers' and pupils' experiences and perceptions of behaviour and discipline in schools' (Scottish Executive, 2004a). This study represents the first of these surveys.

www.pipelineproject.org.au.

The Pipeline Report is a research report looking at the relationship between academic achievement and behaviour. It makes a good point about productive and unproductive behaviours that assist or impede academic progress.

Proactive Teacher Behaviours

Planning for quality learning environments

In this chapter, we begin to explore and practice the practical actions a teacher takes to ensure that their students are actively engaged in learning (and we will continue this in Chapter 5). We are now moving into the instruction components of our definition of classroom management where we stated, '*classroom management involves* **teacher actions** *and* **instructional techniques** *to* **create a learning environment that facilitates and supports active engagement** *in both academic and socio-emotional learning*'. Classroom management and instruction are intertwined as they work together to facilitate learning.

The Positive Learning Framework (PLF) provides an overview that helps us to identify explicit behaviours and actions that teachers do to develop quality learning environments. Quality learning environments do not just happen, nor does effective management of student behaviour. Effective teachers work hard at developing an environment where students learn and feel safe enough to risk a wrong answer. In this chapter, we will focus on preventative elements in Phase One and Two of the PLF. We will address how teachers' prepare for a class before the students arrive, looking at how they analyse their expectations of the students and how the class will operate regarding rules, entry and exit behaviours and routines for working. The chapter will also look at how effective teachers set up the physical environment so that it is welcoming and set out in a way that is conducive to learning. Next, we will view the 'Beginning' components (Phase Two of the PLF) of lesson design and look at how effective teachers convey clear lesson outcomes as well as motivating students to learn.

Positive Learning Framework: elements covered in this chapter

Prevention: self awareness and management plan	Prevention: lesson design
Before each class	*Beginning*
• self awareness	• whole-class attention (C2S)
• proactive thinking—indiscipline will happen at some stage	• clear outcomes conveyed to students
• caring and welcoming classroom	• motivation 'hook for learning'— set induction
• classroom layout and resources	• advanced organiser
• high and specific expectations	• recall prior knowledge
• rules, routines and procedures	• level of student engagement

What is engagement?

There is widespread use of the term *engagement* in educational literature. In your teacher education course you may come across the term in regards to you being engaging or the need for engagement in boys' education, for example. Teachers need to differentiate the curriculum to engage low-ability students or difficult students and in some universities, the term appears on student evaluation forms discussing the level of engagement for different lecturers or tutors. Engaging students in learning is an obvious component of a quality learning environment. Let us briefly outline what the term means in this text.

As a concept in classroom management, engagement has evolved from reactive responses built on reward–punishment and control and coercion to student-centred classrooms that focus on learning, self-regulation and socio-emotional development. Engagement is a complex concept. Early research into the topic identified teacher pedagogy and time spent on academic tasks as main factors influencing student engagement. Newman, Welhage and Lamborn, (1992) see engagement in academic work as the student's psychological investment and effort directed towards work. Corno and Mandinach, (2004) viewed it as more of a disposition than a set of specific behaviours.

The range of explanations highlight that the concept of engagement is multifaceted and involves factors of student disposition as well as the pedagogy of the teacher. Reeve (2006), who built upon the research of Fredricks, Blumenfeld and Paris (2004) and Furrer and Skinner (2003), outlined in detail the student element of engagement—identifying engagement as consisting of a student's behavioural intensity, emotional quality and personal investment in their involvement during a lesson. In Reeve's model (2006), engagement is expressed in a student showing attention, effort and persistence. We need to add teacher instruction to this explanation. It is through deliberate teacher actions that encourage participation and the development of competence that students are engaged in meaningful learning. Engagement is a product of student's attention, effort, emotions, cognitive investment and participation and teacher actions that encourage participation and the development of competence.

Research by Csikszentmihalyi and colleagues (Hunter and Csikszentmihalyi, 2003; Shernoff, Csikszentmihalyi, Schneider and Shernoff, 2003) looked at the level of engagement of secondary-aged students. The researchers had the students record their activity and feeling states eight times during the day by using wristwatch devices. Most of the day was spent in non-interactive activities and only a small percentage was spent in activities that involved discussion or group work. The researchers used student interest, enjoyment and concentration as a measure of engagement. The students reported higher levels of engagement in group activities compared with lectures, exams or viewing in-class videos. The students felt more engaged in tasks that they felt competent in completing but that were challenging. Csikszentmihalyi (1996) stated that people engrossed in an activity involving concentration and creativity were in a state called *flow*. The students' involvement and engagement in flow activities was different from what they experienced when working in activities they found too easy or too difficult. The different levels of engagement is striking, with only 42 per cent of students reporting that they were attentive in easy and non-challenging activities compared with 73 per cent saying they were paying full attention in activities that were challenging and required more skill. Engagement is a product of teacher actions that encourage participation and the development of competence with student disposition of attention, emotions and cognitive investment. As we progress through the text, we will refer to this rich understanding of engagement that involves student dispositions and teacher actions.

Before the year starts

Effective teaching in the first few weeks

There is much energy, excitement and anxiety at the beginning of our first year of teaching. Most teachers feel anxious about the year ahead, about who will be in their class and if they will be organised enough. A successful start to the school year takes time, preparation and personal reflection. What do we need to do before the students arrive? Before we look at specifics, we will review the research to see what effective classroom managers do to ensure a smooth and successful start and how they maintain this throughout the year.

One of the benefits of the 'process–product' research in the 1980s was that it identified teacher practices that appeared to be effective. This research (Berliner, 1989; Brophy, 1989; Emmer and Evertson, 1981; Fisher et al, 1981) greatly enhanced our understanding of effective teaching by examining student-achievement outcomes associated with different teacher behaviours and management approaches. One of the significant findings identified what effective teachers did to get the school year off to a good start. This research on the beginning of the school year was predominantly carried out by Emmer, Evertson and Anderson (1980) and Evertson and Emmer (1982). Their studies supported earlier research by Kounin (1970) and Flanders (1970) and involved Third Grade and Junior High studies. Emmer, Evertson and Anderson (1980) found that a Third Grade classroom that appeared orderly and functioned smoothly resulted from teachers who had thorough preparation and organisation at the beginning of the school year. From day one and through the first week, important issues such as helping the students to get to know classmates, having a clear schedule and procedures for lunchtime and recess were constantly referred to. As the weeks progressed, the full range of procedures and routines were explained, which meant that students were not initially overloaded. These teachers taught procedures to students as they taught academic content. The authors noted that effective managers displayed three major groups of behaviours.

1 **Effective managers conveyed purposefulness**. Time for learning was maximised and that students were actively learning (rather than passively being quiet). Students were held accountable for completing tasks and time was scheduled to review learning.
2 **Teaching students appropriate conduct**. Teachers had clear expectations and students knew what behaviour was not tolerated. Students were taught specific behaviours, including specific learning behaviours (such as following directions in an activity).
3 **Maintaining student attention**. Teachers were vigilant for students exhibiting signs of boredom, confusion or inattentiveness. The class was arranged so that all students could see the front, lessons had distinct beginnings and endings and the teachers had the capacity to gain whole-class attention when required.

These effective teachers maintained this activity in the early weeks by constantly maintaining their expectations.

The Junior High Study (Evertson and Emmer, 1982) identified the following characteristics of effective teachers.

1 **Instructing students in rules and procedures.** These teachers explained their rules clearly and 'installed their procedures systematically'.

2 **Monitoring student compliance with rules**. The more effective teachers consistently monitored the students and intervened to correct poor behaviour. These teachers reminded students of the rules or described appropriate behaviour when giving feedback more often than other teachers.

3 **Communicating information.** These teachers gave instructions clearly and had the capacity to break down complex tasks into easy to follow steps.

4 **Organising instruction**. These teachers maximised student attention through well-planned lessons which had smooth transitions and lesson momentum.

The findings of these authors are as relevant today as they were when the research was conducted. Effective teachers are preventative in their planning, are skilled in instructional techniques, have well-thought-out responses to student misbehaviour and importantly (although not mentioned in this research) they are positive and respectful. One last positive finding in the research completed by Evertson and Harris (1999) was that when a group of teachers took part in professional learning workshops in effective management principles before the year started they were able to establish better-managed classrooms characterised by less disruption and more on-task behaviour than teachers who did not receive the training.

The research by Moskowitz and Hayman (1976) compared first year teachers with teachers identified as 'best'. What they found was that the experienced teachers took their time to set up an atmosphere in the class that was relaxed, they let the students get to know each other, they smiled, praised students and joked with them in the early days of the school year. In contrast, the beginning teachers they observed gave the class less orientation, were nervous and started teaching content very quickly. In other studies of the first few weeks of school, the effective teachers went to lengths to establish an orderly working climate where students knew each other and the expectations of the teacher. In the first week of school, for both the best and the first-year teachers, the behaviour of students was similar. In the next two weeks, the behaviour remained low-level for the best teacher but escalated for the first year teacher to become disruptive behaviour and remained that way for the year. In the best teachers' classes the behaviour also escalated but not to the high levels in the other class.

The beginning of the school year is very complex. There are so many practical tasks to do when the students arrive, especially taking into account how we, as teachers, feel inside! However, what we know is that the effective teachers give the students a roadmap to navigate the classroom, academic activities, behaviour and routines that will occur in the class. Remember, this class is new for the students as well as for you. This class has never been constructed in this way before with you as the teacher. You are setting up a new ecology. Effective managers at the start of the year are confident and clinical (we will explore the term 'clinical' further in Chapter 6). Nothing in the research suggests the best teachers were domineering, coercive or punitive.

Critical reflection

The research findings discussed above have a number of messages about effective teacher practices for the beginning of the school year. What are the key messages that you take from the research?

The messages from the research identify teacher attitude and disposition and teacher actions. One of the 'human' elements involved in being a recent graduate is the enormous emotional energy, anxiety, excitement and expectations that are swirling around inside you as you begin to teach your first class. It is difficult to predict what you will feel on the first day but let us have a go at predicting how you could feel and acknowledging how you currently deal with these feelings or emotions. This will give you an idea of what is happening when you have thirty students staring at you on day one!

We have given one example. See if you can complete the table for three or four emotions you expect to feel on the first day of teaching. If you have a close peer group at university, share your responses to see how others will cope with their first day of teaching.

Teacher attitudes	Teacher actions	Feeling/ emotions Day 1	Usual response	Action plan
• prepared and positive • need for connections, verbal and non-verbal	• have expectations written down • know how class is set out, how students enter and routines and so on	• anxious—will it go okay? • nervous—not knowing what to expect	• when nervous I speak a lot and very quickly	• recognise my response and have a written reminder 'SLOW DOWN' on lesson plan, along with expectations and class guidelines and so on
• need for group cohesion, develop community	• get to know you game • name game • what is around the school quiz	• unsure—will it work? • can I manage the whole group doing an unstructured activity—eager for success, fear it may not work	• get annoyed with those who purposefully ruin it—speak harshly, put downs	• recognise my need for it to go well and the student to like me and hold back on any sharp response to those who don't see it as important

One of the frequent statements I hear from pre-service teachers working in specialised or subject-specific learning spaces (early years, Music, Physical Education, library classes, Languages, Science, Design and Technology and so on) is that 'our space is different'. It is true that different spaces have different demands on teachers. However, the findings from research mentioned earlier from the Third Grade and Junior High Studies apply across learning areas and year levels. To reiterate, the effective strategies included:

- conveying purposefulness
- teaching students appropriate conduct

- maintaining student attention
- instructing student in rules and procedures
- monitoring student compliance with rules
- communicating information
- organising instruction.

In some of these areas, there is another layer to expectations around Occupational Health and Safety issues that are not negotiable. For example, if you are working in a wood or metal workshop you will have protocols for machinery use as well as personal safety protocols that include wearing ear plugs, safety glasses, a leather apron and closed-in shoes or boots. In these areas, accessing materials is also guided by protocols in lifting heavy objects, weight limits and the use of trolleys. The same would apply in Science laboratories or Home Economics kitchens wherever there are dangerous resources needed for teaching that subject.

A good point is made by Williams (2000), a music teacher who suggests to other choir teachers that they should cater for the developmental needs of the students and see these needs as assets, rather than something to fight against. Teachers can use students' developmental needs in teaching. In working with little children, teachers need to be aware of their attention span and level of social skilling. With upper primary or secondary classes the students' physicality, energy and need for peer acceptance requires teachers to construct a learning environment that uses these assets to engage them in learning.

Establishing class guidelines

As we have read above, there is good research evidence, as well as common sense reasons, that as teachers we need to establish rules and procedures in our classrooms. The reality is that just because we have rules, this does not mean that students will behave. Often when teachers feel under pressure from student behaviour the natural response is to set more rules or harsher punishments. In fact, this will only make the situation worse. What we need to do, in this section, is to put rules and procedures into a context and then describe ways that they can be developed in your class that enables students to 'buy-in' and have ownership of them as well as owning the consequences of their actions.

Any discussion on rules or student conduct in schools is always going to stimulate robust discussion among the staff. We all acknowledge that students need rules and that they need to follow them for an orderly learning environment to exist. How can there be any argument? There is argument because we all have our own ideas on what constitutes appropriate behaviour, we have our own beliefs on how children and young people should speak and behave, we have all been to school and experienced previous teacher expectations and rules that 'worked for me'. The area of rules is on one hand simple (we need to have them) yet on the other very complex (which ones do we select?) because we are confronting our beliefs and assumptions developed from the way we were raised and educated. From this viewpoint, it is easy to see why finding consensus among staff can be difficult.

Critical reflection

Values line

What is a values line?

A values line gives students an opportunity to place themselves in a line according to their opinion on a particular statement. Designate one side of the room as 'strongly disagree' end and the other side of the room as 'strongly agree'. Announce a contentious statement on a topic being discussed and then ask the students to place themselves along the line according to their beliefs about it. Ask students to substantiate why they chose a particular position.

Activity

This activity can be done individually or with a group of friends or other pre-service teachers.

1   Using a selection of four or five of the following statements, where would you place yourself on the values line according to your beliefs, and how would you 'defend' your position for each statement? If you have others involved, find an area you can use that has enough room

for people to move along an imaginary continuum. Can you convince others to shift to your viewpoint?

Statements:

- Students know the rules when they come to school, if they do the wrong thing they should be punished.
- It is the teacher's responsibility to teach students how they want them to behave in their class.
- Some students only learn when they are punished or harshly treated.
- Punishment controls the undesirable behaviour but doesn't teach the desirable behaviour.
- Students should follow the rules and not question them.
- Democracy is not workable in the classroom—the teacher needs to set the rules and tell students what will happen if they break them.
- Zero tolerance sets a standard that all students should follow no matter the behaviour or student.
- A quiet class means everyone is working.
- Children should do as they are told when they are told.
- Disruptive students should be excluded so others can learn.

2   Can you identify the foundation of your agreement or disagreement with peers? Understanding your beliefs and assumptions is crucial to responding respectfully to students when they misbehave rather than reacting out of an emotional response.

3   How might these beliefs be reflected in your management plan?

Students are emphatic that they want teachers who are able to maintain order, provide limits for behaviour and develop an environment in which they feel safe (Pomeroy, 1999; McDonald, 2001; Munn and Johnstone, 1990; Rogers, 1991 and Davidson, 1999). In other research, students wanted teachers who were cooperative (supportive, caring) as well as dominant (authoritative, leader). As mentioned previously, teachers need to provide love and limits. Students also respected teachers and found it easier to follow a rule if they knew the rationale behind the rule that they were being asked to obey. The literature on student perceptions of effective teachers highlight that students want teachers who are authoritative without being inflexible, threatening or punitive. Inflexible, punitive teachers are seen as unfair and uncaring.

Establishing classroom guidelines in your class

In developing a management plan, most teachers will include a section preventing student misbehaviour. Part of this section will be around the need for 'rules'. In developing your own rules, you will need to decide on the style or approach you will adopt for your rule creation. Will you develop rules (Weinstein and Mignano, 1993), a code of conduct (Albert, 1995) and class constitution (Freiberg, 1998)? Will you base them on a rights and responsibilities (Rogers, 1998), an understanding, or by guiding student behaviour (Porter, 2003)? You will need to decide this based on your educational philosophy and how you view student capacity to self manage. Your decision about your approach will affect how you frame your rules and the process you use to develop them. We have adopted an eclectic approach that is closer to a mix between Freiberg's constitution and Porter's guiding approach, as we believe that guiding is about working in partnership with students in a way that is educative and prosocial. Guidelines act as reference points for students to develop considerate and prosocial behaviour. Guidelines also give teachers the necessary freedom to respond to students in a manner that best suits their need(s) rather than prescriptively following pre-ordained responses.

The Positive Learning Framework incorporates the following beliefs in creating our classroom guidelines. These include:

- preventing student indiscipline
- developing responsibility and ownership for self-discipline in students
- raising expectations of behaviour where students assume greater autonomy
- developing caring and communal learning environments.

The thinking behind our guidelines requires us to involve the students. No teacher enters a classroom without any ideas on how the class will operate. In a negotiated process of developing class guidelines, the teacher needs to have a clear understanding of his or her standards of student and teacher behaviour. In our experience, the teacher's ideas and the student's knowledge of what helps a class create a positive learning environment are very similar.

A suggested process for developing class guidelines could include the following approach, which initially focuses on expectations and student experiences of successful classes.

EXPECTATIONS OF THIS CLASS

Using a 'Think, Pair, Share' or a 'Placemat' strategy, ask the students to identify what they are expecting from this class this year. What do they wish to achieve in the time that we will be together? Ask them to identify from their schooling experience (Year 1 students will have pretty good insights into this as well) what happened in classrooms where they learnt, felt safe and enjoyed. Record the responses on a table drawn on the board.

EXPECTATIONS OF ME

Again, use a strategy that involves the whole class. Ask the students to identify the teacher behaviours that they appreciated in previous classes, teacher actions that made learning possible and were fun, engaging, helped them as students and so on. Complete a table on the board. As you write up the expectations, it is a good idea to discount any that are unrealistic, not possible or that get in the way of learning—for example, no homework, 20 minutes free time every lesson, no assessments, play outside all day and so on. This can be a delicate act, as you don't want to appear insincere in asking for their opinions and then rejecting what they say. The key here is the positive learning focus of the questions, 'How will this help us to learn?'

MY EXPECTATIONS OF YOU

This allows you to state, clearly, positively and simply, your expectations of the students. These will need to be prepared before you enter the class.

CLASS GUIDELINES

Given what you have written up on the board about what constitutes the elements of a quality learning environment, you can now ask the class:

- What do we need to do to make this happen?
- What guidelines can we develop to assist us in our learning, growing in self-discipline and responsibility as well as leadership together?
- What is important to us in this class? Ask students to work in pairs or groups to come up with guidelines.

A useful guideline here is to focus on the values or principles that the class can operate under. Once the value or principle is known, then the description of what that value looks like in the class can be developed. In the classroom, we can also have 'safety' as one of our values. Safety in this class involves emotional as well as physical safety. In the discussion with the students, we explore what safety means and how we know if we have a safe classroom. From this discussion, the students help frame the rules under the value of safety. For example, under safety we may include 'everyone can "pass" on an answer'; 'use helpful and supportive language with peers' and 'I will support others in learning'. The way the values are framed depends on your style but the essence is that the students need to know the rationale for the guideline and are allowed to have some buy-in in its construction. If the value is not known then the behaviour or descriptor can be seen out of context and seen as overly bureaucratic, or worse, as unfair.

For younger students, it may be necessary to provide them with the values or principles and work with them to come up with what this behaviour 'looks like', 'feels like', and 'sounds like' (Y Chart) in your class. In the primary years, teachers may wish to focus on listening behaviours. You may have as your value or principle 'listen to other class members' and have the students work out what this behaviour will look like—one person speaks at a time (sounds like), raise our hand when we want to contribute (looks like), support the speaker with eyes and ears (feels like). Student involvement in the development of the guidelines and clear understanding of the rationale behind them will help students develop ownership of the class. These guidelines are a source of assistance to students developing responsibility for their behaviour and learning in the class.

Critical reflection

Different approaches to rules in class

In this section, we have discussed a process of establishing expectations and behaviour guidelines in the class. Before we move on to offering a range of approaches, let us focus on what your thinking is towards rules.

Working with a peer or group of students, discuss the following:

1   What is your preferred approach to establishing rules?
    a   rules
    b   code of conduct

    c   class constitution

    d   rights and responsibility

    e   guiding student behaviour.

2 Can you identify the differing assumptions that underpin each approach?

3 What expectations of student achievement and behaviour would you outline for your students?

4 What expectations of your own behaviour would you expect or accept from students?

5 Can you list and explain four expectations you would have of a class?

6 What values underpin your approach to rules?

Reframing discipline—punishment, consequences or solutions?

Before we move on to how we respond to student misbehaviour, let us look at the need to rethink or reframe discipline from a reward–punishment scheme to a more democratic approach that supports student autonomy. Often when the topic of discipline is raised early on in a professional learning session the participant is looking for specific tactics that result in 100 per cent instantaneous obedience. However, punishment is very overrated as a behavioural intervention with all students and even more so with vulnerable students (we will explore the use of punishment and interventions with vulnerable youth in Chapter 6). The conversation with teachers on this topic is often difficult as the use of reward-punishment schemes is widespread and is can be self-reinforcing. The effect of reward–punishment schemes is to set up teacher–student interactions that are based around receiving some reward rather than any real change. Within a class, these schemes fail to meet the needs of individuals and rely more on punishment than any real positive behaviour support for the students. As the culture of the class develops, the onus is on maintaining obedience rather than teaching responsibility and prosocial skills. As Alfie Kohn (1999) comments in the quote below, the wide acceptance of reward–punishment schemes is a cause for concern and, due to its continued use, often goes unquestioned. Teachers and parents see it as common sense. They are not aware of the evidence opposing such an approach and fail to look for alternatives that are more positive.

> There is a time to admire the grace and persuasive power of an influential idea, and there is a time to fear its hold over us. The time to worry is when the idea is so widely shared that we no longer even notice it, when it is so deeply rooted it feels to us like plain common sense. At the point when objections are not answered anymore because they are no longer even raised, we are not in control; we do not have the idea; it has us (p. 3).

The starting point in developing a corrective or guidance element to a behaviour management plan is to start with our beliefs and assumptions about students' locus of control, the intentions or outcomes of discipline and how we understand behavioural mistakes (in contrast to academic mistakes). One way to highlight the range of approaches to discipline is to contrast two different styles. We will contrast an autocratic or controlling style with a democratic style of discipline. The two styles are in opposition to each other, as the autocratic style uses rewards and punishments as a way to control the students. Control is external. The democratic or guidance style is aimed at developing autonomy through self-regulation and internal control. The term 'guiding' is used by Gartrell (1998) and used in early childhood education as well as childcare literature about behaviour. The emphasis in these settings is to guide children so that they learn to direct their own actions. The process is internal and is in sympathy with a needs-based or resilient-based intervention that builds on the students' capacity to self-manage and grow in autonomy.

Reward–punishment approaches reward behaviours that adults deem important and reinforce through teacher praise, time for a special activity, stickers or treats. We can also hope to stop behaviours that are not deemed appropriate by punishing the student in the hope that others will see the punishment: removal from activity, verbal reprimand or isolation from the group, and act more appropriately. The belief here is that behaviour is controlled externally. In contrast, the democratic view is that students will make decisions about their behaviour based on their own needs. These students will ultimately decide, rightly or wrongly, to choose a certain behaviour based on the knowledge that it will meet their needs (Brendtro, Brokenleg and Van Bockern, 1990). The controlling approach is to deal with the students here and now behaviours that are observable and to ignore the emotions and thinking that are motivating the behaviour.

Autocratic and controlling style vs. an authoritative and democratic style

In developing your management plan, one of the areas that needs to be addressed is the aim or outcome of your behaviour interventions. What is it that you want to achieve with your approach? The autocratic or controlling style aims to get the students to conform and comply with adult directives. When students do not, we use labels such as non-compliant, naughty or, for older students, oppositional defiance disorder. If you were to ask teachers who work within a reward–punishment scheme what the aim is they will often say it to teach self-discipline or teach respect. The naughtier the student, the more discipline is needed to teach respect. All we do is increase the punishments or lengthen the time with no real change in behaviour. Often the standard cited for self-discipline in this context is that the students will behave when the teacher is absent. However, it is not certain if the students are behaving because of their internal controls or out of fear or 'internalised compliance' that the teacher will return and catch them being naughty.

The democratic style attempts to develop in students a sense of right and wrong. Then students choose to behave out of this sense rather than out of fear. This is what Alfie Kohn calls 'autonomous ethics' rather than 'internalised compliance' (1996). Using the democratic style, it is anti-democratic to expect blind obedience to adults. Blindly obedient students are not the citizens we need in society—rather we need active citizens who understand right and wrong and act accordingly. An autocratic style goes against the broader goals of education and the research into resilience that views problem solving and critical thinking as assets. The advances in our understanding of learning (cooperative and collaborative, different styles, social constructivism) also run counter to the notion of compliance and the view that students are little adults or empty vessels waiting to be filled with appropriate knowledge and skills, which are achieved through behaviourist methods of reward and punishment. This is in stark contrast to Bronfenbrenner's bioecological view (described in Chapter 3) that views children as integral parts of their ecology who co-construct their identities and knowledge.

The final point of comparison (although there are more areas we could look at, such as causes of misbehaviour, intent of student behaviour, and so on) is to look at how both approaches view the nature of children. In your management plan, you are asked to describe how you view the nature of students. This level of reflection is helpful as most teachers will select an approach to discipline based on their beliefs or assumptions about children. One of the intended outcomes of your plan is to make your beliefs explicit, as they will underpin your approach. A democratic or guidance view of children will view them as reasonable and rational beings who will respond appropriately and thoughtfully when treated with respect, dignity and equity. A controlling style will view children as predominantly misbehaving, needing to be rewarded when they behave—'reinforced' so that they don't slip back to naughty ways—and punished if they behave in ways adults deem wrong.

Problems with rewards

The use of teacher-initiated rewards has been a controversial area in managing student behaviour. The controversy is over the effectiveness of rewards and the controlling or manipulative intent in their use.

Table 4.1 Problems with rewards

Problem	Reasons
Rewards can impact on self-regulation and self-esteem	The use of rewards to inhibit behaviour does not foster internalisation of self-control (Kohn, 1993; Leper, 1983).
	The use of rewards is highly controlling as the teacher determines the behaviours they approve of and how they are to be rewarded. This does not allow for student autonomy or the fundamental and universal need for independence. It also teaches young children that the opinions of others are more important than their own. The offering of rewards for good behaviour can be viewed as bribery.
Rewards can impede learning and academic progress	The use of rewards to increase student motivation may in effect work against developing intrinsic motivation. Students can become too focussed on earning extrinsic rewards—'What's in it for me?' (Deci & Ryan, 1987; Lepper & Greene, 1978).
	Students can become too focussed on obtaining teacher approval or watching the teacher to see if he or she 'sees me being good' to the point of distraction from learning.

	Hoping to please or behave in ways anointed by the teacher as 'reward worthy' can stifle students' creativity or risk taking in learning. Students often pick up that the reason that rewards are offered for certain activities is because the set activity is boring or not interesting (overjustification hypothesis). There is no need to reward work when the activity is interesting. The use of rewards can impact on the quality of work students produce.
Rewards can increase disengaged behaviour	For some students, they may believe that they do not have the ability to meet the teacher expectations and, therefore, will chose to misbehave. This is magnified when the number of rewards available are limited. It is possible that the teacher's intention to reward a specific behaviour can be viewed by the student as socially alienating within their peer group. For example, the teacher may praise or randomly reward a student who finds the attention embarrassing rather than rewarding. Some students can react out of the need to 'save face' in front of peers. Some students can grow to resent being manipulated by rewards and will misbehave to reassert their developing autonomy.
Rewards can be unfair and promote student inequality	Students will see through rewards that do not carry 'currency' or are not justified by the student's actions. The intention of the teacher may be to include the student, however, others may see it as unfair and the teacher's praise loses credibility. It is difficult to distribute verbal praise and rewards equitably and fairly across a class. Some students will purposely appeal to the teacher so as to be rewarded while others who do not can receive less attention. If some students continually miss out on teacher attention they may become disengaged from the learning in the class. In some classrooms rewards, group points, or progress charts can create unhelpful competition. Children will behave to get the points and if there are limited rewards others will miss out.
Rewards can protect teachers from student feedback and stifle effective teaching	Using rewards can shield the teacher from receiving feedback from the students that the work is boring or not engaging as the students fear missing out on a reward. Constant use of rewards can stifle teacher innovation and creativity in teaching strategies to engage students in learning. Their use can sustain less effective teaching practices (Grossman, 1990; Ryan, 1979).

The use and construction of consequences

Consequences are very hard to construct and carry out in our schools. The next time you are at a school, watch and listen for the different types of consequences that are displayed around the grounds, how a teacher administers a consequence and the student reaction to the imposed consequence. It is easy for consequences to be a subset of punishment, in that they are an imposed stimuli used to reduce a target behaviour (Elias and Schwab (cited in Evertson and Weinstein, 2006). Gordon (1989) refers to the concept of logical consequences as 'nothing less than a euphemism for external control'. Alfie Kohn in his book *Beyond Discipline: From Compliance to Community* (1996) questioned how reasonable and related logical consequences were and whether students who receive them see these consequences as an alternative to punishment. Kohn sees logical consequences as 'punishment lite'. Nelson Lott and Glen (2000) view consequences as focusing on the past and making students pay for their mistakes. However, the critical difference between consequences and punishment is intent or the spirit in which the consequence is given and the way the teacher speaks with the student. Let us look at a few of the more influential writers who promote the use of consequences.

In democratic classrooms, Hoover and Kindsvatter (1997) suggest that interventions for student misbehaviour should be framed as a 'reasonable consequence', which is an intervention that is developmentally appropriate with a learning focus for the student. Reasonable consequences are intended to allow the student to see the connection between the behaviour and the consequence that goes beyond the final straw. If students have been reminded of a rule or asked to stop talking during individual work time and continue to talk, then the consequence is being applied because they ignored the reminder and not for the talking. Reasonable consequences are based on the assumption that the student has the capacity to see the behaviour is wrong through reason, mutual consideration for learning in the class, justice and communal responsibility to promoting a learning environment. A positive outcome is for the student to learn acceptable behaviour from the interaction. It is possible that from the student's point of view the outcomes of reasonable consequences are no more than the outcomes of punishment. A positive learning experience of the consequence is largely due to previously established negotiated guidelines for behaviour and the underlying message that is conveyed by the teacher that they care and are supportive.

Linda Albert (1996) promotes the use of the 'four Rs of consequences' in her Cooperative Discipline program. She believes that consequences need to be:

- *related* to the behaviour
- *reasonable*—the consequences are appropriate to the behaviour
- *respectful*—conveyed in a respectful and non-blaming manner
- *reliably* enforced and followed through by the teacher.

Curwin and Mendler (1988), the authors of *Discipline with Dignity*, believe that there are four types of consequences:

- *Logical*: the consequence is logically related to the misbehaviour and allows the student to make right the wrong.
- *Conventional*: are consequences that are commonly in use such as the loss of time at breaks, being sent to the office or cleaning up after making a mess.
- *Generic*: this is possibly the most potent—in 'choosing', the students select from three or four options in response to their misbehaviour, or in 'planning' the students plan out the consequences that they think are most appropriate to change their behaviour.
- *Instructional*: where the behaviour is targeted and teaches the student to behave properly.
  We often share a good example of this in professional learning sessions. A student swears in class and states that they can't help themselves, as it is part of youth culture. However, when they work part time at McDonald's they never swear at customers through the drive through.

Barbara Larrivee best encapsulates the positive requirements of consequences when she states that they need to be:

- logically related to the behaviour
- deliberately planned and delivered
- emotionally neutral
- rational and depersonalised
- conducive to developing self control and
- protecting self esteem (from Larrivee, 2005, p 202).

As you can see, much has been written over many years about the use and abuse of consequences. For consequences to be effective, they must flow naturally from the approach that the school and teachers have towards students and learning. If the approach is more about control or autocracy then the consequences may be no more than thinly veiled threats or 'punishment lite'. If the view is that students can develop responsibility and the consequence is but one support mechanism that will assist the student to develop autonomy then they will more than likely perceived in this way. Reasonable consequences need to be in the best interests of the student. They need to provide the teacher with enough options that allow them to implement a consequence and still treat the student as an individual. Consequences are related, logically, to the class guidelines and are constructed in such a way that they help the student to develop his or her self-discipline.

The one important element that we would include in consequence development is to add an unspecified 'other' option. This allows the teacher the flexibility to use consequences to meet the needs of the individual student. All students are different and their motivations for misbehaving can be different. Therefore, set consequences may not be the most appropriate given the student, behaviour and context. Most schools that support consequences publish the school or classroom rules with a set of consequences that are to be followed if a rule is broken. Often there are five or six consequences listed, from minor actions increasing in severity up to suspension or exclusion. In working with challenging students, our experience is that they can look at the consequences and calculate how many times they have to misbehave to achieve their aim of being asked to leave the room or of being suspended. Having 'other' as the sixth consequence allows the school or teacher the flexibility to base the consequence according to the need of the student. We do this all the time in offering academic support to children in class. We have differentiated literacy or numeracy activities that target specific learning difficulties. We need the same for behaviour. We need the behaviour interventions to target specific student needs if we are to achieve greater growth or change in student behaviour. If the class guidelines are negotiated as suggested in the PLF, it is natural to ask the student questions such as 'what do we do now?', 'how do you propose we move forward?', 'I am not sure how to respond to that behaviour, can you help me here?' or 'we have a problem that we need to solve before I can get back to teaching'. We will explore more the language of de-escalation in Chapter 6.

Solution-oriented approaches

From early childhood settings to senior school settings some authors advocate that we need to move beyond consequences to solutions or more relational responses that incorporate restorative practices. In a framework that centres on relationships and developing learning environments characterised by care and trust, this advice seems appropriate yet challenging in our current schooling structure. Nelson, Lott and Glen (2000) in their Positive Discipline model refer to the 'three Rs of solutions': related, respectful, and reasonable. They believe that consequences can have the connotation of making the student pay for their misbehaviour whereas a solution-focused orientation seeks to assist the student in developing autonomy and seeing problems as opportunities for personal growth. Curwin and Mendler (1988) also viewed their use of consequences and indeed student misbehaviour as opportunities for teacher professional learning. The other benefit of a solutions orientation is that it develops student responsibility, as the student is a part of the solution and the solution can only move forward through respectful conversation with the teacher.

It is interesting that the further we move away from a reward and punishment approach, the more the student is involved and the central factor becomes relationships. 'Restorative justice', an approach that revolves around relationships in seeking a resolution, was introduced in Australian schools in the 1990s. Restorative practices (the alternative phrase used in schools) evolved from restorative justice. The first pilots were closely related to the 'community conferencing' model used in juvenile justice settings in New Zealand and Australia. Restorative approaches stress the importance of relationships over rules. In fact, the central tenet is to restore the relationships between people when these have been damaged by inappropriate or hurtful behaviour. In the early years of restorative justice, some authors referred to it as 'relational justice'. In this context, the community plays an important part as the harm to relationships occurs within a community. A restorative approach shifts the emphasis from managing behaviour to building and repairing relationships.

The need to repair relationships is based on the understanding that our greatest socio-emotional need is to belong and be connected with others in a community. Disconnected youth are prone to anti-social behaviour. Over time, these students become wary of adults and fearful of attempts to reconnect them to a community. This is especially so if they have experienced repeated failure and rejection in the school community. Within a restorative framework, there are consequences or strategies aimed at young people taking responsibility for their own actions. In a restorative environment, the consequence is not 'done' to the wrongdoer but involves all those affected. A restorative perspective is different from one where students believe that consequences are done to them, which encourages students to try to avoid detection to avoid the consequences. In a sense, we are encouraging dishonestly and selfishness. It is a bit like taking the back streets driving home after too many drinks to avoid detection or slowing down when we see a speed camera only to speed once we are past. Communities are essential in a restorative approach. In these communities, students and teachers work together to consider the consequences of their behaviour on each other and take responsibility for this behaviour. In taking responsibility, we need opportunities to explain how we feel and how another person's behaviour has affected us. We all need someone to listen to us, even more so when we are in conflict. How often do we hear students or colleagues complain that nobody listens to them, they feel undervalued, not respected or unappreciated? Strategies used in a restorative approach attempt to build a sense of belonging, a sense of concern for others and the opportunity to heal the damage that the misbehaviour has caused others. A restorative approach incorporates four key questions:

- What's happened?
- Who has been affected?
- How can we involve everyone who has been affected in finding a way forward?
- How can everyone do things differently in the future?

Restorative practice in schools

Restorative practice in schools is an emerging field of study that aims at restoring and building community with disconnected youth. Restorative practice in schools has its origins in restorative justice, which offered a new way to look at criminal justice that focussed on repairing the harm caused by crime to people and relationships rather than punishing offenders. Restorative justice began in the 1970s with mediation between the victim and the offender. This mediation grew in the 1990s to include communities of care where friends and families of both parties were included in a collaborative problem-solving process called 'conferences' and 'circles'.

As an approach to managing student behaviour, restorative practice is similar to any other program aimed at student engagement and behaviour support, which requires time and expertise of staff. Incorporating restorative practices is more about influencing the social climate of the school community rather than a set of discrete strategies aimed at specific behaviours. Brenda Morrison from the Australian National University identifies three levels of restorative practices within a school—from primary and secondary interventions to tertiary interventions.

The primary levels of interventions involve a comprehensive set of lessons taught across the school years, covering topics about conflict resolutions, positive communications and relationship building. The elements centre on essential skills for effective communication including active listening, successful negotiation and an understanding of diversity. Within the community setting, the aim is to enhance members' understanding of the value and role of members in the community. Morrison's evaluation of programs in Australia and America highlights that at this 'primary level' integrated curriculum of social skills and conflict resolution strategies fosters prosocial behaviour, increases the likelihood of students using positive means to resolve conflict, improve relationships with teachers and widen students' circle of friends. In some of the restorative practice programs student academic achievement levels on standardised tests improved.

One of the earliest practices borrowed from restorative justice in the community to be imported into schools was conferencing or peer mediation. Conferencing has been used in schools for decades as a restorative practice. In schools, conferencing has developed into 'peer mediation' where students trained in negotiation facilitate a process to assist students in dispute to negotiate. The facilitator engages the other students in a process that allows them to explain their thoughts, express their feelings, develop options for moving the dispute forward and reach a mutually beneficial solution. Morrison's evaluations have found that some programs of peer mediation have been successful, while others have not been as effective. Morrison believes that the less than favourable response from some peer mediation has been the result of using a single process to do too much and possibly these programs have not been faithful to the tenets of conferencing.

Schools and systems have responded to this issue of a single process by incorporating other processes to support peer mediation. Schools have included 'circle-time' or problem-solving circles to deal with the day-to-day concerns as a class or within the school. These can be facilitated by students or teachers and they allow students to collectively problem-solve issues. Establishing a process or school/class culture for identifying a problem and working collectively to resolve it can have great benefits. When a student exhibits challenging or explosive behaviour, it can be 'problematised' with a view to seeking a solution, instead of punishing the student or dishing out a disconnected consequence. We will explore the language to use in this style of conflict resolution in Chapter 6 when looking at de-escalating conflict in the classroom.

The concept of conferencing and problem solving is carried through to the tertiary level. In this level, the common feature of the circle is an increase in the level of support needed and the number of people involved including parents, professionals or specialist services.

It is interesting to note that a number of public school systems in Australia have adopted restorative practices in their schools. The Federal government's Safe Schools Framework (2004) gave schools the policy support for initiating programs to increase the level of safety in the school. A confluence of policy, practice and research came together under the Safe Schools Framework. Resilience research also supported protective factors in schools as well as local school-based initiatives to increase student and teacher safety.

Restorative practices, democratic approaches to discipline and strength-based programs can only be successful if they are supported across the whole school by the staff and administration. These approaches are doomed to fail if left to the counsellor or one or two teachers. The school needs to support staff in resourcing them with knowledge, skills and a range of strategies that promote pro-social behaviour. Success is further enhanced when it is integrated into classroom teaching and the practices are seamless across the school. Finally, any whole-school approach needs effective data on which to base policy and interventions. Schools collect inordinate amounts of data, however there needs to be a targeted use of behavioural data that supports new initiatives. Professor Ted Watchel, President of the International

Institute for Restorative Practices Graduate School, refers to a report on the effectiveness of restorative practices that highlights the importance of a coordinated and whole school approach.

> When systematically employed on a whole schools basis, restorative practices transform negative school environments by engaging students in taking responsibility for making their schools better. Restorative practices stands in stark contrast to the prevailing reliance on punishment employed in today's schools.

The International Institute for Restorative Practices completed a review of schools who are implementing restorative practices to see if they have made any improvement to school climate. The report 'Improving School Climate: Findings From Schools Implementing Restorative Practices' (2009) highlights the benefits of restorative practices as reported by schools. The report's findings are from schools in America, Canada and the UK. The report is not formal research but is a collection of reports from practitioners commenting on the impact of the restorative practices from their point of view. Taken together, the many voices make a loud noise in favour of the practices they have tried. One deputy principal who is responsible for 'discipline' comments that:

> Restorative practices changed the way I view discipline, as assistant principal my task was to assign blame and levy a penalty. That didn't sit well anymore. The goal is for students not to repeat misbehaviour. Now I see my task as helping them, and it's done through building relationships (Hollahan, R. cited in Improving school climate: Findings from schools implementing restorative practices. International Institute for Restorative Practices. 2009. p. 11).

The Bessels Leigh School in Abingdon, England is a school for boys aged 11 to 16 who exhibit social, emotional and behavioural difficulties. The school believed the traditional approach they had used with the boys was not working, as the students' characteristics and the problems they presented with had changed. In 2005, they decided to adopt the International Institute for Restorative Practices restorative practices approach. The staff and the boys worked collaboratively to establish behavioural 'norms' for circles and for appropriate behaviour so that the school was safe. The Principal, John Boulton, is quoted as saying:

Restorative practices have had a very real, positive impact on our school. The change is clear to the staff and boys. Restorative practices has empowered staff to take control of situations, raise issues, question behaviour and examine relationships with the boys and with each other (Boulton, J. cited in cited in Improving school climate: Findings from schools implementing restorative practices. International Institute for Restorative Practices. 2009. p. 27).

Teachers' experience of a relational view to behaviour management highlights how a focus on needs enables schools and classroom teachers to move away from controlling behaviour to building on students' strengths and their capacity to respond responsibly. Being sensitive to student needs and abilities is part of setting high expectations and being aware of the need to motivate students in learning.

High expectations and student motivation

Although we have looked at establishing expectations as part of the class guideline procedure mentioned previously, it may be useful to briefly describe what these are and how they can be a part of your motivation strategy. Establishing expectations are part of our overall preventative approach and they can also be used in our interactions with students who are struggling with getting involved in class work and who are hard to discipline. 'Hard to discipline' students are mentioned because research shows that the majority of students who are not motivated to learn are also hard to discipline. There is a connection between behaviour and lack of motivation, although which factor is the cause is debated from numerous perspectives. In relation to engagement, we can say that displaying inattentive and disruptive behaviours is not helpful to achieving academic success. Let us look at what unmotivated students do and how teacher expectations can assist in re-engaging them in meaningful learning. We will address the key components of expectations, which include:

- offering hope
- ensuring achievement for all students
- presenting mistakes as learning opportunities
- acknowledging effort
- using student choice to motivate.

Offering hope

As mentioned previously, the research by Emmer, Evertson and Anderson (1980) highlights that effective teachers convey a sense of purposefulness and get the most out of the time available in class. Successful teachers are clear in setting their expectations. In the Positive Learning Framework, this incorporates student input. High expectations are about conveying hope to the students. In an address Bonnie Benard gave to teachers in Sacramento, California in 2006, she noted that students thought teachers who set high expectations showed they cared for them. Within the high expectations was a belief that the teacher was expecting responsibility but also that the teacher was saying that the student can succeed. The students therefore believed they had hope and were motivated to learn. It is very easy for any of us to give up trying if we believe there is no hope of success. Imagine if you felt that you no chance of passing the teacher education course you are studying, or that your lecturers conveyed to you that you were really underachieving and in fact were not cut out for teaching but you could continue if you wanted to! Not many would stay, yet for school-aged students they have no choice but to stay. From this perspective, it is possible to see how students who come to school excited and motivated can soon learn to be unmotivated if not nourished in a dynamic and supported learning environment.

Hope also extends outside the classroom. Often adolescent learners question 'why are we doing this' or decry 'I won't need this when I leave school'. For the student struggling with motivation issues, these sentiments are real. We need to link the learning to meaning for the students. We need to find real-world applications for the work we are setting. The timeframe for this can be short as most students will not have a ten-year plan but might only see the future as next week! Effective teachers will understand this timeframe and work within it for their students. One way to engender hope is for the students to see the love and joy you have for teaching or the subject you teach. Students will pick up your body language, what you say, how you structure lessons, the way you deliver lessons to assess your level of enjoyment and love for your teaching. Your enjoyment will be infectious and possibly enough to assist an unmotivated student to engage in learning. Displaying this level of enthusiasm can be difficult if you have recently graduated and are asked to teach outside your area of expertise or year-level preference. You may not have the passion you have for other areas of teaching but it will help if you find something to like in what you are doing and convey this to the students. They will quickly pick up if you don't enjoy it and then they won't enjoy it either.

Ensuring achievement for all students

Expectations are about expecting all students to achieve. This expectation is reinforced on day one in your class and continually throughout the year in assemblies, newsletters, parent evenings and reporting. In expecting all students to achieve, teachers and the school need to provide support and opportunities for this to happen. As you can imagine, some students require more support than others do and ensuring achievement for all students relies on the teacher knowing their students to help build upon their strengths as well as cater for the range of intelligences (Gardiner, 1985) and learning styles. Finding the right level of challenge in academic tasks for a heterogenous class is not easy but is essential in motivating students to learn. If the task level is too low then students lose motivation and if it is too difficult students will give up. Students are more likely to be engaged when the set task matches their ability.

Presenting mistakes as learning opportunities

When students are engaged and are participating in activities, they will make mistakes. Mistakes are important learning opportunities. Mistakes tell the teacher that students are risking answers and grappling with understanding the topic and these are important elements of learning. Mistakes are a positive part of the learning process when set within a supportive learning community. Acceptance of learning mistakes is supported through mutual respect and valuing others opinions. This environment of support is facilitated by the teacher. There are many times during the day that we are confronted with incorrect or partially correct answers or statements by students. How we respond to these statement is crucial in developing a sense that it is okay to get something wrong and that the teachers has recognised the student's effort. Mistakes also inform the teacher what sections of the lesson content need to be re-taught or emphasised. A guiding principle in responding to student responses is to maintain the dignity of the student and your own if you feel under threat by confronting, silly or rude answers.

Acknowledging effort

It is important to acknowledge and emphasise the effort students make. This follows on from the culture of it being okay to make mistakes, as rarely is anyone's first attempt perfect. Most professions have inbuilt mechanisms for checking and correcting first drafts. In a sense, a mistake can be read as a first draft that needs more work. There is no need for shame, recrimination or embarrassment as we all make mistakes and we all need support to develop our answers further. This notion of a first draft is difficult when we come to formal assessment tasks. However, it may be possible to structure the assessment in such a way that facilitates the students presenting their best work for that set of outcomes you are assessing. At university, we distribute one of the final exam questions to students in the first lecture. Students have all semester to develop a position paper in response to the set question. Students can submit their paper throughout the semester for assistance and can even hand in a full essay that will be returned with comments, suggestions and ideas for further reading. The choice is up to the student. This approach is like the approach taken in computer software development where there is an easy entry level with the capacity for depth of development by skilled users—'low entry and high ceiling'.

Using student choice to motivate

Students develop in responsibility and autonomy when given the power to learn. Choice is often a scary thought to some teachers as they see it as undermining their authority and role as teacher. The opposite is true. The more input the student has in selecting content material, assessment type or style and how topics could be taught, the less need for exerting power in negative or disruptive ways. Offering choice is a good option for unmotivated students. For example, you set homework that includes six questions on a passage they read in class then ask the student to choose 'the best three they like'. Instead of the students struggling to do any of the six it is pretty certain that they will each do their chosen three.

Offering a range of options for assessment also helps make the student feel they are making choices about their learning. When assessing a topic or concept it may be possible to offer them a few options that demonstrate their level of understanding. You could first ask them how they could best demonstrate this knowledge to you and then, as a class, develop an assessment process. One example from a teacher at a professional learning session illustrates this idea of choice. The teacher was teaching History to a Year 10 group on the Second World War. The school did not have a history of good academic achievement and had its fair share of vulnerable students. In discussion with the students, he proposed that he put a position statement to them: 'Hitler was not responsible for the Second World War' that they had to solve or defend over the term and present their position in a range of formats developed by and agreed to by the teacher and class. The student presentation had to meet the set criteria and essential elements for all responses, however, the students could present their information in the form of essay, drama, film, web page or poster. He reported that the level of engagement from the students was unparalleled and changed the dynamics of the class—he was not battling to get students to work but was more of a facilitator in checking progress and affirming the students in their efforts. For this teacher, giving the students power enabled him to have more influence over their work and allowed him to interact in a more personal and affirming way with his students.

Classroom routines and procedures

Effective teachers establish routines for their students systematically and clearly. Class routines and procedures are more effective with students when they are explicit and explained carefully in the first few days of the school year. The aim of class routines and procedures is to enhance the learning environment. They are meant to increase academic engagement by lessening opportunities for disruption and off-task behaviour. As a beginning teacher, you can find it overwhelming to identify the routines and procedures needed in a class, let alone to develop a response to situations as they arise. However, the rationale for developing routines and procedures is similar to the development of class guidelines mentioned earlier in the sense that they are here to assist us to develop a quality learning environment. Some procedures and routines are not up for negotiation, however, the rationale and reason for them needs to be carefully explained to the students. The table below outlines a range of common procedures and routines involved that beginning teachers will need to be aware of and have planned for. The table attempts to cover a broad range of routines and procedures from K–12 but it is not exhaustive. We have not completed all the teacher responses and it is worthwhile as a beginning teacher to develop a response yourself for these behaviours. Some of these elements in the table below are highlighted in this chapter and in Chapter 5 for more in-depth explanation.

Table 4.2 Classroom routines and procedures

Lesson sequence	Routine or procedure	Classroom specific	School-wide
Beginning of the class	Entering the room		Attendance roll to office
	Where to place bags and books/ materials needed		Set rules for bags on hooks, lockers
	Getting whole-class attention	C2S	
	Greeting and attendance roll		
	Students previously absent	Absent slips to go on teacher's desk	Record of absences
	Late students	Late note to teacher	Signed note from office
	Distribution of resources, worksheets, motivational material	Student leaders or assigned roles	
Middle of the lesson	Student attention during whole-class instruction	Listening behaviours— 'I know you are listening when you are looking'	
	Asking questions	Signal for attention or response	
	Assigning groups and roles	Each member has a role and responsibility in group	

Middle of the lesson (cont.)	Acceptable noise level	Teacher reminder of noise, periods of quiet used in activities	
	What to do when finished work early	Get worksheet from the independent work activity box	
	Using the bin or pencil sharpener	Pencils sharpened before class, if needed ask and one at a time at sharpener or bin	
	Leave class for toilet, office, library, extra support, counsellor, chaplain and so on	Authorised pass from teacher to leave room If required, note from support teacher or librarian requesting student	All student need authorised 'pass' when out of class
End of lesson	Reviewing lesson outcomes		
	Whole-class attention	C2S—everyone needs to pay attention	
	Returning of resources	Resources and workbooks back to proper storage places by students rostered on	
	Collecting student workbooks		
	Homework in diaries	Before packing away students write homework in diaries quietly	
	Bags packed (if in class)	Wait for bell or signal lesson has finished	
	Say thank you and good bye		

Other activities	PA announcements	Students seated and quiet	
	Guests in room	Whole-class greeting	
	Fire drill		
	Assemblies		Student assemble in set positions with teacher
	Watching DVDs or computer use		

Beginning a lesson

Once you have done your pre-planning, as outlined in the table above, it is time to begin your lessons. Once your students inside the classroom have taken the roll, you then use your C2S to get whole-class attention. You wait until you have full attention from all students and then are ready to begin the start of lesson sequence. In this sequence, we are using an amalgamation of Madeleine Hunter's (1994) lesson design and Gagne's (1985) nine events of instruction. We are not attempting to offer a full account of Gagne's nine events nor Hunter's stages of lesson delivery. Rather we are highlighting certain elements of a lesson that assist us in managing a learning environment, which facilitates student engagement and minimises student misbehaviour. One of these strategies is how we motivate our students so that they are 'ready' and 'wanting' to learn. This motivation is called the Establishing Set or Set Induction (Burden, 2003) or Hunter's Anticipatory Set (1994).

ESTABLISHING THE LEARNING SET

Establishing the learning set is the initial activity that a teacher does to motivate the students to want to learn. In one sense, it is the 'hook' or trick to get the students involved in the learning you have planned. This initial activity sets the scene for the lesson, the learning that they will be engaged in and establishes the expectation of success. Set induction helps the students to see what the lesson is about by linking the lesson to common interests or to an experience shared by the class. The term 'set' refers to the state of readiness (set) of the students for learning in the lesson. The set activity helps to create curiosity and interest in learning that relates to the students' lives.

The set can be brief or more involved and can take up to five or ten minutes. Whatever the type of set used, Burden (2003, p. 170) highlights a number of criteria that a set needs in order to be effective. These criteria include:

- creates interest in what is to be taught
- is connected to the lesson
- is understood by the students
- is related to the students' lives, a previous lesson or a common shared experience.

Creating interest requires active participation. Ensure that all students are involved from the start of the lesson. A set won't work if you have only a handful of students paying attention. There are many examples of what this activity may look like and the range is only limited by your imagination (and levels of energy and time). Remember that the young people in our classrooms live in a culture saturated by pictures and sounds mixed together in an amazing array of technology. Bearing this in mind can help in coming up with ideas or visuals to motivate learning. Some examples may include:

- Act out a *MasterChef* episode (you could actually cook!) when teaching procedure in writing with Year 2s—follow the recipe as a procedure. This is an actual example from two Year 2 teachers at a recent professional learning seminar.
- Show a news item on local or international racial conflict as a discussion starter for a topic on racism.
- Read a picture book about numbers before a maths lesson in junior primary.
- Give every student a card with physical characteristics on it (four legs, fur, omnivore and so on) as students enter room in a science lesson on classification.
- Present PowerPoint slides of politicians and government buildings for a quiz to start a topic on Australian government or politics.
- Come dressed in period character and have the students interview you for a history class. You could ask a colleague to get the students in and seated and inform them they have a special guest today and then your

colleague introduces you. I used this strategy in a Year 4 class and came in as Louis Pasteur and, another time, appeared as a child worker in the industrial revolution for a Year 9 class, where I was interviewed by a pre-service teacher on school placement.

Whatever the activity, it needs to be *connected to the lesson*. Some of the examples above take more preparation than others. It could be that the motivational activity is a question on the whiteboard for class discussion or a simple review of previous learning. Reviewing yesterday's lesson is always good practice and provides a good link for the lesson you are starting. This in itself can be motivation to get the students interested in learning. However, the important point is that the set activity is no more than a fun activity or icebreaker if it does not lead into the intended learning for the lesson.

As with all lesson content, it needs to be *understood by the students*. The initial activity needs to be constructed in a way that the students understand that it is connected to the lesson. This connection may take several minutes if the students are excited and engrossed in the activity but as the activity unfolds, the connections should become clear. This clear connection allows the activity to be referred to in the lesson as a learning experience, for example, 'remember when we were following our *MasterChef* recipe for honey crackles we started with the corn flakes'.

The set induction needs to be *related to the students' lives, a previous lesson or a common shared experience*. The students will be motivated to get involved if the activity relates to their lives or if it has some relevance to them. Also, some activities can follow on from a shared class experience such as an excursion, guest speaker, camp or a big event in the local area.

When these criteria are met, a good start to the lesson sets the tone for the learning to come. The next step in our lesson flow is to make explicit the learning to follow.

Stating the learning outcome of the lesson

Once you have motivated the student and 'hooked' them into learning, orient the students to the nature, purpose and importance of the learning in the lesson. One way to assist students in seeing the purpose and importance of the lesson and to highlight the main ideas, concepts and vocabulary to be covered is to use an *advanced organiser*. Advanced organisers help students to frame the learning in the lesson, and can be written or verbal instructions that indicate the content and activities being presented. In the advanced organiser, we would include the lesson objectives, learning goal for the lesson and the intended learning outcome (there are a range of labels for what we are trying to achieve). A step-by-step outline of the lesson sequence can be included with the allotted time beside each activity if desired. In this way, students can see the purpose of the activities and how they link to the intended learning for the lesson. In the classroom management and instruction unit taught at university to pre-service teachers, we use an advanced organiser for each session, which is written up on the whiteboard. Once it is written up we then ask the students if they wish to add anything (questions from their readings, news reports on behaviour, school experiences or reflections on learning to date) and then begin the session. Student feedback has been overwhelmingly positive to our advanced organiser and university-level students comment that they feel supported in their learning when they know what is coming up in the session, how it relates to the weekly outcome and what is required of them.

When the advanced organiser is part of a set routine in the lesson with the lesson outcome clearly stated, it assists the students in evaluating their learning for the lesson against the stated outcome. 'Today in the lesson we have covered …', 'three things you should have learnt today are …', 'what we know today that we didn't yesterday is that …' 'tomorrow we will …' A clearly set-out advanced organiser that is part of every lesson gives the students a learning routine and makes the lesson safe in its predictability. It can also be motivating in that one of the activities listed can be very interesting and motivate students to get involved and complete the earlier activities in order to get to the one they find most exciting. As part of our classroom layout, a section of the whiteboard can be ruled up permanently as the 'lesson today' section with a heading on the top of the board so that the lesson outcome can be clearly displayed for the students. Depending on your students' age level this can be written into their workbooks or files as part of the lesson routine you have with them. This then provides a good structure for the students to review their learning at the completion of a topic, term or semester.

In Chapter 5, we will describe the processes for the middle of the lesson and how to effectively end a lesson, but first we will explore student movement, one of the important areas where student misbehaviour can increase and we can lose valuable teaching time.

Dealing with student movement (transitions)

Any student movement increases the likelihood that students will misbehave. One way to deal with this is to have a sequence of instructions that you follow when speaking with your class. Kounin used the term 'transition' and since he coined the phrase research has indicated that transitions are a source of lost learning time in classrooms. Research by Burns (1984), Gump (1982) and Rosenshine (1980) highlight that over thirty transitions happen in a day and they found that this movement accounted for a loss of 15 per cent of learning time. Doyle (1984) noted that effective teachers foreshadow movement and clearly tell students when it is to happen as well as actively orchestrating transitions.

The potential for student misbehaviour is increased in transitions. Transitions are potentially difficult because you are asking students to stop one piece of work to move on to another when they might not have finished or they are enjoying this piece and they 'know' they will not like the next activity. Students may also use the movement to remind them that they *need* to go to the toilet, to get something from their bag, to have a drink or to say something to their friend. Student movement can include:

- entering or exiting the class
- moving from mat time to desk work
- moving to activity centres in the classroom
- moving to form groups
- getting resources
- resource distribution
- changing subject topic
- leaving the room mid-lesson
- going to the library.

One way to improve transitions is to use a sequence developed by Bennett and Smilanich (1994). They outline a three-part procedure to maximise efficiency and reduce potential for student misbehaviour. The sequence involves *when* (the students will move), *what* (will they do), *who* (will do it).

The student movement sequence	The rationale
1. Cue to Start (C2S)	The transition must begin from a sense of order
2. A statement of *when* the student moves	Always start the transition with *when*. Using other words may result in students moving before you want them to.
3. Tell the students *what* you expect from them	The *what* is the essential part of the transition it tells the students what they are going to do and what is expected of them
4. A statement of *who* will move	The *who* statement completes the transition
5. The direction to move	To achieve your objective
6. Monitor the move and be close to where the action is likely to be	Preventative action will reduce the likelihood of misbehaviour
7. Provide specific and positive feedback	You want to maintain and support students' positive transition behaviour

This transition sequence is taught to students at the beginning of the year. Other transition sequence approaches involve the teacher cueing in the students' attention with either a hand signal or performing a sequence preceding the instruction to transition. For example, the teacher may ask student to tap their heads, touch their nose or shake their hands before telling everyone to move back to their seats, or get out their maths books.

The transition sequence above builds upon some of the teacher actions you practiced as part of Chapter 1 in the practice activity on C2S. These actions include your *C2S* (short statement to get students attention, hand gesture, clapping or singing depending on the year level taught) *proximity* (moving toward a student or students), *looking* or scanning the room, ability to be on the alert with '*withit-ness*' and the use of a clear and confident voice. These teacher skills are essential in effective classroom management.

Skills review for beginning a lesson

In beginning your lesson, you would have included the following skills or teacher actions:

- connecting (with students outside the class or as they enter)
- C2S
- proximity
- pause
- scan
- name
- look
- 'withit-ness'
- possibly a planned ignore for a student slow to pay attention
- politeness.

You will have used these skills just to get the students in the classroom and to gain their attention. This is before you start your motivational set or lesson review! When viewed in this way we can begin to see how active effective teachers are in developing an orderly learning environment. Identifying these skills is a good source for reflection when a start to a lesson does not go well or when we struggle to settle the class. On reflection, we can go through the various skills to see what was done well and what may have contributed to the difficult start.

Teacher perceptions of misbehaviour

Why is it that in different classrooms, some actions are deemed as misbehaving while in others they are ignored? Why is there a marked difference in teacher understanding or perceptions of what constitutes misbehaviour? Why do 'good teachers' appear to have little misbehaviour and when they do intervene their response appears to be a 'good fit' to the behaviour whereas in less effective teacher's classrooms misbehaviour is often dealt with harshly or inappropriately?

Complete the table below (starting with1 through to 4 even though the table is not set out in that order), either by yourself or with a peer. List the 'low level' misbehaviours that continually happen in the classroom that will require a teacher response. Once you have listed a range of behaviours, try to identify the teacher response to these behaviours. If working with a peer discuss the responses and possible differences in opinion.

Practice activity

Complete the table as outlined below from 1–4.

Preventative strategy	Low-level behaviour	Teacher thinking and/or emotional response	Corrective strategy Low-level teacher behaviours
4. Identify the proactive teacher behaviours that could be used to (possibly) prevent these behaviours from happening	1. List a range of low-level behaviours that will require a teacher response—for example, student talking, turning around, tapping a pen	3. Hypothesise the teachers thinking or emotional response to these behaviours—how would you feel and what might you be thinking?	2. Identify the teacher response—what does the teacher say and do to respond to this behaviour?

Critical reflection

Teacher action plan

Using the content from this chapter, develop an action plan for 'developing a quality learning environment'. Identify the strategies and teacher actions that you will contribute to your classroom management.

This action plan will assist you in developing the practice section in your management plan.

A possible framework is to use the sections of the Positive Learning Framework presented at the beginning of the chapter and put action points next to them (template below). This is also a useful strategy for revising the main points in the chapter and book so far.

Teacher action plan

Prevention: management	Action points	Prevention: lesson design	Action points
Before the class:		Beginning:	
self awareness		whole-class attention (c2s)	
proactive thinking—indiscipline will happen at some stage		clear outcomes conveyed to students	

caring and welcoming classroom (connecting)		motivation 'hook for learning'—set induction	
classroom layout and resources		advanced organiser	
high and specific expectations		recall prior knowledge	
guidelines, routines and procedures		level of student engagement	

Developing my classroom management plan

In this chapter, we have discussed the proactive behaviours that effective classroom teachers display in organising their class for learning and ensuring students are engaged.

1 How does the content of this chapter inform your teaching philosophy?
2 In establishing 'rules' in your class how much student involvement are you comfortable with and why?
3 What is your view on consequences and will your plan include reasonable consequences?
4 Will you incorporate any restorative practices and how do these relate to or support your philosophy?
5 What elements of this chapter could assist you in your practice section?
6 Do you think that it is feasible to start every lesson with the outcome on the board using an advanced organiser? Is this a practice you intend to incorporate into your plan?

Summary

Effective teaching is a deliberate and planned approach on behalf of the teacher to develop a quality learning environment where all students are actively engaged. A significant amount of preparation needs to happen before students arrive on the first day. These quality learning environments are characterised with a sense of purposefulness, have clear and high expectations for student achievement and agreed behaviour guidelines, and provide positive and restorative responses to conflict woven into teacher/student interactions.

Respectful learning environments move beyond rewards and punishments. If students are to grow as responsible citizens then they need to experience and learn responsibility in the classroom and school. Reward and punishment schemes do not meet the needs of students nor do they facilitate the development of prosocial behaviours that enable student autonomy. The development of responsible and autonomous students is linked to our instruction. The way we structure our lessons and involve the students is crucial.

We have also seen in this chapter the practical skills that teachers use in the beginning parts of a lesson as outlined in the Positive Learning Framework. In the next chapter, we will move onto the middle and ending of a lesson and see how teachers manage group work and other instructional strategies to actively involve students in learning.

FURTHER READING

Advancement Project and the Civil Rights Project, 2000, *Opportunities Suspended: The Devastating Consequences of Zero Tolerance and School Discipline Policies*, Harvard Civil Rights Project, Boston, MA.

Bohn, C. M., Roehrig, A. D. & Pressley, M. 2004, *The First Days of School in the Classrooms of Two More Effective and Four Less Effective Primary-Grades Teachers*, University of Chicago Press, Chicago.

Burden, R. 2000, *Powerful Classroom Management Strategies: Motivating Students to Learn*, Corwin Press, Thousand Oaks, CA.

Casella, R. 2003, 'Zero Tolerance Policy in Schools: Rationale, Consequences, and Alternatives', *Teachers College Record*, Volume 105, Number 5, pp 872–892.

Dunbar, C. & Villarruel, F. A. 2002, 'Urban School Leaders and the Implementation of Zero-Tolerance Policies: An Examination of Its Implications'. *Peabody Journal of Education*, 1532–7930, Volume 77, Issue 1, pp 82–104.

Fredricks, J. A., Blumenfield, P. C., & Paris, A. H., 2004, 'School Engagement: Potential of the Concept, State of Evidence', *Review of Educational Research*, 74(1), pp 59–109.

Fredricks, J. A. & Eccles, J. S. 2006, July, 'Is Extracurricular Participation Associated with Beneficial Outcomes? Concurrent and Longitudinal Relations', *Developmental Psychology*, 42(4), pp 698–713.

Libbey, H. 2004, 'Measuring Student Relationships to School: Attachment, Bonding, Connectedness, and Engagement', *Journal of School Health*, Vol 74, 7.

Stinchcomb et al. 2006, 'Beyond Zero Tolerance: Restoring Justice in Secondary Schools', *Youth Violence and Juvenile Justice*, Vol 4, pp123–147.

Sugai, G. & Horner, R. 2002, 'The Evolution Of Discipline Practices: School-Wide Positive Behaviour Supports', *Child & Family Behavior Therapy*, 1545–228X, Volume 24, Issue 1, pp 23–50.

Wong, H. K. & Wong R. T. 1998, *The First Days of School: How to be an Effective Teacher*, Harry K. Wong Publications, Mountain View, CA.

WEBSITES

www.mdrc.org/publications/419/full.pdf

Akey, T. M. (2006, January). School context, student attitudes and behaviour, and academic achievement: An exploratory analysis.

http://youthviolence.edschool.virginia.edu/pdf/JEA%20Guidelines%20article%20 2003.pdf

Dewey G. Cornell article on guidelines for responding to student threats of violence from the Curry School of Education, University of Virginia.

www.teachers.tv/video/1416

Behaviour management guru Sue Cowley works with primary school teachers on issues of pupil behaviour, stress and school rules.

www.education-world.com

Suggested activities to involve students in creating classroom rules and fun ideas for getting the year off to a good start.

www.sreb.org/programs/hstw/publications/pubs/02V47_AchievementReview.pdf

'Academic achievement in the middle grades: What does research tell us?' A review of the literature.

http://findarticles.com/p/articles/mi_6929/is_1_35/ai_n28521093/

A phenomenographic investigation of teacher conceptions of student engagement in learning.

www.lessonplanet.com/search?keywords=anticipatory+set&rating=3

Search anticipatory set lesson plans to find teacher-approved lessons by grade and rating.

Developing Safe and Accountable Classrooms

Learner outcomes

After reading this chapter, you should be able to:

- acknowledge the importance of engaging all students with a range of abilities in learning
- explain how to maintain a learning environment that is varied, safe and accountable
- identify strategies to develop student self-responsibility
- understand the importance of instructional strategies in a productive classroom
- frame questions to assist in developing safe and accountable classrooms
- recognise the importance of working with parents

Key terms

Class meetings

Cooperative learning

Competence

Individual accountability

Mastery

Safe classrooms

Social cohesion

Teaching for thinking

Think time

Teaching in a quality learning environment

In Chapter 4, we began to explore how to establish a framework in the classroom (routines, expectations and behaviour expectations) that assists the teacher to engage students in meaningful learning. Let us assume that you have developed your behaviour expectations and have taught your routines and procedures. The students are in the class and ready to learn. The decisions you make and the strategies you use to engage them in learning is the point where instruction and management meet. In this chapter, we will look at a sample of instructional techniques you could use to support the type of learning you believe to be important for your students. This chapter will focus on a range of instructional strategies outlined in the middle phase of the Positive Learning Framework. In particular, we are interested in addressing how we:

- engage all students with a range of abilities in learning
- maintain a learning environment that is varied, safe and accountable
- develop student self-responsibility.

The assumption that underpins this chapter is that all students need to experience success in their learning. It is very difficult for students to see any worth in their class work if all they experience is failure. These students will not be able to sustain focus and are more likely to misbehave. Can you imagine turning up to university or work every day to be confronted with failure? It is unlikely you would keep going back. Unfortunately, for school-age students they have a legal obligation to be at school, education or training. This is why it is imperative we make our learning environments places students feel safe in.

The universal need of 'mastery' recognised by Brendtro, Brokenleg and Van Bockern (2002) or 'competence' acknowledged by Stanley, Richardson and Prior (2005) highlights how important it is for students to experience success in learning so that they can recognise that they have talent or are competent. Effective teachers have the ability to enable even struggling students to experience success. As effective teachers, we need to structure our classes and deliver content material so that students experience success and are motivated to involve themselves with peers in active learning. This chapter will address the skills and strategies aimed at achieving this level of engagement and success in learning.

Engaging students who have difficulty with learning

The strategies mentioned in this chapter are appropriate for all students including those who have difficulty with learning. The strategies outlined in this chapter and in the textbook are universal in their design and thinking. For some students in the class, you will need to make reasonable adjustments to make the learning inclusive of their ability levels. We have advocated this same approach in responding to student behaviour. As leaders in the class, we need to know our students, connect with them, work with them equitably and respond to their needs. There may be times when you will need support. There may be situations where you require help with specific strategies and expertise for students who need high-level support. If you need help from someone with this level of expertise, then collaborate with specialist staff and ask for support. Seek resources (in the school, at the department level or in the community) to assist you to engage this student in meaningful learning in your class. When working to improve student behaviour we need to be curious about the many ways we can engage students in learning and reflect on what is helping or impeding this student's learning. Often the starting point in including students who have difficulty learning is to ask yourself to what degree you believe they should be included and how much effort you are willing to put in to achieve this level of inclusion. The answers to these questions will affect how you respond to students with additional needs as well as help clarify the kind of class you want to establish as a teacher.

This chapter will address instructional skills and strategies aimed at achieving student engagement and success in learning.

Positive learning framework: design phase

Prevention: lesson design

Middle
- teaching/learning strategy—active student involvement
- collaborative learning strategies
- group work
- student movement for resources
- questioning and responding to student answers
- promoting student success

Ending/closure
- check for understanding against outcome
- evaluation expectations
- lesson summary
- link learning to outside of classroom
- next lesson—what we will be doing next lesson is …

Do not waste students' time!

One point that is not made explicit in teaching or educational texts is a simple message to not waste students' time. Most people loathe having their time wasted. Think of the lectures or tutorials that you opt out of. What is your overriding opinion of these sessions that make you not attend? More than likely, it is a waste of your time and, as a waste of time, you believe that it is not worth the effort. In a professional learning session, teachers will begin to be oppositional or purposely argumentative when they believe that the content is irrelevant. Some will vote with their feet and not return after lunch!

When we think that something is a waste of time, we begin to feel resentful at 'having been forced to go'. We can also feel disrespected or that our abilities are not acknowledged. When people begin to feel disrespected then they will misbehave or opt out of the experience. The difficulty in the classroom is that students are a trapped audience—they have to be there. Students will react to their time being wasted by misbehaving or by deliberately not engaging in the learning. Both outcomes are not helpful to the student, you, or any member of the class. Wasting students' time is not an upper primary or secondary specific problem. It occurs across all age-levels of schooling. Students will perceive their time as wasted if they do not see a purpose for the activity, if the activity is going on far too long, if it is an activity that is a 'hobby' of the teacher's and does not relate to previous learning or if it is just another exercise that is aimed at keeping them busy.

As part of the Critical reflection activity on page 16 of Chapter 1, you were asked to identify the behaviours of effective and ineffective teachers. Revisit your responses—I would guess that wasting time is not a behaviour you would have identified. In reality, an effective teacher would have done the opposite: they would have been very engaging to the point that you couldn't get enough! That is the kind of teacher our students deserve and need—the kind of teacher I hope this text is assisting you to become.

Critical reflection

Using the 'no time wasting' concept

Recently, I had the opportunity to discuss this concept with a group of teachers. One of the teachers was particularly keen to share her story as she used this concept with her lower secondary classes (she was teaching in a Middle school). She commented:

In the first few days we are together, I outline to my class how I will approach my preparation and teaching of lessons. I explain that I will prepare my lessons so that I can assist all of the class to join in and understand what we are learning. I explain that I will not give them material that is worthless or of no point. I will not waste their time with work that has no purpose or function in learning. If we do it, we do it for a reason. If the students are unsure of the reason, they can ask and I will explain. I hope to do this background rationale introduction before topics and briefly when we do some activities, but if I forget the students can remind me and that is fine.

I also say that we will have homework as part of our learning in this class. I try to explain the rationale behind the homework I set and how at times we will use it to catch up, but I will try to keep this to a minimum. I also say that I will not give homework if I have none to give. I will not give homework for homework's sake. When we have homework, it is for a reason and therefore I expect it to be completed in full. I will not waste their time.

I also explain my approach to my class is that I want every student to do well. I will work hard at assisting all students to do well and achieve academic levels that they are proud to receive. Even if the student doesn't want to achieve or is having a slight dip in confidence about the work I will work harder to ensure that they pick up and get back on board with the learning. I tell my students that they will have to work very hard to 'fail' my class, as I will be working very hard for them to succeed.

What I have found with this straight talking about time wasting is that the student responds very positively. They understand the concept of time wasting and they have experienced a lot of time wasted (waiting for Mum or Dad, having to go somewhere they don't want to go, going to 'boring things' and having to do work they felt was of no importance). For me, it also helped have a common language in the class so that if someone was not working as well as I thought then I could comment about their 'wasting time' and the need to get back to work. It works for me and the students appreciate the honesty and capacity they have to be involved in this discussion.

1   What is your initial reaction to this approach? Do you think it is a valid approach or one that you could use?
2   How do you think this approach makes the students in the class feel? How might a student who struggles with academic tasks or who sees little value in school feel about it?
3   How could this concept assist you in having a conversation with a student who is not participating or engaged in your lessons? Could it help or hinder you?
4   This teacher used it for upper primary and lower secondary students. Could you use this approach for lower primary students? If so, how would you present it and would you need to change anything?
5   How would you frame this concept for a parent information evening or in a letter you send home to parents at the beginning of the year telling them about you and your approach to teaching?

Safe and accountable classrooms

Effective teachers go beyond teaching for knowledge and recall. Expert teachers use instructional strategies that develop deep understanding of the topics taught as well as 'teaching for thinking' (Eggen, P. and Kauchak, D., 2006). Teaching for thinking requires students to hypothesise, be curious and take risks in answering questions. For this level of engagement, students need to be accountable for their learning and the classroom needs to be safe.

Accountability is the responsibility of both the student and the teacher. Students need to be held *individually* accountable where they are responsible for being involved in lessons and learning the material taught. Students need to know that the classroom is a place of learning and that the expectation (discussed with the students on day one) is that when we are in the classroom, we are about learning. For this level of accountability, the teacher needs to take deliberate actions. These actions include conveying to the students the purpose behind the work they will be engaged with, and providing instructions on how and when the work is to be completed. It is possible to discuss and negotiate the 'how' and 'when' with students as an aid to increasing ownership and motivation with the work. Students will require monitoring, encouragement and feedback on their progress. In developing accountability, we are also developing student self-responsibility in academic progression as well as behaviour. We will discuss cooperative learning later in this chapter, along with Johnson's (1989) use of the term 'individual accountability' within cooperative learning. Johnson expands individual accountability by proposing that students, as group members, need to be accountable for the group's learning, not just their own.

Students will grow in individual accountability in a safe environment. Students will not learn in a hostile or fearful class where they do not feel emotionally safe. Maslow (1970) identified physical needs (food, shelter etc.) and safety as pre-requisites before other needs can be met. Students will not learn if they fear they will be bullied or ridiculed as a response to their classroom involvement. An emotionally safe classroom is one where a student feels they can risk a creative answer, take an alternative opinion, say something completely wrong and 'pass' on an answer. A safe classroom needs planning and ongoing teacher assessment. Students can feel more vulnerable when transitions occur that require them to move to another room or activity. Often when making transitions there is potential for students to misbehave or to physically threaten other students. Using the skills outlined in Chapter 4, we can reduce the likelihood of this happening. We can use our strategies of proximity, looking, pausing, scanning, saying their name, ignoring, humouring and the instructional strategy of questioning to maintain a safe and accountable classroom.

Once a student feels emotionally safe, we are more likely to develop an environment where they feel they belong. A student that feels safe finds it easier to trust others. In our safe and accountable classrooms, students will feel part of the group, experience their talents and efforts being appreciated and develop positive social bonds with other students. It would be very hard for a student who felt safe, experienced success and was a trusted member of a group to be unmotivated. This is a quality learning environment.

Selecting teaching strategies

Developing a quality learning environment is a personal enterprise. How we teach is, to a large extent, based on who we are. In the assumptions that underpin this text, we have mentioned that the way we manage will be influenced by the way we think about management. The same is true for instruction. How we relate to the students and what activities we select to achieve set objectives will depend on what we bring to the classroom as human beings.

There is no one way to teach. There is no one way to become an effective teacher. A key element of being effective is to understand your strengths and preferences and select strategies that complement your style. There are numerous teaching models on the market. Some will appeal to you and others won't. What is more important is having an understanding of the range of strategies and selecting ones that best suit your teaching style and personality. The qualifier here is that we cannot give you a set of strategies that will work with every student every time. Marzano (2007) in his book *The Art and Science of Teaching* reinforces this point when he states:

> The best research can do is tell us which strategies have a good chance (i.e. high probability) of working well with students. Individual classroom teachers must determine which strategies to employ with the right students at the right time. In effect a good part of effective teaching is an art. (p. 5)

In this next section, we focus on questioning. As a skill, questioning is integral in developing student engagement and accountability. It is also a broader teaching strategy we can use to intervene when students are off-task, and to enhance student self-responsibility.

Questioning for engagement

Questioning as a skill can assist us in engaging students in learning. Part of establishing this skill is keeping safety and accountability central to our thinking so that we can actively engage every student in learning. It is sobering to note that 80 per cent of questions asked in the classroom are answered by 20 per cent of the students. Framing questions to use with a class requires the teacher to consider how to:

- increase higher-level thinking
- promote active learning for all students
- encourage students to use think time
- respond to students' answers
- ensure equitable distribution.

Increasing higher-level thinking

Student responses to our questions allow us to judge the depth of student understanding during the lesson. How we ask questions will determine the level of thought in the response. Bloom's Taxonomy (Bloom, Englehart, Furst, Hill, and Krathwohl, 1956; Anderson and Krathwohl, 2001) has been used extensively for designing higher- or lower- order questions. I am sure you would have come across Bloom's Taxonomy and others like Aschner's, Guilford's and Krathwohl's in your education studies or curriculum areas. For those that have not heard of Bloom's Taxonomy, it includes:

- knowledge—recall
- comprehension—explain
- application—apply your understanding
- analysis—compare/contrast
- synthesis—look at something differently
- evaluation—judge based on evidence.

If we ask simple recall questions then we would expect students to recite facts. If we ask more complex questions about evaluation then we would expect a more involved response. What we know from the literature is that teachers tend to ask more descriptive or knowledge questions (Applegate, Quinn, and Applegate, 2002) and fewer higher-level questions (Dillon, 1988; Wragg, 1993; Wragg and Brown, 2001). A knowledge question could be, 'Who won the AFL Premiership last year?' or 'What is a verb?' If we are aiming at deep learning with our students we need to incorporate higher-level questions. A higher-level question would be in the synthesis or evaluation category of Bloom's taxonomy and could be 'Do you think the Old Man was right in going out to sea for that one last time?' (based on reading *The Old Man and the Sea*, by Ernest Hemingway). 'Construct a speech to give at his wake.' Another way to develop higher-level thinking is to promote student questioning, rather than relying solely on teachers to generate questions.

Developing higher-level thinking

Working with a peer or university colleague, identify two different age groups or year levels and construct one question for each category of Bloom's Taxonomy. You can construct them together or individually and then compare each question. The categories are:

- knowledge
- comprehension
- application
- analysis
- synthesis
- evaluation.

1 How did you find constructing the questions at either end of the taxonomy?
2 What was different in constructing knowledge questions compared with evaluation questions?
3 Think back to a lesson you have taught and see if you can identify the number of knowledge questions you asked compared with synthesis or evaluation questions. How could you change this next time you taught that lesson?
4 What did you notice about the language and level of difficulty in the different age levels you selected?

There can be barriers to encouraging higher-level thinking and questioning in the classroom. Some pre-service or early career teachers often ignore higher-level questions because most questioning is spontaneous and higher-level questions are more difficult to construct off the top of your head. Having a range of questions written down is a good way to ensure you are developing deep learning with your class. In addition, when students are asked more difficult questions, we are often less certain what their responses will be, which can cause anxiety. With low-level questions we are more certain of the types of responses and often believe that more students will be able to answer. One of the concerns in the early years of teaching is knowing the content. Higher-level questions require a good command of the content and we can avoid them if we fear not 'getting it right' or not being able to deal with the student responses or level of curiosity from the class. Finally, students may not have had good exposure to higher-level questions and do not have good models to draw upon to answer confidently. Despite the possible barriers, a quality learning environment incorporates deep learning and the development of deep knowledge. This deep learning needs to be planned and involves the use of activities and questions that actively engage the students in higher-level thinking.

Promoting active learning for all students

Once again, we must mention our goal of engaging students in 'meaningful' learning. Active learning is not mere busy work. Just because the students are quiet does not mean they are engaged with the content or are learning. When you are asking questions or discussing a concept, just because a student is looking at you it does not mean they are following what you are doing or thinking about an answer. In Chapter 4, we explored the concept of engagement, which involved teacher actions and student disposition—effort, attention, cognitive investment and participation. We can assist in student engagement through the style of questions we ask and, importantly, whom we think should respond. When we ask a question, we need to decide whether we have all students respond or whether students can choose to respond when or if they are ready or interested.

We can increase the chance of engagement with how we frame the question. If we ask questions such as:

'Can anyone tell me…?'
'Who can tell me …?'
'Does anyone know…?'
'Joseph, what is the…?'

we are not likely to engage most students. When these types of questions are used as the main source of questioning, it provides an environment for the students to opt out of learning. For instance, when a teacher asks, 'Can anyone…' a student automatically sighs with relief because they are not that 'anyone'. Global questions like these do not encourage student accountability. Questions that begin with a student's name do not engage students because as soon as the student has been named the others can sit back and ignore the answer because they weren't asked.

A more inclusive way to frame questions to promote active participation might include the following style of questions or stems to questions:

'No hands please, I would like you to think to yourself first then be prepared to share your answer when I ask. What are the ...'

'Yesterday we explored the workings of the water cycle. Discuss the processes involved with your partner for a minute then I will ask several of you to share your discussion.'

'I would like you to think to yourself for 30 seconds then share your thinking with your partner and then I will invite several of you to share your answer. Who can judge what is wrong ...'

What these questions invite is student participation. They also are safe as they allow the students to think first or check their understanding with another student before answering publicly. What this style of questioning also highlights is the amount of time we give students before they respond to questions. These questions allow the student time to think.

Questions for active learning

Reframing questions for maximum participation is a skill that needs to be practised.

Working with a trusted peer or university colleague, use a *Trivial Pursuit* card to select a question and reframe it to encourage maximum participation. Read out your reframed question to your partner to get their feedback.

1 Were there common elements to each question beginning?
2 Did you find that some questions got too wordy, where you tried to explain every point? Were the questions engaging? What do you need to do to make them engaging?
3 Could you use this style of questioning for every question you asked in a lesson? If not, when would you most likely use this style of questioning?
4 With your partner, discuss what you are learning about safe and accountable classrooms through the work in this section on questioning.

Practice activity

Using think time

One of the most common mistakes in questioning students is not to allow them thinking time or 'wait time'. Research highlights that teachers wait less than 1 second from asking a question to a student responding (Rowe, 1986). Ideally we should give the students at least 3–5 seconds think time. Rowe (1974, 1986) identifies three benefits to providing think time:

- Students give longer and better answers.
- Voluntary participation increases, and fewer students fail to respond.
- Equitable distribution improves, and responses from cultural minorities increase as teaches become more responsive to students (Cited in Eggen, P. and Kauchak, D. 2006, p.67).

In Chapter 6, we will go into more detail about the amygdala, the brain's sentry, and its role in student behaviour, especially that of vulnerable students. However, the role of the amygdala in responding to situations where it recognises a threat is applicable when looking at questioning. When a student is put on the spot to respond to a question they do not know the answer to, they may feel threatened and respond in a fight or flight way. It is easy to see how students will respond aggressively or in a manner that distracts others from knowing they are under threat of failure! Students will want to save face with their peers. We can assist them by using inclusive framing of questions and by how we respond to student answers.

Responding to student answers

How we respond to student answers can determine whether a student continues to be engaged or whether they shut off from the lesson. Expert teachers have the capacity to 'orchestrate' a question and answer session or discussion that is fluid and engaging for all the students. These expert teachers do this with a range of student responses and not necessarily with just correct or sensible responses. Skilled teachers have the capacity to maximise the level of engagement by understanding why the student has responded they way they have. As beginning teachers, we need to be able to respond to student answers in a way that continues the learning. Barrie Bennett and Carol Rolheiser outline a number of possible responses and teacher responses in their text *Beyond Monet: The Artful Science of Instructional Integration* (2001, p.65). They identify no response, partially correct response, silly response, guess, incorrect response, and correct response. Let us look at how we could respond to these situations while maintaining maximum engagement.

As a teacher, sometimes you ask a student a question and get no response. Think of times at university when a lecturer asked you a question and you did not know the answer. Why didn't you respond? There could be a range of reasons. Maybe you were not paying attention, you didn't understand the question, you did not feel safe and decided not to make yourself vulnerable with a wrong answer, or you didn't hear the question. These could be the student's reasons as well. When you get no response, helpful language could include 'I may have worded that question in a pretty confusing way so let me try again' or 'I think Raymond is telling me that I may have asked that question in a confusing way so I will ask it again more clearly.' If there is silence, you could re-phrase the question in a way that involves the students in a think/pair/share activity (explained later in this chapter). Another strategy is to give students the option of 'passing' or an escape from answering this particular question. When using the 'pass', make sure students know that they will be required to answer another question that they feel comfortable answering later in the lesson.

Sometimes students will get the answer wrong or only partially correct. Often when this happens, it could be our question is too convoluted or has too many parts and the students got lost in the words. It is often necessary to re-state the question in parts or break it down into manageable chunks. If part of the answer is correct it is good to highlight the part that is right and encourage others to assist answering the rest. We could say 'Kaylah you are spot on with Germany being involved in the First World War but the others you mentioned weren't involved, so I was wondering if anyone else could build upon Kaylah's answer and mention some other nations involved in the First World War?' With an incorrect response it is helpful if you can find some element of the response that is noteworthy, for example, 'I like the way you have tried to work this out, well done', 'A good guess but not correct; can others have a go?', or 'No, that is not correct but I am pleased to see you have a go at this question, thank you'.

At times, we will receive a silly response. It could be that the student doesn't know the answer and is putting on a brave face for the class, wants attention or is intentionally disruptive. The motivation could be anything. However, the main thing is to maintain the learning focus of the class.

If you have a good relationship with the class, it may be possible to laugh and then re–direct attention back to learning. When this happens, we try and play the answer with 'a straight bat' and not get caught up into worrying about the appropriateness of the answer. We have often used 'I am not sure that what you suggest is possible but if it was it may assist humans to live more sustainably', 'I am not sure I would have used those terms but the last idea you mention is close to our topic and makes sense', or 'I am not sure I agree with you on this but lets see what the class thinks'. You will need to be confident that the class are on your side and you have the capacity to get them back to learning despite a few distractions.

Practice activity

Responding to student responses

It is important to keep developing a 'language of discipline' as we work through the text. Responding to student responses can be challenging. It is helpful to have practiced some responses that you can use automatically when you are in the middle of a lesson.

Write a reply to the following student responses and then say it aloud.

- In your Year 2 class, you are doing a recount activity on the recent science excursion. You ask one student to speak about the experiment the scientist did with bi-carbonate of soda and vinegar. The student looks straight at you and does not say a word.

- In your pre-primary class, you are working on the topic of 'families'. You ask a student to tell you one good thing that they like doing with their family. The student avoids making eye contact and says, 'We don't do anything'.

- In your Year 7 Maths class, you are working with two-dimensional shapes to see if it is possible to put a line of symmetry through them. You ask one student to comment on whether this is possible with a particular shape and they respond with a silly joke that makes a number of students laugh.

- In your Year 10 History class, you have posed the discussion topic, 'Hitler is not responsible for the Second World War', and asked the students to develop an argument. You ask a question about the role of America and a student answers the question correctly.

- In your Year 9 Home Economics class, you have been focussing on Italian cooking and are currently constructing a menu for the class to work on. You ask one student to identify ingredients a well-known dish you have discussed before but they can only identify a few and guess the rest, which are wrong.

1   What elements of this activity did you find challenging? Can you explain the difficulty?

2   Was it easy to keep the concepts of safety and accountability in your thinking? How can these concepts assist in the type of responses you make?

Ensuring equitable distribution

It would appear an easy task to ensure that you distribute your questions around the room and invite participation from all students. It is a simple idea but it can be difficult to do. The term 'equitable distribution' comes from Kerman (1979) to describe a pattern of questioning where students are called on as equally as possible. When students know that they will be required to answer a question at some stage and that questions are distributed equitably it increases their motivation and achievement (McDougall and Granby, 1996). Equitable distribution is part of the accountable classroom, 'we are here to learn'. This is quite different from the previously cited research that highlighted that most questions in a class are answered by only 20 per cent of students. Distributing questions equitably requires ongoing monitoring by the teacher as well as energy to sustain student motivation and enthusiasm.

Freiberg and Driscoll (2005) describe a questioning technique devised by Freiberg (1992, 1999) called the 'Go Around System'. This system is aimed at helping teachers gain equity in question distribution. The teacher goes around the class and asks the students in order 'tell me one idea you learned from yesterday or from today's class without repeating another student's answer'. As the teacher goes around, if a student cannot think of an answer, he or she can pass. Students who pass raise their hand and must answer another question before the activity is finished. The students who pass are asked questions in between the other class members responding. Freiberg and Driscoll (2005) highlight that students find it a fair system because they all get a chance to respond and have the option to pass or come back later to a question they may have forgotten the answer to. This system ensures students are listening and engaged as the ones who have responded keep focussed to see if another student repeats their answer and those who have not yet responded know that they have the safety of a pass or can answer later on.

Cooperative learning strategies and tactics

Placing students in groups as an instructional decision has been a part of classrooms since education began. Grouping students is a way of reducing the whole group to a more manageable size, which allows us to teach a few students at a time. As classrooms continue to grow in diversity, placing students in groups is a common practice for all year levels. Although common practice, it is still an area marked with problems and it presents the teacher with specific management issues, instruction decisions and resource and environment challenges. Placing students in groups can often be seen as natural and the 'done thing', yet it is not as simple as putting them together and expecting them to learn. Often we have witnessed the pre-service teacher go into a class determined to use groups in their lesson, because they had covered this in their course, only to find themselves struggling to control the class and get them on-task to complete the set lesson. Working in groups and using instructional strategies aimed at group interaction is a skill that needs practice and planning. Robert Slavin (2002), a leader in the research and practice of cooperative learning, identifies that to be effective we need to be 'intentional teachers', where we reflect on our practice and make decisions on our instruction based on our knowledge of learning and our learners.

Research on cooperative learning

The research on cooperative learning is vast. We do not intend to summarise the whole field or convey the message that it is a simple practice. Cooperative learning is a complex and sophisticated approach that needs careful implementation and highly developed teacher skills. In this section, we are aiming to give you practical instructional management skills associated with grouping students for learning.

Cooperative learning is 'a form of instruction in which students are organised into groups to complete assignments collaboratively, to assist each other, to solve problems, to share materials, and to participate in discussions' (Emmer, Evertson and Worsham, 2003, p. 110). It is this group nature, involving social interaction and the need to problem-solve, share ideas and acknowledge others' opinions, which makes the approach to instruction appealing. A positive element of this approach is that it is aimed at engaging student in meaningful and varied learning.

The research on cooperative learning often highlights the positive bene-fits of increased student engagement. The use of small groups offers students a greater potential for active participation rather than being passive recipients of information. Often, students who struggle can benefit from leaning with other more able students. In this interaction, the students are developing their interpersonal skills. When a group works well the student also receives affirmation of their efforts and contributions to the group. Importantly the research helps us realise that just because students are in groups does not mean they will learn. A number of strategies can be used to enhance the effectiveness of groups (Emmer and Gerwels 1998; Cohen 1994; Slavin 1995). The strategies we will outline include most of the essential compo-nent of groups outlined by Johnson and Johnson (1999).

Johnson and Johnson (1999) have identified essential components that need to be included in your planning of activities when using groups. Effective groups have the following components:

*   *Individual accountability*—making sure that all member of the group are responsible for their own learning and the learning of other members of the group. This is a crucial element because a group will not function and learning will not occur if it is dominated by one student, or if several members are allowed to hide, leaving one student to do all the work.
*   *Face-to-face interaction*—the students have maximum opportunity to con-tribute to the group. Students are encouraged to support, encourage and help other members in the learning task. For this to happen, students need to be sitting in small groups (of two to four people) close enough to hear each other and see each others' faces.
*   *Interpersonal and social skills*—the students' social, communication and problem-solving skills that enable them to work effectively in groups. Students need to be taught these skills and to have them continually affirmed for groups to work effectively. It is easy to see how important it is to have developed a sense of safety in our classrooms for students to work collaboratively together.
*   *Positive interdependence*—students' working positively together and being accountable for the learning of the group members. This element may not happen because of the students' different personalities, different ideas of the task, and their own opinions on how tasks should be completed.

- *Group processing*—the metacognitive process of reflecting on group work to see how the group could be improved academically and collaboratively. With this reflection, groups can grow to be more effective.

Cooperative learning strategies

In this section, we will explore the decisions teachers make to ensure that groups work efficiently and are engaged in learning. As we look at these teacher actions, we will describe several cooperative learning strategies that could be used to enhance the safety and accountability within the class. These tactics are only a selection from a number of cooperative learning strategies from authors including Spencer Kagan, Jeanne Gibbs, Robert Slavin, Barrie Bennett and Carol Rolheiser. We suggest you find some of these authors' texts or programs to extend your repertoire of skills and strategies to enhance student learning in your classroom. If used effectively, you will reduce the likelihood of students being off-task and possibly misbehaving. Some of the strategies you can use are:

- 'human bingo' and 'find someone who' (group cohesion activities)
- inside/outside circles
- value line and four corners
- placemat
- think/pair/share
- graffiti.

'HUMAN BINGO' AND 'FIND SOMEONE WHO ...' (GROUP COHESION ACTIVITIES)

Johnson and Johnson's basic elements of groups provide a litmus test of strategies to use with the class. When using a strategy or tactic it is good to see if it is supportive of these elements. However, before we look at some of these strategies and apply them to a class setting, we will need to do some preparation and make some basic operational decisions. One of the first steps in deciding to work in groups is to develop a climate of cohesion and cooperation. In Chapter 2, we looked at making individual connections with students. It is also possible to make social connections with the class. There are a multitude of resources out there for developing positive group dynamics and group cooperation. Some of the activities that we have used from the early years to university level include 'human bingo' or 'find someone who ...' The latter requires the students to 'find someone who' has, for example, the same number of family members, uses the same toothpaste, whose birthday is the same and so on. These items are put onto a sheet and students have to walk around the room in silence or talking quietly trying to sign off their items. This is a great way for students to get to know each other in a short amount of time.

INSIDE/OUTSIDE CIRCLES

Working together as a group outside the class can be a powerful way to bond students and teacher together. We have mentioned several ideas already, such as decorating the classroom on the weekend, fundraising or working for a charity on a weekend or one day in school if the 'appeal' is on a weekday. This is a great way to help students become more generous. Students can also introduce each other, or, using an 'inside/outside circle', talk about their hobbies, interests, family, favourite holiday or anything that suits their age-group. An inside/outside circle is where the class is divided into circles with one circle on the inside facing out and the other outside circle facing towards the inner circle. Students are given a set amount of time to introduce themselves to the peer opposite them and then the inside circle can move so that they are facing a new partner. This is a great way to promote interaction at the beginning of the school year or whenever you need the class to discuss a topic, idea or activity.

The second decision to make when using groups in cooperative learning is the size of each group and which students are in what group. The natural temptation is to listen to the students who want to work with their friends. At times, this may be acceptable, however Johnson and Johnson (1999) found that these groups are less focussed on the task than teacher-selected groups. Cohen (1994) believes that smaller groups are more efficient and allow for more interaction and engaged learning time. Most writers in this area agree that small is better with only two to four students in a group. The third important decision is your role in cooperative learning. Managing multiple groups is complex and requires planning and teacher actions. Cohen (1994) found that teachers were more successful in cooperative learning situations when they delegated authority to the groups to enable more interaction among group members. We will explore the role of students as leaders in the next section and how such involvement leads to students developing responsibility. The second part of the teacher role involves the teacher's ability to give clear instructions and directions about the objectives and to structure the group's activity.

VALUE LINE

In her 'Tribes' program, Jeanne Gibbs talks about the value line, where students put themselves on the line or continuum from 'strongly agree' to 'strongly disagree'. We use this strategy a lot when working with teachers in schools and with university students around issues in schools or classrooms. There are a few variations, but the idea is that students place themselves on the line in response to a question read out by the teacher. The teacher then asks the students to explain why they positioned themselves where they did. It is good to sample a range of responses so that students see the breadth of responses in their class. This is a good activity to highlight the diversity of stances on common teaching issues. These often exist in a teacher group that has to work together. Some unity of purpose needs to come from this diversity, though this can be difficult to achieve. This strategy can be used from students of all levels. We have seen it work in lower primary classes around the topic of sharing or treating each other with respect. The teacher has read out a statement and students move to a spot and then say what they think about the issues. Used this way, it can be a good visual guide to how students in a class feel about issues like sharing or bullying.

FOUR CORNERS

An expanded version of the value line is 'four corners'. Four corners is great for stimulating a debate on a chosen topic. To do this activity, read out a statement and then ask the students to move to a corner that best represents how they think about the topic or where they stand on the topic. The corners can have paper labels with 'strongly agree', 'agree', 'disagree' and 'strongly disagree'. Once students are in their selected corner they can then be called upon to explain why they chose where they are. This is great, for example, to use in a Year 5 class that has been studying Australian landforms, focussing on the features and location of mountains, waterways, desert, and coastal plains. You could ask students which feature is most important to Australia and have them explain why they have chosen this feature. This can be done for other topics, such as energy or sustainability, which are taught at varying levels of complexity from Year 1 through to the final year of school. Teachers can use this technique with a novel or storybook and have students move to where they think the most important character is, or where the most pressing problem in the book is, or they could have the corners represent solutions to a problem and have the students move to the solution they believe is best suited to solve the issue.

PLACEMAT

The placemat strategy allows students to work individually as well as part of a group on an issue or topic under investigation. The placemat offers safety to students as they will first have time to write down what they think and then have the chance to share their response and listen to others. After completing this step, the group offers feedback. This strategy is not only safe but also gives students the opportunity to be accountable.

For the activity, you need to provide a placemat—that is, a piece of paper that is big enough for each group to work around. This could be butcher's paper or an A3 sheet. The paper is divided into the number of people in the group. Four is ideal, but more is possible, as long as you realise you are increasing the complexity and management with more members. There is a central circle or square in the middle of the page. Group members brainstorm ideas in their section. The middle square is for common points or for forming the groups' response once all members have had their chance to share ideas. See Figure 3.3 on page x for a placemat template.

Placemat is a helpful tool for introducing a new topic. For example, if you are starting a topic on Australian government or Australian history, you could ask the students to write down what they already know and then identify common areas of existing knowledge in the middle square. You could also use this activity when you have a documentary or DVD that you want the students to watch. They can write down ideas or observations in their section during the DVD and then share what they found. If you conduct class meetings, then you can use the placemat to seek consensus or discuss what your class thinks are the most important issues around a problem that they have identified. Each group can then report on what they have discussed.

THINK/PAIR/SHARE

The think/pair/share activity is one of the simplest cooperative learning strategies to use and yet it can be tricky to implement correctly. When the students are in groups, they are asked to *think* to themselves, and then with the person next to them (*pair*) *share* their answer or ideas. Although it sounds very easy and as if it will happen automatically, this strategy still requires guidance to ensure accountability. It could be that one person dominates the sharing or does not listen actively to what is said or the two talk about something completely off-task. One way to increase accountability is to use a group-forming tactic. An easy one is 'lettered heads'. Students 'letter off' in their pairs as either A or B (this is the same as numbered heads used for forming groups or pairs). After they have had time to think, the A speaks for a minute and then you ask B people to paraphrase the first answer back to A. Repeat for B, then explain you will randomly call on pairs to share an answer. Think/pair/share helps make students feel safe as they have the chance to think first, rather than be asked on the spot and they have the additional safety of listening to another student's response and together offering an answer. The strategy increases individual as well as group accountability as all students are involved.

GRAFFITI

Graffiti is a brainstorming activity that involves the whole class. This strategy can be used at all levels. In groups of three or four, students are given a piece of paper with a topic on it that can be different or the same as another group's paper. For example, it could be that you are studying the ancient world and want the students to identify as much as they know about ancient civilisations such as Egypt, Rome, Greece and China. Students write down as much as they know about one element (for example, Rome) on their sheet of paper in two minutes. You then ask them to move to another topic sheet and to brainstorm all they know in two minutes again. This is repeated until all groups have returned to their original sheet. When they get back to the sheet, there are a number of things they can do: prepare group responses, develop questions to ask, identify common myths, errors or truths. Use different coloured markers for each group. This will help you identify a group who have not grasped the concept properly or who have purposely written silly or inappropriate answers. As a preventative technique, how will you respond when a student puts down a silly answer? It will happen and you will need to respond positively and work to re-engage the student or group into the activity.

We mentioned in Chapter 1 that students come to school from diverse backgrounds, interests and capabilities. Engaging a class of diverse learners requires planning and skill. Included in the planning is our own position on what we are trying to achieve. We believe that quality learning environments promote student responsibility and leadership. The classroom should be a safe place to risk a wrong answer as well as a place of learning where students are accountable for their learning and the learning of their group. The suggested strategies outlined in this section can be used by effective teachers to promote meaningful learning for all students. Assisting students in becoming responsible members of the class and developing the ability to be personally responsible is made possible through involving them in the planning, learning and teaching in the class. The next section explores how we can do this in our class.

Applying cooperative learning strategies in your class

Working with a peer or study partner, construct several sample lessons where you include cooperative learning strategies. Select a focus or objective from a topic you have taught or will teach and identify the age group. In this practice activity, it is important to articulate your 'teacher dialogue'—what you will say and do to achieve your intended outcome. Use the lesson design format you are required to use at university and develop lesson plans that you can use as part of your school placement teaching requirements.

In your lesson, you will need to address the following instructional issues:

1   Is your class ready for group work? What will you need to do to prepare them for collaborative work in groups? Outline the strategies or processes you would use to develop a positive social bond in the class.
2   What size are your groups? Does this suit your room or learning environment? Are there any constraints or physical limitations you need to take into account?
3   What is the group membership? How will you decide the membership of the groups?
4   How will you form groups—write out exactly what you will say and do.
5   When they are in groups, identify a cooperative learning strategy you would use that enhances student and group accountability.

Keep what you have developed as a resource you can use when in schools. If others have done this or it has been part of class activity share the resources you have developed to build your teaching resource portfolio.

Practice activity

Helping students develop as responsible learners

The approach taken in this text and set out in the Positive Learning Framework emphasises student self-discipline and the creation of caring learning environments with a high degree of social decision making. Students need to be an integral part of the classroom, and active participants rather than passive observers. As Freiberg (1999) says, they must move from being 'tourists to citizens'. Developing student responsibility will not happen spontaneously in any classroom. In fact, it requires a shift in thinking and practice from teacher-centred to more student-centred learning environments. The process of developing students who are a responsible and accountable part of developing a supportive learning environment involves strategy building, self-control and conflict resolution. To promote the role of the students in the classroom we will need to seek student input into how the class works, how lessons are taught and assessment processes. A number of strategies to achieve this have been included in the above section and in Chapter 4, however, one strategy that we have not previously mentioned that affirms the value of student input is classroom meetings.

Classroom meetings

One approach that a number of writers have identified as a good forum for encouraging authentic student voices is holding scheduled class meetings (Glasser, 1969; Gordon, 1974; Kohn, 1996; Nelson, Lott and Glenn, 2000). As a strategy, class meetings are not new. The focus on getting students involved to solve problems or discuss how the class is progressing has been part of a number of recent approaches that refer to it in different terms. For instance, 'circle time' has become popular in primary classrooms. Irrespective of the title, the essential elements are that students learn to voice an opinion and take ownership for what is happening in the classroom. The structure of these meetings can vary. Some teachers 'call' for topics or issues to be tabled the week prior to the meeting and an agenda is worked out. Some teachers will have a suggestion box or meeting folder where students can place items for the teacher's attention. The follow on from an agenda approach is that decisions, when reached, need to be revisited to see if the solution is still valid. In this way, students learn that solutions are not set in stone and that the life of the class is dynamic and circumstances may change. We advocated this approach in Chapter 4 when looking at 'rule creation'. It may be that some rules have reached their use-by date and need reworking.

One decision the teacher needs to make is who will chair the meeting. This will depend on the age of the students and your personal style. Some teachers do it themselves or have a rotating chairperson so every one gets a chance to chair the meeting. You need to decide if students will take on the roles of secretary, timekeeper, resource person, arranging the room or if a small group will be responsible for developing the focus or agenda for the meeting. Whatever the process you select, it is important to recognise that the students are developing highly sophisticated problem-solving skills and that this will take time. Jones and Jones (2001) highlight that, while it will take time, third grade students can run their own class meetings with support from the teacher. Jones and Jones (2001) support a process whereby the students gradually assume more responsibility as they grow in confidence and capacity to work collaboratively. A 'meeting job roster' can assist this process.

Class meetings as a strategy do not always involve high-stakes problem solving. There are great social benefits in getting the class together to share their stories, or using the gathering to decide on how the room could be set up for the next topic of work, help in planning for the science excursion or music excursion as well as reflecting on how the class is developing as a safe and accountable place. The students can also use class meetings to develop more ownership of the intended learning. Within this context, teachers can discuss the next sequence of work and the proposed assessment with the students. Students may suggest parts of the assessment or develop ideas, questions or processes. An example of this is giving the students a choice of how to present their information for an assessment. They could do it through an extended written answer, write a simple play, create a poster or learning resource for the class, or some other idea that they can negotiate with you. The learning outcomes are still achieved except this time you have a lot more enthusiasm and student motivation to do the assessment.

Classroom leaders

When we were talking earlier about cooperative learning we mentioned that more responsibility or involvement given to the students in groups can yield a better level of engagement than teacher-directed processes. The same thing is true in the day-to-day workings of the classroom. In developing responsibility, we need to give the students opportunities to be responsible. We also think it is important for the student to take responsibility and ownership of their learning and classroom. An easy way to do this is to have the students be leaders of specific jobs in the class. For example, when we change from literacy to art the leaders responsible for the art equipment know that they need to get the art materials out and distribute them to the class. The literary leaders are aware that they need to pack away the books and games used in the session. When we take the roll and are required to take our list to the office a student could be responsible for this. This leadership role happens in classrooms across the world. However, what is different from 'getting a student to do a job' is that in this class we see it as a leadership role because they are responsible for assisting learning and maintaining the classroom environment (packing away). At the beginning of the school year, we talk about them getting involved and being leaders. A roster is drawn up and students rotate through the jobs during the year. Each leadership role lasts for four or five weeks so students get two changes per term. This is just another example of how the students can be involved and contribute to developing a positive learning environment. The concept of student leaders is not just for primary classrooms, although it is easier to sell the idea to them. If it is part of the way we do things around here then it is easy to say to secondary classes 'this is what we do in our class and all of us will be classroom leaders over the year'.

Working with parents

With all these approaches, it is important to convey the rationale and practice to parents. Let us look at how we can involve parents in supporting you in your efforts to promote a quality learning environment.

Barriers to parent involvement

One of the areas of school life that recent graduates find threatening is working with parents. Often we are not taught how to work with parents or how to address parent conflict. It is true that a number of the skills identified in working with students are transferable to working with parents. We would suggest that the skills and strategies outlined in the next chapter are just as valid when working with parents as they are with students. We know this to be the case as we have used these strategies in parenting evenings and courses we have facilitated. Before we look at the importance and strategies to engage parents let us look at some of the reasons why parents are reluctant to get involved or may come across as antagonistic towards teachers and the school.

School is not a fun or successful place for all people. Some of the parents of children in our schools do not have positive memories of school nor of teachers. For some parents, schools are places of failure, both academically and socially, and there is nothing there that brings any joy to them. In fact, the sights and sounds of a school may bring back awful memories. Often the way these parents cope is to avoid getting involved or setting foot onto the grounds to avoid these memories.

Parents and families are under stress. Parents need to work to survive and they do not have the time to drop everything and get to school. For some, their priority is to work to feed their family. School or their child's behaviour is a low priority. As a teacher, it is important to recognise this level of pain so that we can connect with the parents and understand their situation. Out of this understanding and connection, it may be possible to work together in different ways. A related issue, mentioned in Chapter 2, is the lack of support we give to working parents, in particular mothers. After working a full day, it is difficult for them to assist with the project on endangered animals when they have to get dinner ready and bath the youngest. If we add in, for a minority of parents, another layer of stress or complexity such as substance abuse, then it is very difficult to find any space in the parent's life for education. This is not to say that the parent doesn't want what is best for their child. However, it highlights that, as teachers, we need to find alternative ways to work together to help the child.

A growing problem is the changing level of expertise in parenting skills. Experienced early childhood teachers are united in their observation of how the expectations and skills of the parents have changed over the years. Teachers are often confronted with an attitude of 'if it happens during school time it is your problem, as I have to deal with him all night.' Or parents comment that they 'can't get her to go to bed before 10 p.m. or make her behave'. These barriers need not be insurmountable. Let us explore some ways that we can make our classroom and school welcoming to parents.

Encouraging parents to be involved

Parents are no different to students who want to feel welcome in the classroom or school. One way to make parents welcome and at ease with you is for them to experience how you are caring for their child. They need to know that you will listen to them and you value their opinion. One way to do this is to make contact with parents early on in the school year. This can be through phone calls or through a newsletter, note or class paper. If you choose to phone them it is a good idea to have some positive feedback about the student. Another idea is to have a newsletter and class paper as ways to communicate information about you and how you will work with the class this year. It is a good idea to inform the parents about what you hope to achieve this year, how you intend to teach, how you will manage the class and what processes you will use if a student has any problems. This does not have to be written out formally but can be done as a newsletter or front page of the newspaper with some student artwork. The parents will love the fact that you have made an effort to inform them about what will be happening and that you will seek assistance throughout the year with parents. This communication alerts parents that you will be making contact and that together you are partners in assisting their child to thrive in your class.

In the newsletter, it is a good idea to ask for parents to drop in to the class and school. This doesn't have to be a formal day set aside or placed on the school calendar but an invitation for parents to come to class to see what happens. While they are visiting, let them join their child for lunch! It is amazing how student behaviour improves markedly when a parent is in the classroom. If parents can't come then let them know that grandparents can be involved. Intergenerational cooperation is wonderful for the students. Grandparents can also be a great source of knowledge and wisdom in the school. If dropping in is too difficult then, as a class, schedule times for parent involvement. This is crucial in upper primary and secondary as after the first few years parents can get lost in the ether, never to be seen again. Often it is in these years the students need as many supportive and caring adults as possible.

A criticism often levelled at teachers is that the parent never knew what was happening or was not given feedback (McDonald & Thomas, 2003). Parents have a point, as finding out from an adolescent how they are going at school can be very difficult. Parents need feedback that is frequent and meaningful. A quick phone call to alert a parent to your concern over a student's behaviour is a very effective way of getting support and tackling the problem before it becomes unmanageable. Parents also appreciate the early notification. It is always worthwhile to establish a process of communication that is sustained throughout the year over and above the usual parent evenings or reports. These can be simple 'well done' notes or class newsletters that go out twice a term noting achievements and successes.

Working with parents is a necessary part of teaching and is integral to effective classroom management. In working with parents, we need to:

- view them as being on our side and as team members, not adversaries
- respect the knowledge they have of their child
- understand parents who struggle with coming to school because of past experiences
- appreciate the effort is takes to come to school—a parent's visit may entail shifting around home and work schedules and possibly making childcare arrangements
- identify an issue, come up with several solutions and have evidence or work samples to support your concerns
- be aware of community resources that are available for parents seeking assistance and support.

Working in partnership with parents

This activity is intended to give you practice in problem solving with parents. We often do not get much practice in working with parents in a teacher education course, however, it is a vital element in teaching and it requires highly developed problem-solving skills.

Working with two peers or study group members, use the scenarios below to have a conference or interview with parents. In the scenarios, you will need one peer to be the

Practice activity

teacher, one the parent and one an observer. The observer's role is to offer descriptive feedback on what they heard and saw. The teacher needs to focus on the problem or issue to be discussed and to outline possible solutions. Remember to be aware of 'how' you are saying what you are saying—eye contact, tone of voice, body language, facial expressions and so on.

Scenario 1

Laughlin's quality and quantity of work has been dropping off lately. Last week he did not hand in his science homework sheet and he was easily distracted in class. He has not progressed much in his Society and Environment assignment, which is due in two days time. At the end of today's lesson, he asked if he could hand it in next week. He knows that you have already allowed two other students who were sick for a number of days to hand their projects in late.

Scenario 2

You find Aleisha's attitude to learning negative and when you try to get her involved, she often responds rudely. On numerous occasions, you have asked her to return to her desk to complete work where she has muttered under her breath how much she hates this class. You have put her in a supportive group with friendly students but this is not working. Yesterday she openly refused to work and threw her books on the floor. When her mum arrives to meet with you, her opening remarks are, 'I am not sure us meeting will do any good as she does not like you. Once she hates someone there is nothing you can do'.

Scenario 3

One of the practices you have in your Year 2 classroom is for the students to work out of an exercise book for homework. The students know that when they get to class in the morning they place the book on your desk for you to check during the day and they get it back after lunch. Victor is an energetic student who does his best in most activities. You always find checking his work tedious as he is in not good at writing and often uses drawings instead of words. On several occasions, he has done a story for you instead of what was set for homework. Today when you are checking his work, you notice that he has written some swear words in his story. You are very surprised that Victor would do this, because you have spoken to him before about language in the playground. When Victor's father arrives, he pushes across the teacher's desk a doctor's note saying that Victor has ADHD and says that is why Victor swears.

Case studies

In these case studies, these teachers are having difficulty with organising and presenting instruction. As a teaching and learning expert from central or district office, you have been asked to assist these teachers in improving their instruction. Using the information and concepts in this chapter, outline strategies that would be helpful in overcoming these problems.

Case study 5.1

In Mr Pickering's class, there always seems to be a group of students that require extra explanations or who just don't get the work set for them. Mr Pickering gets frustrated during his lectures when students keep asking questions about what they need to write in their workbooks. When homework is set students ask more questions on material that he has covered in the class. Sometimes he has to explain again something he has just covered in the class. During some classes, Mr Pickering has to raise his voice so that students can hear him because there is so much talking from groups of students.

Case study 5.2

Ms Averill is the literacy specialist in the lower primary classes. As the class after lunch is about to start she uses proximity, standing near two students who are talking. The students stop and Ms Averill begins her lesson. As the students are getting their pencils out, Ms Averill hands out the resource sheet. She explains that the lesson will focus on the activity on the sheet and that students will be working in their reading groups. Ms Averill then asks 'Who can tell me what the pussy cat in the story is trying to tell the other cats?' As some students call out and others put their hands up, she exclaims 'Oh, I nearly forgot to mention that tomorrow we will be going to the library for a puppet show by a professional storytelling group'. The students are excited and after a little while, Ms Averill returns their attention to the sheet on their desk. 'Before we move to groups I want you to do the missing words activity'.

As the students begin to write down words, two students come into class late with a note from the office. Ms Averill calls out to them across the room to come here and asks 'Why are you late?' The students begin a long story of what they were doing in the office and how they were the only ones who saw the soccer ball hit the light and they saw which Year 5 had done it and they had to speak with the principal. The rest of the class stops their literacy activity. Several students ask questions of the two late students. Ms Averill stands up and says, 'Right, where were we? Yes, let's get into our groups and finish off our activity sheet. Before we do can anyone tell me what the answer was to the first missing word space?' One student responds with an incorrect answer. 'Mackenzie that is not right, you must have been asleep, can anyone else tell me?' No one puts their hands up or calls out. Ms Averill continues, 'Well, then let's get down to work. Don't forget the puppet show tomorrow'.

Developing my classroom management plan

In this chapter, we have discussed the need to establish learning environments where students experience success. In quality learning environments, students feel emotionally safe and are individually accountable for learning. We have also suggested that cooperative learning as an instructional approach provides the teacher with a range of strategies to engage students through collaborative group work. This chapter raises a number of questions that you will need to answer or address when looking at your role as the teacher and how your students learn. Below are some questions that may help you to imagine how this approach to instruction and learning will work in your classroom.

1   Is the concept of 'not wasting time' appealing to you or workable in your approach?
2   To what degree do you think we need safe and accountable classrooms?
3   To what degree is a safe and accountable classroom the teacher's responsibility and to what degree are the students responsible?
4   Is cooperative learning an approach you could use? To what extent will your class be collaborative?
5   Is the social engagement of students important to your classroom and teaching?
6   To what degree, if at all, will you involve students in the planning, teaching and assessment of curriculum content?

7   How important is the involvement of parents in your class? How could you use this resource?

8   If someone were to visit your class, what would they expect to see if you followed a collaborative approach to learning with your class?

9   What will visitors see when they visit your class and what would they say about your approach to teaching?

Summary

All students need to achieve success at school. Planning for student engagement, and the strategies and tactics we use to achieve this engagement, highlight where classroom management and instruction meet. Classroom management and instruction are two sides of the same coin. Planning for instruction and being aware of what we are trying to achieve through the instructional strategies we use is important to making our classrooms safe and accountable. Students need to feel emotionally as well as physically safe in our classrooms. We want students to risk answering questions, to be curious about learning and have the capacity to collaborate with peers in learning. We want students to have the capacity to problem solve, work in teams and grow in responsibility. Cooperative learning as an approach to instruction assists us in this task. In particular, we looked at the strategy of framing questions. We also explored some common group-forming strategies and instructional techniques that are aimed at facilitating students' development as active learners rather than passive recipients of teacher knowledge.

Students will need support to develop as responsible learners. Students will need opportunities in which to practice responsibility and leadership. We can give students opportunities for responsible development in our classes. When we see our students as partners in learning and involve them in learning, the opportunities for involvement open up. We can invite their thoughts and enlist their help through class meetings, cooperative learning strategies, problem-solving processes and leadership roles in the class. In this partnership, it is vital to involve parents. Parents are important allies in developing self-regulated learners. We should involve parents whenever we can in the classroom and have them support our efforts to enhance learning.

Developing a quality learning environment where deep thinking occurs requires careful planning and decisions about how the students will learn. Once these decisions have been made it is up to us to use a range of instructional strategies to actively engage the students in learning. However, even with this planning and level of expertise there will be some students on some days who chose not to learn as best they could. How we respond to these students and re-engage them in learning in the lesson and in future lessons is the focus of the next chapter.

FURTHER READING

Arrends, R. I. 1998, *Learning to Teach*, McGraw Hill, New York.

Bennett, B. & Rolheiser, C. 2001, *Beyond Monet: The Artful Science of Instructional Integration*, Bookation Inc., Toronto.

Cohen, E. 1992, *Restructuring the Classroom: Conditions for Productive Small Groups*, Wisconsin Center for Education Research, Madison, WI.

Freiberg, H. J. 1999, *School Climate: Measuring, Improving and Sustaining Healthy Learning Environments*, Falmer Press, New York.

Gardner, H. 1993, *Multiple Intelligences: The Theory into Practice*, Basic Books, New York.

Good, T. L. & Brophy, J. E. 1994, *Looking in Classrooms*, Harper Collins, New York.

Hunter, R. 2004, *Madeline Hunter's Mastery Teaching: Increasing Instructional Effectiveness in Elementary and Secondary Schools*, Corwin Press, California.

Johnson, D. & Johnson, F. 2000, *Joining Together: Group Theory and Group Skills*, 7th edn, Allyn & Bacon, Boston.

Johnson, D. W. & Johnson, R. T. 1999, 'Making Cooperative Learning Work Theory into Practice', *Building Community through Cooperative Learning*, Vol. 38, No. 2, pp. 67–73.

Kagan, S. 1994, *Cooperative Learning*, Kagan Publishing, San Juan Capistrano.

Lang, H. R., McBeath, A., & Hebert, J. 1995, *Teaching: Strategies and Methods for Student–Centered Instruction*, Harcourt Brace, New York.

McDonald, T. & Thomas, G. 2003, 'Parents' Reflections on their Children Being Excluded', *Emotional Behavioural Difficulties*, Vol. 8, No. 2, May, Sage Publications, London.

Morgan, N. & Saxton, J. 1994, *Asking Better Questions*, Pembroke Publishers, Markham, ON.

Slavin, R. E. 1999, 'Comprehensive Approaches to Cooperative Learning Theory into Practice', *Building Community through Cooperative Learning*, Vol. 38, No. 2, pp. 74–79.

— 1987, 'Cooperative Learning: Where Behavioral and Humanistic Approaches to Classroom Motivation Meet', *The Elementary School Journal*, Vol. 88, No. 1 pp. 29–37.

Stevens, R. J. and Slavin, R. E. 1995, 'The Cooperative Elementary School: Effects on Students' Achievement, Attitudes, and Social Relations', *American Educational Research Journal*, Vol. 32, No. 2 pp. 321–351.

WEBSITES

www.tribes.com

Describes Tribes Learning Communities, safe and caring environments in which kids can do well.

www.instructionalintelligence.ca

The focus of instructional intelligence is on enhancing student learning through quality teaching. It is the integration of what we know about how students learn, the curriculum to be learned, instruction, assessment, personal change and systemic change.

www.kaganonline.com

Dr. Kagan created simple 'structures' that allow teachers to guide the interaction of students. Kagan's structures not only lead to greater cooperativeness; they have proven positive results in many areas, including greater academic achievement, improved ethnic relations, enhanced self-esteem, harmonious classroom climate and the development of social skills and character virtues.

www.co-operation.org

The Cooperative Learning Center is a Research and Training Center focusing on how students should interact with each other as they learn and the skills needed to interact effectively.

http://olc.spsd.sk.ca/DE/PD/instr

Instructional strategies determine the approach a teacher may take to achieve learning objectives. The site includes five categories of instructional strategies and explains these categories.

www.humboldt.edu/~tha1/hunter-eei.html

Outlines what is generally referred to at the Madeline Hunter Method with an explanation of the meaning of the terms and a fuller development of the Hunter method.

http://tonyl.files.wordpress.com/2006/06/Noble%20MI%20tool.pdf

'Integrating the Revised Bloom's Taxonomy with Multiple Intelligences: A Planning Tool for Curriculum Differentiation.'

www.educationoasis.com/resources/Articles/working_with_parents.htm

Working with parents – advice from teachers.

Re-engaging the Disengaged Learner

Learner outcomes

After reading this chapter, you should be able to:
- identify the common behaviours experienced in the classroom
- describe the negative effects of zero-tolerance philosophy and punishment for vulnerable students
- understand the key components of a whole-school approach to discipline
- explain a range of strategies to defuse and de-escalate conflict in the classroom
- recognise the opportunity for professional learning from incidences of conflict.

Key terms

Amygdala
Consistency management and cooperative discipline
Language of de-escalation
Pain-based behaviour
Positive behaviour support
Punishment
Reframing
Zero tolerance

Introduction

Psychiatrist Edward Hallowell believes that young people who display challenging behaviours signal a deficiency in connections with other humans. As teachers, we should not overestimate the power we have in making connections with students and how affecting these connections can be. Schools actively promote, in their policies if not in practice, the development of prosocial behaviours. It is not possible to develop prosocial behaviours in young people through a lesson on civic friendship or respect for others, rather, prosocial behaviours are internalised by students through interactions with others and bonds with caring adults who model these desired behaviours. Often what helps students who feel alienated from school is one teacher who really notices them.

Students who consistently challenge teachers' authority in school are in the minority, but they demand a large percentage of the school's resources and personnel in working with them. It is amazing to see how a small Year 4 student who is having a bad day can have the attention of the Assistant Principal, Principal, their Teacher and possibly the Teacher Assistant in trying to get him or her back in class. That is a lot of people tied up on one child. We are not suggesting that this student is not worth the attention but rather, we use the example to highlight that these students are resource intensive and that change will take time and expertise. Influencing and changing challenging behaviour is difficult and cannot be sustained through quick-fix solutions or imposing zero-tolerance policies. Students who challenge authority are trying to influence the world around them and are highlighting that something important in their lives is not quite right. As Allen Mendler states in his book on power struggles:

> Essentially, kids who misbehave are telling us that their basic needs are not being met. Although we need to have specific, short-term strategies to handle inappropriate behaviour, good discipline is linked to our understanding of the motives that drive students to act inappropriately and the solutions that address these basic needs (2005, p. 5).

In this chapter, we will focus on the small percentage of students who consistently challenge authority. We will explore the motivations for this behaviour and positive ways of working with vulnerable students. The approach outlined is positive and views conflict as an opportunity for professional growth. This perspective can be challenging as conflict can be uncomfortable and difficult to deal with, especially if we have the view that 'students need to follow what I say because I am the teacher'! We will also explore strategies that promote and teach responsible behaviours within a whole-school context. In the Positive Learning Framework we will be concentrating on the third column, in particular the moderate to crisis response to students as outlined below.

Positive Learning Framework

Moderate-level responses
- circle-time, conferencing
- identifying motivation, identifying the 'game'
- empathetic statements
- offering escape routes
- offering choices
- giving students responsibility for actions

Escalating/crisis response
- awareness of escalation phase
- de-escalation/defusing strategies
- crisis-response strategies

Restorative responses
- skills for connecting, clarifying and restoring relationships

Before we begin to explore positive ways of viewing challenging students, let us briefly acknowledge that the majority of behaviours we will face in the classroom are low-level indiscipline and not the often sensationalised anti-social or aggressive behaviours.

Common classroom behaviours

One of the oft-quoted fears of beginning teachers is that the students will behave 'really badly' and will be 'out of control'. It is these fears that keep pre-service teachers awake the night before school placements. Media reports of violent and out of control students in schools does not help and does not reflect what actually happens in schools. The percentage and prevalence of students who consistently challenge authority is small. The Elton Report (1989) in England highlighted the prevalence of low-level behaviour in its report. The Elton Report was commissioned by the government in response to newspaper articles on the rise of violence and thuggery in schools. The report highlighted that the newspaper reports were exaggerated and that the real issue was persistent indiscipline (mildly disruptive behaviour) that inhibited academic progress. This is reflected in comments made by teachers who leave the profession, who cite behaviour as one of the main reasons for their decision to leave, but do not specify anti-social or aggressive behaviour. The behaviours that wear teachers down are the low-level consistent behaviours of talking, being out of seat during work time, passing notes, not completing work, turning up late, general apathy and inattentiveness.

Research commissioned by the Scottish Education Executive Department (2004) compared results from previous teacher surveys to find out what extent misbehaviour in Scottish schools was increasing and what the nature of the misbehaviour was. The survey data highlighted the problems of low-level indiscipline similar to the Elton Report. Recent research in Western Australia (Angus, McDonald et al) identified 'inattentiveness' as the behaviour that impeded academic progress most frequently cited by classroom teachers. Similar findings are reported by Stephenson, Linfoot and Martin (2000) who reported on behaviours that early years teachers in 21 primary schools in Western Sydney found to be of most concern. Teachers identified distractibility and poor listening skills as well as behaviours that disrupted others as the most concerning. Aggressive and anti-social behaviour is not in pandemic proportions as reported in the media, however when these students act out of their pain they demand a different response to reactive punishment strategies that view these students as dysfunctional, disobedient, delinquent, disturbed or even demonic.

Students in pain

One way to view students who are acting out is to view their actions as 'pain-based' behaviour. As humans, we all suffer emotional pain at times in our lives. Growing up in families and being in relationships with others means we have experienced the pain of rejection, been hurt by those close to us or have been in situations where our trust has been abused. When this happens, we are people of pain. Some students have been deeply hurt by mistreatment, racism, religious bigotry or trauma at the hands of adults. Brendtro and du Toit (2005) quote a Native American Proverb that says 'hurt people hurt people'. Students in pain will act out pain-based behaviour. If students have not had their needs met (belonging, mastery, independence and generosity) they will be in pain. As teachers, if we do not understand or know what is going on inside the student we will react to the behaviour instead of responding to the needs. Remember the diagram of the pyramid or 'ice-berg' in Chapter 1 and the need to look under the surface of the behaviour. Another way to understand this concept of pain-based behaviour is to reflect on times when you have been hurt by others and how you reacted to the people who hurt you, to yourself or to others. It is often those closest to us that experience our pain-based behaviour.

In working with vulnerable students, we need to look for the thinking and emotions behind the behaviour (refer back to Figure 1.3 on page 14). As teachers, we need to understand the motivation for their actions. Students who act out are in emotional pain because they have unmet needs. In schools, this is challenging as we often respond to the outside behaviour when it occurs in front of twenty-five other sets of eyes rather than looking for what really motivates the behaviour. The preceding chapters in this text lead toward an understanding that views students positively and encourages us to recognise their thoughts and feelings rather than react to their behaviour. When we continually react to students, it is easy to use deficit labels and view them as being crazy, dysfunctional, or criminal. In a school setting, these students need caring adults who respond to their needs, not react to their behaviour. When schools and education systems react to the behaviour or labels based on naïve psychology, they usually resort to suspension or exclusion as a course of action. Often the justification is based on taking a tough stance on violence or because the school has a zero-tolerance policy. Whatever the justification, the end result is the disposing of the student.

Critical reflection

Reframing limited frameworks

Reframing is a technique whereby you provide *new words for difficult situations*. It is a way of seeing a situation from a different, more positive, perspective. For example, if we were cut off in traffic by another driver, we could view this person with anger and see the driver's actions as inconsiderate, dangerous and unlawful. However, if we discover that they are rushing to hospital as their passenger is about to have a baby we begin to view the same behaviour with understanding.

Your reframing must convey the attitude to the student that he or she is more important than their behaviour. Reframing is about highlighting the person's strengths rather than the specific outcome. This skill is difficult and needs practise, as we do not want it to sound sarcastic.

Try and reframe these student behaviours:

- A student comes late to class and is often unprepared.
- John repeatedly takes Amy's pen.
- Ashwin has a temper tantrum and knocks over a chair.
- A student talks excessively to others.
- Michaela is the 'class clown' and tells five jokes per lesson.

John Seita says that, 'Pessimism is a pathway to failure with challenging kids'.

Punishment and zero tolerance

Punishment doesn't work with challenging students

Students who display pain-based behaviour often evoke an aggressive or coercive response in adults. In the school setting, we often react more to our frustration rather than respond to the students' needs. Punishment is a good example of adults showing their frustration at not knowing how to respond to students' behaviour. Punishment comes from the Latin word 'poena' that translates as 'pain'. Punishment is adults inflicting pain on students to control their behaviour. It is difficult to see how fighting pain with pain will result in positive behaviour change. Yet punishment approaches and discourse are common. In some staffrooms, it is common to hear staff talk about increasing the level of punishment for challenging students, as the first level 'didn't work'. Instead of asking, 'why does this behaviour continue in spite of the punishment' we instead ask, 'what kind of punishment will work?' The effectiveness of punishment comes into sharp focus when working with students who continually challenge us. Punishment works for students who want to please their teachers, although for lasting positive behaviour change, there are more appropriate responses than punishment. Punishment does not work with students who do not trust adults or have weak connections with adults. Inflicting pain on pain is not going to assist these students' abilities and capacity for responsible behaviour. In reality, what tends to happen is that punishment tends to teach troubled students to become sneakier so as not to be caught, to fight with adults who inflict this pain or to retreat into a world of self-blame.

Punishment has a long history in Western society. In society, punishment regimes have been established in response to threats. Social order is necessary and we punish those that threaten that order. The thinking continues with school students who challenge this order—they need to be punished, we think, or excluded from the school. Even when we know that these approaches do not work, we often resort to punishment as a 'necessary evil' in disciplining students who do not respond to normal behaviour management approaches. Punishment does not lead to educational gains, rather it is a more potent means to maintain social order and reinforce the authority of adults. Over time punishment regimes become sanitised with responses like 'teach them respect', 'they need discipline', or 'administering consequences'. When a behaviour incident in a school is sensationalised in the press we often hear these terms, or the paper reports that what is needed is more 'boot camps' or harsher penalties. The editorials report that in having these boot camps these young people will learn 'respect' and 'discipline'. These responses are more civilised than saying we are going to inflict pain on you. The reality is that these students will develop respect and responsible behaviour in connecting with trusted adults who respond to their needs and not in an environment that offers a concentration of negative peers. An emerging trend in Australian schools that follow the punishment rhetoric is to use the term 'zero tolerance' as a response to disruptive students.

Zero tolerance

The philosophy of zero tolerance has infiltrated education systems and schools. Politicians seeking election try to woo voters with a 'tough on crime' stance and a zero-tolerance policy for young offenders. When the media report an incident in a school, politicians and education officials are quick to respond to public outrage by adopting a zero-tolerance philosophy. We are not advocating that violence be tolerated in schools—rather, we oppose the way that political expediency triumphs over educational policy. In fact, there is compelling evidence that 'get tough' approaches do not match educational principles and, when applied in a school setting, often lack commonsense. Zero tolerance, as it was initially designed, was meant to protect children from guns and drugs in school. School safety is a critical issue and in Australia, as in most countries, schools are one of the safest places for children. However, this policy has been diverted from its original purpose, and, as a result, some students have had their educational opportunities reduced and their chances in life limited due to imposed criminal status. In addition, if you are in a minority ethnic group or have additional needs you are more likely to bear the brunt of zero-tolerance policies.

Zero tolerance was developed in the United States after a number of high profile, extremely violent incidents in public schools. Education systems and government tried to redress this situation and to make the schools safer. What transpired was that education districts and systems adopted the 'take no prisoners' approach to discipline that was being used in the country's criminal system. In 1994, The United States Congress passed the *Gun-Free Schools Act*, which required states to pass legislation including provision for a one-year expulsion for students carrying a firearm on school property. Inherent in the legislation was that states would lose federal funding if they did not comply. The legislation was aimed at preventing very dangerous and criminal behaviour by school-aged students with mandatory sanctions. The mandatory sanctions that emanate from the legislation became known as zero-tolerance policies. In the United States, school districts have broadened the zero-tolerance policies to include many more types of behaviour and student misbehaviour that pose little or no safety concerns to other students or teachers. The result is that a range of student behaviours have been included under the umbrella of zero tolerance that have nothing to do with drugs or violence. One example reported in a Harvard report from a national summit on zero tolerance titled *'Opportunities Suspended: The Devastating Consequences of Zero Tolerance and School Discipline Policies'*, uses the example of a large district in Maryland who 'suspended 44 000 students for non-violent offences of "disobeying rules", "insubordination", and "disruption"' (2000, p. 2). It would appear that some students are being arbitrarily removed from school for actions that could have been handled differently if alternative behaviour management methods were used.

One of the hallmarks of a positive discipline approach is that it is developmentally appropriate to the child's maturity level. Respectful discipline involves adults supporting the needs of the students as well as setting high expectations for positive behaviour. From a developmental perspective, teacher guidance will be geared toward the child's changing needs as they mature. An adolescent will need a teacher to be more of a mentor and advocate, whereas in the early years teachers will need to teach more social and behavioural skills along with boundaries. Central to this support are trusting relationships with adults. The Harvard Report (2000) highlights that one need students have that must be met 'is their need to develop strong, trusting relationships with key adults in their lives, particularly those in school' (p. vi). Zero tolerance environments make developing trust difficult and motivate the student to respond angrily or to avoid the punishing adult. This is exacerbated when the students feel that the punishment is unfair or unjust. When teachers apply 'automated' punishments, which do not take into account any other possible influences or circumstances, students feel there is a two-tier order to the school and one that says, 'do as I say not as I do'. Adolescents have a heightened sensitivity to fairness and part of adolescent development is to develop a sense of justice and an understanding of how people should be treated. In the adolescent years, students look for identity in the group, however, they crave individualised discipline interventions. In using zero-tolerance punishments, we lose a golden opportunity for a 'teachable moment' in which to guide students in understanding respect and an opportunity to demonstrate trusting authoritative figures. M. Lee Manning, Professor at Old Dominion University, highlights that when adolescents experience these negative lessons, or when these teachable moments are lost in this developmental phase, they are likely to last a lifetime.

Schools need to use all available resources to ensure that the school is safe and to develop a school climate conducive to learning. The 'Safe Schools Framework' (MCEETYA, 2003) provides a broad outline of how this can be achieved. However, the key is developing effective programs that have a clear evidence base of success. In a climate of fear or perceived threats to safety, schools may resort to a 'get tough' stance that embodies a zero-tolerance philosophy as an intuitive model to deal with issues of safety and student behaviour. For some principals and members of the community, it makes sense that strict punishments be used to enforce order and to send a clear message about acceptable standards of behaviour. It follows that it makes sense to remove disruptive students will increase student learning and strengthen a climate of academic success. Yet the evidence tells us another story. Exclusion of challenging youth does not increase the time on academic tasks in classrooms. As Skiba and Rausch cited in Evertson and Weinstein (2006) in their chapter on Equity and Effectiveness of Zero Tolerance:

> There is no evidence that zero tolerance makes a contribution to school safety or improved student behaviour. Rather, higher levels of out of school suspension and expulsion are related to less adequate school climate, lower levels of achievement at the school level, a higher probability of future student misbehaviour, and eventually lower levels of school completion. Finally … disciplinary school exclusion may carry inherent risks for creating or exacerbating racial and socio-economic disadvantage (p. 1077).

Critical reflection

Student suspension in Australia

- What is your opinion about zero-tolerance approaches to student behaviour?
- To what extent do the schools you are placed in use or claim to use (or have written in their behaviour policy) a zero-tolerance stance and how effective is it? What do the staff think and what are some of the reasons staff give in support of such an approach?
- In Australia, Aboriginal students are overrepresented in suspension and exclusion data. What factors contribute to this and how can this trend be reversed? Does your state publish this data and, if so, what are the levels of Aboriginal suspension and exclusion?
- Suspension of students is becoming a 'sanction of choice' in Australian schools. Why is this sanction so popular and what factors contribute to this practice?
- As a beginning teacher, what is your position on zero tolerance and the use of suspensions? What reasons do you have to support your position?
- Comparisons between states in Australia on suspensions and exclusion data is problematic, however, it is worthwhile to view the available

published data from the education department in your state. What are the levels per 100 students? What percentage is long or short term? Is there any reporting of differences between schools or regions?

- Can you identify why education systems use suspension data as an index of the level of students' misbehaviour and how reliable is such an index? What other measures could educators use?

Indigenous students are three times more likely to be suspended, excluded or placed in another school than non-Indigenous students (Bourke, 2000, p. 13). A review of Aboriginal Education in NSW in 2004 highlighted that 60 per cent of Indigenous adolescent males will lose days at school to suspension (NSW Review of Aboriginal Education, 2004, p. 126). The impact of Indigenous suspensions and exclusion is magnified when we include academic performance data. A National Report on Schooling produced by the Ministerial Council on Education, Employment, Training and Youth Affairs identified that Indigenous youth performed significantly lower (20 per cent) on national literacy and numeracy benchmarks with 50 per cent of Year 7 students below the numeracy benchmarks. As students progress through school, the disparity widens. This disparity, or drop in achievement levels, is evident when test scores from Year 3 are compared to scores in Year 7. Students who struggle to meet the national benchmarks will find school very difficult. The link between academic achievement and behaviour is reflected in the suspension and exclusion data coupled with student performance data for Indigenous youth. One of the interesting by-products of suspensions is that, at a time when students need extra support from teachers in a caring environment, they are pushed out or denied the things they need. Importantly, the students lose face-to-face learning time and opportunities to engage in socially appropriate behaviour when they are on suspension.

The evidence is clear that any short-term benefit from suspensions and exclusions is far outweighed by the negative short- and long-term consequences for students, families and communities. However, there is a case for suspension when a student's behaviour threatens the educational opportunity of others in the school. Even the most positive and proactive principal, who may not agree with suspension, will at times have to act in the interest of the school community. There will be times when this sanction is unavoidable. However, in some cases there are alternatives to suspensions that provide far better long-term behavioural and academic outcomes for students. In Chapter 4, the preventative approaches outlined under the banner of restorative practices may assist in students being aware of their behaviour before it reaches a crisis point. All preventative practices and discipline interventions are more effective when they are embedded in a whole-school approach to discipline.

Whole-school approaches to learning and student behaviour

It is common practice for schools and school systems to codify their behaviour policy. Zero tolerance, suspension and exclusion practices, when outlined in a discipline code, are often interpreted as 'whole-school' approaches. In some education systems as well as schools, the stated code of discipline that schools and teachers are to follow are based on these reactionary practices rather than other more positive intervention strategies. Suspensions and exclusions occur when the behaviour management policy is enacted for serious student misbehaviour. The behaviour policy outlines the process to be followed, the number of days allowed and the stages in re-integrating the students back into the school. At this level, these policies only serve the purpose of outlining sanctioned behaviours and punishing students for serious misbehaviour. These current reactionary practices are failing our students. What is required is a coherent proactive and preventative approach to student misbehaviour that is across the school and school systems. Calls for proactive school-wide policies are being heard louder and louder in Australia. The task of developing whole-school approaches is not new. Schools followed a Glasser system in the 1980s that developed a whole-school approach to managing student behaviour. However, like most educational trends these can fade away until someone else sees the need and they become popular again. The challenge for implementing whole-school policies is to get an agreed stance on what elements are needed and how student misbehaviour will be viewed. In particular, how does the school view or deal with students who are vulnerable or whose behaviour is continually challenging? Any whole-school approach needs to be proactive and offer support for all students, especially the vulnerable, as well as enhance the academic achievement of the students. Let us look at two whole-school approaches that are gaining currency in Australia and around the world. We will explore Jerome Freiberg's Consistency Management and Cooperative Discipline and Sugai and Horner's Positive Behaviour Support (2002). In exploring these two approaches, we are intending to highlight the key elements in a whole-school approach and how any approach needs to be positive, respectful and needs-based, and should include instruction and help develop the skills to be active citizens when students leave school.

Consistency Management and Cooperative Discipline

Consistency Management and Cooperative Discipline (CMCD) is a research-based classroom and school reform model that builds on shared responsibility between teachers and students (Freiberg, 1996, 1999). Freiberg's model provides consistent messages for all members of the school community about appropriate behaviour and what it means to be self-disciplined. The program provides support to all staff members of the school over a three year period. The support is through professional learning opportunities, school-based staff trained as facilitators and ongoing research on behaviour and school climate. The program aims to turn 'tourist' students into 'active citizens' by teachers developing active classrooms where students are actively involved in learning and leadership roles.

As the name suggests it has two main components. *Consistency Management* centres on the classroom and instructional techniques and planning by the teacher. The teacher is the instructional leader, developing a supportive and caring environment in which all members of the class can participate. The *Cooperative Discipline* element focuses on the leadership roles of the teacher and student within the classroom. Freiberg believes that if students are given the opportunity for leadership they will become more self-disciplined. In this element of the model, the students are actively involved in the development of a classroom constitution, are responsible for 'jobs' in the room, are involved in solving disputes, and work collaboratively in groups and with the teacher. This means the responsibility of the classroom climate is no longer the sole responsibility of the teacher.

The CMCD philosophy incorporates five themes: prevention, caring, cooperation, organisation and community (Freiberg, 1991). Let us briefly discuss each of these themes as they apply to the whole school context.

Freiberg (1999) believes that *prevention* is 80 per cent of classroom management. He believes that classroom management is about problem prevention rather than problem solving. One of the ways that CMCD assists teachers in this prevention is that it requires teachers to have a plan of how their classroom will operate and to work with the students in the first few days establishing high standards of behaviour. In the first few days, students and the teacher work together to establish rules for learning based on mutual needs, by developing a class constitution. The document is signed by all participants and it may be that through the year a 'constitutional convention' is held to revise the existing constitution. The class constitution may take on many forms, but it needs to be positive, meaningful to the students and have a learning focus. This is similar to the process outlined in Chapter 4 that the authors use in their teaching.

As we have outlined in previous chapters, both from student feedback and resilience research, students want teachers who care. Freiberg (1999) believes that '*caring* is the heart and soul of teaching'. Teachers show that they care about students by listening to them, trusting and respecting them (Rogers and Freiberg, 1994). Bonnie Benard's research supports this caring theme. When she asked students how they know a teacher cares for them, the most common response was that the teacher called them by name and knew something about them. This practice is a very cheap preventative measure for a school! Students view teachers as caring when they share their story and allow students to see that they are human. The class can have 'structures' that support a caring environment in which special occasions are celebrated or acknowledged (for example, noting birthdays, the birth of a brother or sister, the death of a grand-parent or a sporting achievement). In this classroom, it is okay to care for others and caring is encouraged through leadership opportunities in the class.

A *cooperative* classroom is one where teachers and students help each other, share responsibilities and help each other to succeed. Freiberg believes that cooperation leads to ownership and assists in developing greater opportunities for student self-discipline. Students in a CMCD classroom have the opportunity to develop responsibility and hence become active citizens in the classroom. Students develop ownership in the classroom as they become more adept in self-discipline. Freiberg (1999) cites the story of Seventh Grade student Sergio who wrote a journal entry about the day when his teacher was not at school and the substitute teacher was late:

> I feel lucky today because the day has just started and we have already been trusted in something we have never been trusted on, being alone. It is 8:15 and everything is cool. Nothing is even wrong ... (p. 83).

The students took responsibility for the classroom. In Sergio's story, one student took the absentee slip to the office, another reviewed the students' homework with the class and the class was working when the substitute teacher arrived.

In a CMCD classroom, *organisation* is a mutual responsibility that increases learning time and helps students develop ownership and self-discipline. Central to this theme is the students assuming classroom management positions. Freiberg uses the term 'one-minute managers'. The one-minute managers take responsibility for routine classroom tasks. These can be discussed as a class to identify the jobs that the teacher normally does that takes away valuable teaching time. The students apply for these jobs and are interviewed if necessary. The jobs are rotated every 6–8 weeks so that all members of the class get the opportunity to work in specific jobs as one-minute managers. The range of jobs will be dependent on the age and needs of the students. Importantly, the jobs are not externally rewarded nor are students given incentives for doing them. The reward is in doing the job and having interaction with the teacher and their peers. Other elements of the program allow school discretion on the use of rewards and incentives, although Freiberg's model is more about providing opportunities for student self-discipline rather than behaviouristic approaches.

CMCD involves parents and the community as much as possible in the life of the school. It is important for teachers to link the school with the home. It is equally important for the students to interact with positive adults interested in education on the school site. These opportunities need to be carefully orchestrated so that a greater connectedness between the students and the community develops. Freiberg (2002) maintains that it is important that the teachers also know the backgrounds of their students. Teachers need to have skills for cross-cultural conversations and an awareness of the students' cultural background.

CMCD has been replicated in controlled studies over time. The findings from both qualitative and quantitative research show a positive outcome for reforming schools and transforming learning in classrooms. Freiberg and LaPointe, in their chapter on research-based programs in Evertson and Weinstein's (2006) *Handbook of Classroom Management: Research, Issues and Contemporary Practice*, quote research findings that highlight increased academic achievement for students, reductions in office referrals, students truanting from school, and:

> improvements in classroom and school climate, instructional time saved (from 1.4 to 4.4 school weeks), as well as improved attendance and teacher retention in both elementary and secondary schools (Freiberg, Connell and Lorentz, 2001: Opuni, 2002, 2003; Day and Townsend, 2004; Eiseman, 2005).

Freiberg's model moves away from a behaviourist approach that favours rewards and punishments to one that emphasises self-discipline, community and social responsibility. Freiberg's model believes in students accepting leadership roles, developing self-discipline and being allowed freedom to make decisions and choices. This focus on a person-centred approach indicates his move away from Skinner's behaviourism. Freiberg's CMCD model promotes a shift in thinking from intervention to prevention. The shift in strategy is more a shift in philosophy and in how teachers view classroom management. For Freiberg, the view is to create classrooms that are democratic and caring where students and teachers are partners in learning. Through this partnership, students will move from being passive bystanders or 'tourists' in the classroom, to citizens who are developing responsibility and self-discipline.

School-wide Positive Behaviour Support

Positive Behaviour Support (PBS) has emerged as an approach to problem behaviour that had its origins in Applied Behaviour Analysis (ABA) and ultimately from behavioural theory. ABA developed in the 1960s and extended the behavioural principles of positive reinforcement and stimulus control to bring about changes in behaviour. PBS was seen as an effective intervention strategy for children with severe behavioural problems when, in 1997, the US government amended the *Individuals with Disabilities Education Act* (IDEA). The government introduced a new language that required students with challenging behaviours have access to PBS and functional behavioural analysis to reduce behavioural problems in students with disabilities (Sugai and Horner, 2002). PBS can be considered a developing science 'that uses educational and systems change methods to enhance quality of life and minimise problem behaviour' (Carr et al, 2002, p. 4).

PBS developed in the 1980s and 1990s to include the broader social, familial and interpersonal contexts that students are in and to increase the emphasis to all students rather than just those with severe developmental disabilities. Recently, PBS has been used to address the social behavioural needs of students in school settings. This application of PBS, which involves all students, staff and parents, became known as school-wide PBS (SWPBS). Sugai (2007) states that the emphasis in SWPBS is on:

(a) preventing and development of occurrence of problem behaviour,

(b) teaching and encouraging clearly defined behavioural expectation in natural contexts,

(c) balancing school-wide systems of positive reinforcement with typical classroom and school discipline systems,

(d) school-wide data-based decision making,

(e) prioritised school-wide outcome-based action planning that is led by school teams, and

(f) function-based interventions and systems of support for students whose behaviours are not responsive to general school-wide efforts.

Although the terminology (ABA, PBS and SWPBS) can become confusing, all these approaches have a common behavioural base, are data driven and use positive reinforcement.

When PBS or SWPBS is described or presented to teachers, it is usually accompanied by a triangle-shaped graphic that illustrates the continuum of positive behaviour support to students (Figure 6.1). The triangle represents the preventative logic in the approach. Interestingly, the original logic for the use of the triangle was a late-1950s model for preventing chronic illness. In the 1980s and 1990s, the triangle was used in public health, medicine and mental health fields. In the early 2000s, the triangle's representation of a continuum of support was used increasingly in relation to supporting students with special educational and behavioural needs.

The triangle has three overlapping tiers. The 'primary' tier represents 80 per cent of students and is where all students experience a universal set of interventions that are meant to prevent the development of problem behaviours. The next tier is the 'secondary' or targeted tier, for students who need more intensive interventions as their behaviour requires more attention than the primary intervention. About 15 per cent of students are in this secondary tier. The last tier is termed 'tertiary prevention' where 5 per cent of students need specialist, individualised intervention as their behaviour is unresponsive to the primary and secondary interventions.

Figure 6.1 Continuum of school-wide instructional and Positive Behaviour Support

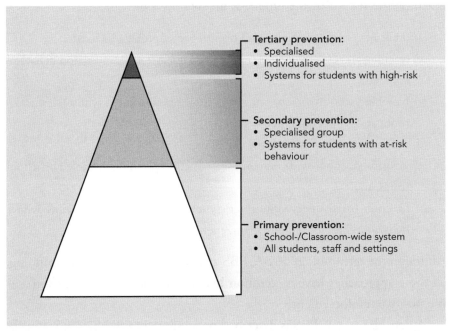

Source: pbis.org

SWPBS is often equated with a curriculum delivery package because, in the primary prevention tier, there may be social skills lessons taught across the year levels to ensure consistency of message. However, as the pbis.org website claims:

SWPBS is NOT a curriculum, intervention, or practice, but IS a decision making framework that guides selection, integration, and implementation of the best evidence-based academic and behavioral practices for improving important academic and behavior outcomes for all students.

As a system-level decision-making process, SWPBS has demonstrated that schools can implement these best practices at the prevention or early intervention level. The strength of SWPBS lies in early intervention, which is crucial in developing safe schools and positive learning environments. The behavioural base to the model allows each level or component to have a solid empirical base or validation. The next step (Lewis, et al, 2006) in supporting the systemic use of SWPBS is to build up the evidence base of its effectiveness as a system across schools, districts and a range of locations. Research on the overall application is emerging. One study by Metzler, Biglan, Rusby and Sprague (2001), and cited by Freiberg and LaPointe (2006), noted that the middle school students reported receiving more positive reinforcement, the referrals to the office decreased, students felt safer at school and levels of verbal and physical aggression decreased.

Selecting CMCD or SWPBS is about school reform and making a commitment to change. It is not possible to use a regime of management stalled in the nineteenth and twentieth century to teach twenty-first-century students. Students prefer flexibility, self-discipline and independence over compliance and control. It could be argued that the biggest shift in developing classrooms that are truly caring, creative and engaging is in how teachers gain new ideas and knowledge on these approaches. This relates to our last assumption that underpins this text: that becoming an effective manager takes experience, reflection, knowledge and time.

Case study

The need to restore a positive learning environment

In this section, we have presented two whole-school approaches that are quite different in their origins and application. Freiberg comes from a person-centred philosophy where students assume responsibility for self-discipline. SWPBS is more prescriptive and has its origins in Applied Behaviour Analysis, which, in turn, has its roots in behavioural theory.

Read the following case study. You have been employed as a classroom management consultant by the school to help them build a more positive school climate and assist the teachers creating quality learning environments. In your advice, detail how you would go about turning this school back into a positive place to learn. Use the concepts from one or both of the whole-school approaches. You can also include some elements from theorists you have been reading to assist you in your consultancy advice to the school.

Consultant Petrina Caporn has been invited to work with Altura Park Primary School. The school's administration believes that the students are steadily growing more disruptive and uninterested in learning. The administration believes the students are rude, rough in their play and disrespectful to each other and staff. What they would like is assistance in making the school a positive place of learning where the children respect each other and staff.

Petrina hears the concerns of the administration and then asks if she could speak with staff and students to get a better idea of the issues. The administration agrees and Petrina begins by talking with some of the teachers.

Mrs Ricciardi is an early years teacher and has been at the school for 15 years. Mrs Ricciardi comments, 'I have seen the behaviour of these students decline over the past few years. The parents don't care about their education; they drop them off and are not interested in getting involved or working with us if their child has a problem. I have noticed that what the parents put in the lunchboxes has changed to all packaged food and no fruit. The students behave as if we need to entertain them all day, they are rude to each other and speak poorly to staff. Most don't know how to behave'.

Miss Woodham is a recent graduate who is teaching middle primary and she doesn't quite agree with Mrs Ricciardi as she says, 'some of the students don't behave that well but it is not too bad compared to my first school where the kids were hanging off the ceiling. I think that the school is trying to be too strict and we need to give the students some more fun and responsibility'.

Mr Doudakis teaches upper primary and believes that 'the student behaviour is not good but I think that the school administration has made the situation worse by adding new rules for behaviour to the point that I do not know what punishment to give for what behaviour as they change nearly every day'.

Mrs Loermans is the library specialist and she agrees with Mr Doudakis that 'the kids can't move without the administration jumping on them and telling them they are horrible or silly. Students come in here and they are hanging out for some fun and interaction, which I provide through the computers, DVD days and different clubs that the students love being involved in'.

Petrina speaks with some students about the school. Petrina finds that the students are not keen to speak with her until she says that no names will be used and that anything they say is confidential. Some of the students comment that, 'they don't trust us here. They think that we will go crazy and burn the place down if were just walking to the library or out to lunch'. Paul thinks that, 'the teachers are pretty boring and the lessons are crap. I am not learning anything except in the science club at lunchtime which is wicked fun'. Sidney thinks that the school is 'run like a prison. We have over 1000 rules in this place. If you tell a joke or move out of your chair in class you get busted and have to do a detention! I can't wait until I get to secondary where they treat you like adults and not babies like here'.

Coping with defiance

The students we are referring to in this chapter are in the minority. These students are what John Seita calls 'adult wary'. They have very good reasons for keeping their distance from adults. Our task as teachers is to connect with them. This is difficult when the student is wary or distrustful of us as adults and teachers. These students present a further challenge in connecting that requires skill and patience. Students' distrust of us can be magnified through race, religion, gender and social status. Sometimes it is difficult to cross a colour line that has a history of mistrust and abuse. This can be a challenge for newly qualified teachers working in schools with a majority of Indigenous students or inner-city schools with a high multicultural population. Despite the challenges, we need to connect with these students if we are going to engage them in learning.

In Chapter 2, we mentioned the brain's sentry, the amygdala, and how our brains scan the social horizon for clues. In working with distrustful students, powerful social signals are communicated with the eyes. We can convey positive and negative emotions with our eyes. It is interesting to note when working with young children that when they draw a human they usually draw stick arms and legs with a big head that is dominated by huge eyes. For these children these are the most powerful conveyers of meaning and emotion. In the classroom, we can send positive signals to students all around the room with our body language; these messages convey to them they are doing well, that they are okay or how pleased you are of their efforts. Students who are distrustful of teachers appreciate the positive messages. Like all of us, these students also want to tell their story to a trusted adult. As teachers, we want to be that trusted adult.

Building trust with distrustful students takes time and patience. One of my learning experiences was working one on one with students who were constantly in trouble in school and were on the road to exclusion, as well as students who had been excluded from another school and were entering the new school. Part of my role was also to work with teachers in developing effective strategies to re-engage these students in meaningful learning. Working with the students was easy compared to the teachers! We will explore more on the difficult nature of changing teachers' practice later in the chapter. However, what these students taught me was that developing bonds with students takes time—if they are rushed or forced, students retreat into behaviours that safeguard them. What the students wanted were brief encounters with an adult that were finished before they felt uncomfortable. Teachers can 'start on the student homepage', and when the students are ready they will take you to other links or pages. In this situation, humour and non-verbal signs that conveyed warmth, and signals that 'this adult is safe and friendly' also worked.

Our needs as teachers and the urge to fix problems

It is natural for teachers who have high levels of care and concern for others to feel the urge to 'fix' student problems. This urge is strong in the early years of teaching, when we are developing our 'teacher self-esteem' as we have the need to be liked, accepted and to know we are good at what we do. As teachers, we also have the need to *belong* to the school and our new role as teacher. We also have the need to seen as having a good level of *mastery* in our teaching and to be *independent* and have power in how and what we do in our classes. In return, we gain a sense of purpose in knowing that what we have chosen to do is right and grow in *generosity* in the school community.

As early career teachers, we can find it difficult to resist the urge to fix the students. This can be the case when students feel they can trust you and they tell you parts of their story. At other times, when, in your role as teacher, you are privy to students' background information, there is the desire to fix or heal the hurt the students have in their life. We all have natural abilities to respond to people in pain, what Taylor (2002) calls the 'tending instinct' where we respond instinctively with empathy and nurturance to people in need. However, as teachers we need to resist the urge to fix vulnerable students' problems and rather to 'get a fix' on the problem. Distrustful students have years of experiences and life events that have led them to interpret and respond to the world in the way they do. These students have developed sophisticated strategies for blocking out teachers' attempts to help or change them. In fact, they think that their previous behaviour has served them well in the past and will serve them better than the options the adults are offering. As teachers, we can offer support to distrustful students because we know that in times of crisis these students will seek out support from people they trust. The problem the student has is a burden and they will look to find people to help carry the load. In this light, we can see the power of the peer group in reinforcing behaviours or outlook on the world. Vulnerable students will speak with teachers they believe they can trust and who listen. It is ironic that in times of crisis when a student most needs support and time with a trusted adult we send them away from school or to isolation to think about their behaviour. Possibly the fear is that by giving them time or attention we will be rewarding poor behaviour, when, in reality, it is a golden opportunity for the student to learn and develop coping skills. How then can teachers connect with these students and respond to them in a positive manner that de-escalates the conflict and turns the event into a learning opportunity for all involved? We will look at strategies that can be used in the classroom and the skills to develop a positive language of discipline while ensuring that both teacher and students maintain their dignity.

Strategies for de-escalating conflict in the classroom

In this section, we will describe practical strategies aimed at defusing conflict in the classroom. We will discuss the range of approaches. The skills and strategies discussed are presented in an ascending order, from preventing conflict through to asking the student to leave the room and working one on one on problem solving the student's return to class. We will discuss the following strategies:

1　using preventative low-level responses
2　being aware of our emotional state and not taking it personally
3　not taking the bait
4　having a private chat
5　listening, acknowledging, agreeing, deferring (LAAD)
6　using language of de-escalation
7　using de-escalating statements
8　offering students a choice
9　removing a student from the class
10　using one-on-one problem solving
11　asking the student for assistance.

As we discuss the strategies, you will be invited to apply your new learning to the practical activities and case studies incorporated in each strategy. These activities are meant to help you develop your language of discipline so do not worry if you feel that you 'can't do it' or 'it sounds silly'. It is important that you hear yourself say these statements so that when you are in the classroom, you can respond automatically rather than stumbling around for what to say when confronted by an angry student.

Using preventative low-level responses

The strategies and skills in this section are built upon the myriad of normal interactions that teachers use to develop positive relationships with their students. In Chapter 2, we outlined a range of strategies for 'connecting' with students. From these connections, we can build meaningful relationships with students. The following strategies follow on from this positive groundwork and are based on the belief that all students are worth it, even the ones that openly challenge our authority. Let us recap some of the foundational strategies that we will have in place in our classrooms (discussed in earlier chapters) that help us to establish caring and quality learning environments. These *preventative strategies* include:

- calling students by their name
- saying hello to each student every day—they count!
- knowing something about the students' interests and life outside of school
- letting the students know about you
- having fun
- setting clear and high expectations
- involving students in class guidelines
- being transparent in your discipline—the students know what will happen next
- treating the students fairly not equally
- teaching engaging lessons.

As mentioned earlier, prevention is the best strategy. Effective teachers who connect with students, attend to their universal needs and develop quality learning environments tend to encounter fewer behaviour problems and lower levels of student disengagement than teachers who do not. However, even in the best circumstances children will test limits and are sometimes uncooperative despite our best efforts. When conflict does happen, de-escalation is the best way forward. There is no 'one size fits all' sequence or approach that will solve teacher–student conflict in the classroom. However, we will suggest some approaches that we and others have used that have helped in de-escalating conflict and in the process have maintained the dignity of those involved.

Being aware of our emotional state and not taking comments personally

Conflict is stressful. Being in a continual state of stress is not most people's preferred position. When a student is angry and refuses to follow instructions or do their work, continually interrupts the class or is disrespectful towards us it is confronting. We need to recognise that student behaviour can at times be confronting and we can feel threatened. The added difficulty with conflict in the classroom is that it is public. The other students are waiting to see what happens and, as teachers, we can feel under pressure to respond in a way that demonstrates our power and role in the school. We need to recognise our natural or emotional response. Often we will feel threatened and angered at the behaviour and feel like we want to lash out and vent our anger at the student. Sometimes we may feel threatened and feel like running away and become paralysed by our fear and need to escape. Recognising the stress we are feeling can assist us to respond in a logical and thought-out way. We need to respond in a 'clinical' and thoughtful way that is respectful of the student but allows us to get back to teaching and the students back to learning. Being 'clinical' is not being cold or aloof; it is about responding in a manner that de-escalates the situation without personal emotions interfering. In the classroom, we can respond in a clinical and respectful manner when we are confronted with an angry student who is swearing and calling us names in an attempt to engage us in conflict. We respond in a way that is supportive of each other's dignity and we calmly use language that de-escalates the conflict. We do not take it personally but respond with previously thought-out responses aimed at getting the class back to learning (while maintaining your sanity).

As a teacher, how we think of ourselves should not be dependent upon what our students think. If a Year 1 child is having a tantrum and lashes out at you with the comment, 'I hate you, you are a bad teacher' or a Year 9 student blurts out that your lesson 'sucks and is boring' you do not need to take these comments personally. We need to stay connected to the students but we do not have to take what they say personally—even if they are uncannily accurate! This can be difficult in the early years of teaching because we might not have a robust view of ourselves as teachers and may not have sufficient experience to counter the comments. Nevertheless, we should not take what a student says and does personally. If on some level we feel we need positive comments from Year 6 students to make us feel appreciated or worthwhile as teachers, then maybe we should rethink teaching—as it may not be as rewarding as hoped. However, it is also true that some of the comments students say can be hurtful, even when you know they are not really about you.

Not taking the bait

Students are very good at getting us to engage with them in conflict. Adult-wary or distrustful students can have highly developed coping strategies, which include skills in getting adults to respond to their comments. At times, it is difficult not to comment back but we need to have the strategy for not taking the bait when it is offered by students. Often, by ignoring the comment the potential for conflict is diminished. Not taking the bait is a deliberate and conscious act we need to take to de-escalate conflict. If some of us are quick to respond or quick to anger then we need to train our ears to ignore the bait. For some teachers this will be difficult. One of the key components of conflict in the classroom is the notion of 'saving face' for both the teacher and the student. Students will work hard at saving face with peers even to the detriment of their relationship with you. An example might be when a student has been moved away from his group to another desk, for talking. As the student moves his books, he mutters under his breath, 'this class sucks anyway, who wants to work'. As the teacher, we need to ignore the bait in the comment. The student has moved and will get on with work so there is no need to engage in a verbal argument over the class being boring. Bill Rogers calls these comments 'secondary behaviours' and also urges teachers not to respond to them. In this incident, it is possible to see how if we responded to the muttering we would have interrupted the lesson yet again and caused the class to lose valuable learning time. In ignoring the comment, the class can continue working.

Another example is when a third student enters the conflict. A concerned student comments, 'Shelby says that this class sucks, are you going to do anything Miss?' Remember we need to keep the learning atmosphere in the room so we do not want to engage in a dialogue with this student. One response could be, 'Thanks for your concern but that is a private matter between Shelby and me'. This sends a clear message: I will not discuss a student's behaviour with others, I am respectful of each student, and it is important to get back to teaching and learning in this class.

There is an important message for the class in not taking the bait. The message is that you will not stop the class or learning for every incident. Your class is a quality learning environment and quality learning cannot happen if we are stopping and starting all the time because of distractions. This also allows you to defer speaking with students until you are ready. For example, when you are moving around the room (proximity) and a student says something that is not appropriate that is heard by all the students you can say, 'I know that we all heard what Chantelle said and I will speak with Chantelle to find out the problem and how we will solve it. For now, I would like people to continue with the activity.' This approach takes the pressure to react or respond to every incident off the teacher and keeps the focus on learning.

Using a private chat

In a conflict or potential conflict, it is useful to keep conversations private and allow the student to save face. One strategy for this that Mendler (1997) developed is PEP which stands for privacy, eye contact and proximity. PEP is were the teacher goes to the student and quietly speaks with them about the behaviour or the result of their behaviour and what the teacher would like them to do. It is done in a way that other students do not hear what is said nor are they party to the conversation. PEP allows you to preserve the dignity of the student and keep the class on track with the set work. One of the pitfalls of PEP was highlighted recently when we were working with a group of teachers and we introduced them to PEP. One of the secondary teachers said that it would not work for her, as she was a coordinator, which meant that she had to discipline students, so whenever she went to see a student they thought they were in trouble. This teacher was right: PEP will not work if the only time you go to see students at their desk in private during a class is to tell them off. Our suggestion to this teacher was to use PEP for positive interactions so that students don't come to fear her presence at their desk.

Listen, acknowledge, agree, defer

The four skills: listening, acknowledging, agreeing and deferring (LAAD) are helpful in diffusing conflict (Curwin and Mendler, 1999). They offer a framework when teachers are confronted by a student. The skills in LAAD can also be applied with family and friends. We have used LAAD in parent workshops as a strategy, not only for use with the children but also as a framework in relating to each other.

Listen	To what the students are saying and not how they are saying it
Acknowledge	To the students in a firm and confident manner that you hear them
Agree	That what the students are saying is or may be true
Defer	Let the students know that you will speak with them about this at a later time

Let us apply LAAD to an escalation of the earlier example of moving Shelby to another desk. After a while, Shelby becomes angry at having to move and shouts out, 'I am not doing any of this stupid work and you can't make me'.

Listening	'Shelby, I hear that you are angry at moving and right now you are in no mood to listen, I will respect that.'
Acknowledging	Use this if Shelby continues to protest, or you could use acknowledging in the first instance, 'Shelby, if I hear and understand correctly you are saying that you are not going to do the work assigned. Do I get that right? Thank you for letting me know'.
Agree	When students use the phrase 'you can't make me', they are pretty well right! All we can do is assist them do it themselves. 'Shelby, you are right, I cannot make you do it, nor is it my style to force you. However I was hoping that you would make the decision to complete the work so you can move on in this topic. Good luck with your decision'.
Defer	This is a great strategy that can give you time to think or calm down as well as direct the attention back to learning. 'Shelby, I think we are headed for an argument, and I don't want that. I would like to work this out with you so let's talk about this after class'. If Shelby does not stay after class this is okay, as you both know that the issue needs to be resolved before the next class. You will need to follow up with Shelby to have that discussion. Often when students are given the option of discussing their problem after class it is enough to diffuse the conflict.

LAAD in action

Working by yourself, with some peers or with study group members, apply LAAD to a conflict you have had with a friend or a student in a school.

1 What is a behaviour that a friend or student does that makes you want to react or that 'pushes your buttons'?
2 When your friend or student behaves in this way, what are the associated non-verbal behaviours that accompany it? Using the LAAD framework write a statement that you could say in each stage of the defusing process.
   a listening
   b acknowledging
   c agreeing
   d deferring

Practice activity

Using the language of de-escalation

The language of de-escalation incorporates the statements we make to students that defuse potential conflict. These statements need to be in your voice and be authentic. Whatever is said, the statements need to show the students that you care and are connected with them and are not taking their behaviour personally. With this positive attitude and with the goal to defuse and re-engage in learning many potential conflicts can be avoided. One component in the language of de-escalation is to use empathy. Gordon emphasised that using empathy to understand students is a necessary precondition to building a community in the classroom (1989). We want to model and actively promote the use of empathy in our classrooms. Colvin (2004) highlights that to be effective, empathy involves two components: recognising that the student has a problem and then communicating this concern to the student. These two parts are seen in the following example, when a secondary student comes into class and puts their head on their hands on the desk looking out to one side. The teacher sees the student (recognises) and says, 'You don't seem your usual self today', 'You look tired or stressed. Do you want to take a few moments before you join us in the activity?', or 'Hi Johanne, are you unwell? Do you think you need to go to the nurse or will you be alright?' These responses are very different from reacting to the student behaviour and escalating a conflict.

The effective use of empathy or empathetic statements is dependent on whether you have connected with the student. Can you imagine if the student first hears you use empathy in Term 2 after a term of not being empathetic? You are bound to get some strange looks or reactions. Empathy follows on from connecting with the student and is a normal part of relationship building. In relationships, we show interest in others, demonstrate concern and have knowledge of their lives. When a student is vulnerable or upset they are more receptive to empathy when it is a part of the normal relationship in the classroom. When working with teachers in professional development sessions we often touch on the use of empathy and a question often arises about letting the student 'get away with it' or 'fairness' to others in the class. In responding, we remind the teachers that we are talking about a small proportion of the class who are quick to escalate to conflict. Other students will know this pattern as they have witnessed this escalation before. The class will be aware of your strategy, as you may have discussed this with them in the beginning of the year: 'when someone is having a bad day I will …' Your aim is to treat everyone in the class according to need. At this time the student needs more time or space to compose themselves before they start work. You will continue to encourage this student to begin work because they know that 'in this class, we work'. The student is not going to misbehave during every lesson for the year. If the behaviour continues, instigate a conversation with the student about working together to solve the problem of avoiding work in class.

Using de-escalating statements

In order to develop a language of de-escalation, you will need to use words that fit with you and your style of communication. Below are samples of statements that can be used to avoid conflict with students. In constructing your statements, keep in mind that conflict is usually public and can be confronting; however, our goal is to re-engage the student in learning.

a   I am interested in what you have to say, but now is not the best time so tell me more after class.

b   Wow, you must be very angry to tackle me like that in the class. I am not sure how to respond so let's meet later to discuss.

c   I would like to know what I did to make you so mad. However, using that language is not helping, so why don't we talk about it after class.

d   I can see you are angry but throwing chairs doesn't solve anything. Let us use words to solve this after class.

e   Your actions tell me you are pretty unhappy or bored with this class. It takes a lot of strength to keep working when you see little point. Thanks for being so strong.

f   I can see that you do not look yourself today. That must feel rotten. Let me know if you need some time out.

Sometimes it is necessary to make short succinct statements to the students that give you time to think as well as placing the responsibility for the behaviour back with the student. These defusing statements are good to use with all student in situations when the behaviour has escalated to a point where you need to confront the behaviour as it is impeding students learning and your teaching. Again, we would recommend that this approach be discussed with the students in the early part of the first week as to how you will respond when students choose to misbehave. Some defusing statements could be:

a   I am not sure how to respond to that. Let me take a few minutes and I will come back to you.

b   Now that you have said that I am not sure what you expect of me in this situation.

c   I do need to respond to that statement but I am unsure how to. Can you help me solve this?

d   When you think of something, can you help me out and let me know what we should do next?

e   What should we do next?

f   Where to from here?

Construct and practice de-escalation statements

Working with a peer or members of a study group, complete the following tasks.

1   Identify a type of student behaviour that 'pushes your buttons' (you can use the same behaviour as in the LAAD activity).

2   Picture the classroom, the class and the student.

3   Select one of the statements above or construct one yourself and say it to the others in the group. Try to be as realistic as possible and say it in a firm yet respectful tone that ensures everyone's dignity remains intact.

4   Construct some statements as a group and take turns saying them. Discuss the body language that would help convey respect and empathy.

Put your defusing statements to the test

As individuals, construct a response to the following misbehaviour based on the language of de-escalation. Imagine you are teaching a lesson that has been less than successful. The students aren't picking up the topic as easily as you anticipated and several irritating events such as persistent talking, books falling on the floor and students not completing their work have also occurred. You are already feeling frustrated when …

1   A student gets up to 'sharpen his pencil'. When you ask him to sit down he responds defiantly, 'All I want to do is sharpen my pencil'. You reply, 'It's not the time for that'.

The student says arrogantly, 'How am I supposed to do my work, then?'

You say …

2 For a good reason you ask a student to shift to another seat. She responds with angry defiance pushing her chair over and yelling, 'I'm not going, you can't make me!'

You say …

3 Kelly, a recognised Year 8 power player, has not taken her book out and you are already halfway through the lesson. You say, 'Kelly, you need to get your book out'. She sighs, mumbles, 'F***', then says defiantly, 'Maths sucks. It's stupid and boring'.

You say …

Offering students a choice

No matter how good or logical you think your approach is, some students will continue to escalate the situation. One strategy that is used and abused in schools is the use of 'choice'. Offering students a choice is one of the most commonly used strategies by teachers who see themselves as more democratic than autocratic. The use of choice has developed out of logical consequences and under the guise of developing responsibility in the student, as discussed by several democratic and psychoeducational theorists (Dreikurs, Glasser, Ginott). Canter also talks about the use of choice. Choice has been used as a behaviour strategy within the boundaries of limit setting. We say that choice has been abused as it is easy to make a choice sound like a threat, ultimatum or punishment. Offering students a real choice where they are taking responsibility for their behaviour takes skill and preparation.

Choice in the classroom is important in developing a democratic learning environment, where students develop their capacity to self-regulate learning and behaviour. Research by Zimmerman (2000) found that students who felt they had a sense of control in the classroom were more likely to be motivated and engaged. Research by Flowerday and Schraw (2000), which set out to codify teachers' beliefs about choice found that teachers offered choice to students in a range of classroom activities including choice of study, reading material, project focus, group membership and submission dates for work. Behaviour was not mentioned. What the study found was that teachers were all for the idea of choice and believed it made a difference, however, it was offered conditionally to those students who had already displayed a high degree of self-determination instead of assisting all students to develop more responsibly. We mention this study as it can be argued that the same is possible for the use of behaviour choices. People agree they are beneficial and fit a more student-centred teaching approach, yet they are offered inconsistently and the students who are offered them are those deemed capable of making the right choice. In reality, choices need to be offered to students who do make wrong choices and who need to be supported in making positive choices that assist them in engaging in learning.

If we are going to use choices as a strategy let us explore the essential characteristics that we need to make them effective. When using choices it is crucial to make them a part of your overall management plan and language from day one. Offering students choices is a short-term strategy to stop behaviour so learning can happen. However, through teacher feedback the process and decision can be used as a positive illustration of the student being responsible and developing positive abilities to solve conflict. The use of choice is set within a whole management framework that is supportive of young people in their development as citizens.

What makes a choice effective is what went before it! If a teacher jumps into offering a student a choice the first time they were caught talking, it is less likely to be effective in both the short- or long-term. Choices will be more effective when offered at the most opportune time. For example, if a student is talking to another student during group work and not completing the task required, the teacher may initially use a range of low-level interventions to get the student back on task. A range of low-level interventions may include (increasing in intensity):

- the look—which implies, 'please stop talking and get back to work'
- the gesture to stop talking (finger on lip)
- proximity—to walk around and stand next to the student; he or she stops talking when you are there

- using the student's name, pausing and reminding the whole class they have five minutes left
- using an 'I statement': 'Kyle, when you keep talking during work time I get annoyed because it stops you and others from doing the work properly.'
- changing the 'I statement' to an 'impact statement' (Larrivee, 2005, p. 127), which appeals more to the students' sense of responsibility as their behaviour is affecting others. 'Kyle, when you keep talking (behaviour) I have to stop helping other groups (impact) and the students in that group have to wait for me to get back to start their work again (those affected).'

Now is the time to offer the student a choice, as he has not responded to your request to stop talking and is, at present, making a poor learning choice. The choice for the student is offered in a non-threatening tone and is done matter-of-factly as part of the lesson flow. You could use PEP or move next to the group and offer him a choice.

'Kyle, I would like you to stop talking and get on with the worksheet' *(state the expected behaviour)*.

'If you choose to continue to talk I will need you to move desks and sit over here by yourself' *(state consequence or action)*.

'I will give you half a minute to decide' *(allow time for the student to decide or pack their things up and move)*

The teacher then moves away from Kyle to another group.

When Kyle moves you thank Kyle for making a positive choice.

If Kyle is still there after thirty seconds you can ask Kyle have you made your decision? If he moves or is quietly working, thank him for the positive decision.

It is important to give the student feedback on his decision and ability to get on with the work during the lesson. This can be done while you are walking around the room and said privately. It may also work when asking for answers to the tasks to invite the student to offer an answer and comment on his ability to make good decisions and how well he has done. Others in the class will know that the student has been shifted during the lesson. Drawing attention to the fact that he did shift and then got on with his work is a good way to reinforce good decisions and to emphasise that, in this class, we are open to discuss behaviour as well as learning. This safe climate in the room is established from day one when we start off with inclusive language about 'our' class. If the use of choice is transparent, it is possible for the students to say 'I know. I know, I have a choice …' and they can self-discipline by shifting or suggesting ways that they can help themselves get back to work. When this happens, the students are internalising a conflict-resolution strategy. They are developing internal process to regulate their behaviour.

As a beginning teacher, we can imagine that you are reading this and asking 'what happens if they refuse to move and stay in their desk defiantly?' First, we do not panic as we have already planned for this in our management plan and are aware of the school's discipline policy. Therefore, we move to another strategy further up the discipline hierarchy.

Removing a student from the class

There will be times when it is necessary to ask a student to leave your room. However, it must be remembered that the student is better off in your room learning than sitting outside the class or waiting at a principal's or assistant principal's office. It is also better for your status within the class to keep students in your room as long as possible. Teachers' authority and power will be quickly eroded if they handball problems at frequent intervals to the Assistant Principal, Deputy, Year Head or Subject Coordinators. The students will quickly pick up that you can't handle them. The decision to remove a student will depend on what you have done before to re-engage the student and the intensity of their behaviour.

There are some occasions when a student's behaviour is such that is makes it impossible for us to teach and for learning to occur in the class. When this happens, it is so important that we treat the students with respect and maintain both your and their dignity in their departure. This can be difficult, as we may be feeling quite frustrated or angered by the behaviour. It could be that inside we are seething and have had enough so we shout across the room, 'Kyle, I have had enough of your behaviour. You know the rules and you have purposely disobeyed them. Get out and go to the principal's office'.

We need to be aware of how we feel and use a calm, clinical manner to ask the student to leave the room. The language used in asking a student to leave the room is similar to offering a choice, in that we want to convey that we are asking the student to leave because they have made a poor choice but also that we want them back as they are a valued member of our class. Standing close to the student, or speaking to them privately, we could use the following words, 'Kyle, your behaviour is stopping me from teaching. You know I respect your opinion and like your presence in the room and wish you could stay, however, I am going to have to ask you to leave. I hope you decide to come back as soon as you are ready to learn'. As you grow in confidence, you may wish to make this request to leave a choice by adding into the second sentence after 'could stay', 'I am going to ask you to make a choice to leave the room or stay and get on with your work. If you choose to go I hope that …'

Removing a student should be the last option. The student will be back, so it is better to make the departure a smooth one and to ensure that the student knows that their contributions to the class will be missed and that you want them back. Students are less likely to want to miss a class if they feel they are an integral part of it. Through our language and inclusive approach, we are developing a sense of belonging for all our students, even those who challenge us.

De-escalating conflict with a positive language of discipline

The following scenario offers an opportunity for you to practice a range of responses to misbehaviour with increasing intensity. At each level, write out what you would say. Read it aloud to see if you are comfortable saying it and that it conveys a confident yet respectful message. Compare your responses with peers to see what they would have said.

Level 1

A student enters your class late and immediately puts his head on the desk. You offer an *empathetic statement* …

Practice activity

Level 2

The student does not respond. You decide to ignore the lack of response and get the rest of the class working. Later you notice his head is still down you offer a *de-escalating statement* ...

Level 3

The student lifts his head off the desk and begins to show more overt agitation, trying to get others off task and dropping books off the desk. He or she eventually gets out of their seat to wander around the room. You decide to *offer a choice* ...

Level 4

The student takes the choice to sit by themselves and work alone but is slow to move. As he or she is shifting books, you hear the student mumble something. You ask the student to hurry up and he or she explodes, calling you a b-tch/d-ckhead and telling you your class sucks and everyone thinks you're a useless teacher so back off!

You clearly see the escalation and choose to attempt to *de-escalate by* ...

1 At level 4 did you keep the student in the class or ask them to leave your room?
2 What is your thinking to justify your actions? How did this compare with your peers?
3 Were there similar reactions to this type of behaviour? Why do you think this was the case?

One-on-one problem solving with students

Our students are exposed to some elements of society that are hostile and that promote a 'might is right' mentality. In our classroom, we need to model respectful ways of communicating and prosocial patterns of behaviour. One area that we can assist our students is in problem-solving behaviour. We can involve them in a process of coming up with ways to change their behaviour to achieve desired aims or goals. Although there are many 'off-the shelf' programs in this area (PATHS, Second Step: A Violence Prevention Curriculum, I Can Problem Solve, Open Circle, Child Development Project—Caring School Community, to name a few evidence based programs), we will present a more organic approach that has evolved out of working with students excluded from school who were enrolled in an alternative education program. The program was highly individual and relied on effective goal setting to change behaviour.

The approach, shown in Figure 6.2 overleaf, works when a teacher and a student problem-solve together. The student identifies a behaviour that is impeding their academic progress or getting them into trouble at school. The behaviours do not have to be at the high end of the scale. They could be simple acts that affect the student's ability to work in the classroom, such as calling out.

The student identifies the *problem behaviour*. This could include getting into trouble with a group of friends, arguing with the maths teacher, not turning up to school, fooling around in the library or having negative thoughts about their ability.

The student then sets a *goal*. It is good to have a short-term and a long-term goal, as behaviour change takes time. For calling out in the classroom the student may suggest they put their hand up or not get into trouble and contribute to the class.

After this, you and the student create an *action plan* (how will you achieve the goal/what will you do). This could involve the student having a card with 'hand-up' written on it or a picture that is on the desk or in their pencil case so that they can use it as a visual reminder to raise their hand. The plan may be to count to four before the student puts their hand up to distract them from calling out.

What might *prevent them from achieving the goal* is a practical and realistic look at what might get in the way. The student may recognise that when they sit next to a certain student they are more inclined to call out, if they do not have lunch they are more distracted, that it could be that they enjoy annoying the teacher in their music class, and so on.

Support refers to whom or what will assist them to achieve their goal. Maybe sitting next to a particular student, sitting up the front or getting organised with all necessary equipment makes them feel more confident.

Review is the frequency that you wish to review with the student. This can happen briefly every day or second day, with a more formal sit-down once a week. The review is to assist the student succeed and look for supports rather than a negative experiences.

Contingencies outline what 'we' will do if the goal is not achievable and outlines the next step in the process. This could involve home support or different interventions available in the school.

Figure 6.2 One-on-one problem-solving approach

Problem (what do I see as the problem?)	Goal (what do I want to achieve?)	Action plan (what do I need to do to achieve my goal?)	What might prevent me from achieving my goal?	Support (name staff and students)	Review

Contingencies (e.g. case conference, time out or review plan)

Asking the student for assistance

Often in resolving conflict or in general behaviour in the classroom we can forget one of the greatest resources available to us—the student. When a student misbehaves we can get annoyed, hypothesise about why they are misbehaving and, when the behaviour persists, we can offer an intervention that hopefully will stop the behaviour. When the behaviour persists we can get annoyed, increase the level of intervention or ask for help from the school leadership team. What we often miss is asking the student.

An incident that illustrates this gap occurred when I worked with a secondary school teacher who was Head of Department/Learning area and doing a PhD. This teacher explained how he had one student who, after about ten minutes of class time, would lift up his pen and drop it onto the desk. He would continue this action until the teacher took the pen away. The teacher would merely take the pen, say nothing and continue teaching. The student was compliant and didn't seem to mind that his pen was taken away. In the discussion, the teacher said that the student didn't need the pen as he didn't do any work and was failing in his class. The teacher was concerned about this student and when he checked with other teachers, found that this student was failing all his other classes as well. The teacher felt vindicated and continued to take the student's pen when he dropped it on the desk. I asked the teacher if he had any theories as to why the student dropped his pen every lesson. The teacher said he thought he might be bored or just didn't want to do any work as he knew he was going to fail anyway. I retold the story I had just heard to see if I had the story correct and at the end asked the teacher if he knew what the student thought his motivations were or if the student could help in understanding the pen dropping every lesson. The teacher went quiet and stared at me as I had said something unbelievable. He paused and then slowly said that he had not asked the student and, in fact, hadn't thought to ask. In this teacher's approach to discipline over a number of years, he had ignored the main resource we have at our disposal—the students. When we involve the students we are assisting them to develop responsible behaviours and their capacity to self-regulate behaviour.

In working with all youth in a school setting, it is preferable to involve them in the solution to conflict. One of the big shifts that the teacher described above needs to make to include students is to change his belief that this student's needs should conform to the teacher's rules. This change will move the conflict—involving the student in resolving it so that they are active participants in their own personal development. When we involve students in problem-solving conflict we are developing their capacity for moral and ethical behaviour towards others in the school, home and society. In this light, conflict can be seen to be positive and with skillful facilitation can be used in the class as a source of growth for students and teachers.

Conflict as professional learning

Student conflict can be a source of professional learning. In reflecting on our performance, we can use an incident as a way of analysing what happened and what part our actions play in escalating the situation. Through this reflection, we can see how the technique or approach used was not successful with this student and we begin to see a pattern of escalation that led, for example, to the student slamming the door on the way out of the room. When a technique or approach fails, we tend to blame others or ourselves for the poor result. However, blame is not helpful in assisting us get a better fit between the technique we use and the needs of the student. What is helpful is reflecting on what happened and what could be done differently to create a positive outcome next time. It is sobering to realise that the defiance vulnerable students give to you as the teacher is probably not as bad as the aggression they may be receiving from someone important in their life. Unfortunately, students with challenging behaviours can be so resentful that is difficult not to see them as repugnant. However, in working to develop caring and respectful learning environments there are no disposable children.

It is also worth reflecting on the way that we categorise or label students. These labels usually stem from the ways we see the world and the frameworks we use to view student behaviour. It could be that, at times, we are operating out of a limited set of frameworks. Reframing is a useful way of broadening the frameworks we currently use. Students can make good decisions; however, they may not have learnt how to make them consistently. It may be that the student has not yet understood how a different decision will make the response from others more positive. Teachers often use labels to categorise students. These labels can support and affirm students or demonise and blame them. For example, the student labelled as lazy, could be reframed as, 'yet to find value in my class' or the defiant student is really a student, 'who sticks up for himself'. In this approach, we can give credit for the motives of the students, while still disagreeing with their methods. In the 'lazy' student example, we could say, 'I can see that you have lots of priorities in your life so let see how we can make study one of them'. Earlier in this chapter, we used this skill in one of the critical reflections to highlight how the use of reframing can be a positive approach to student behaviour. Reframing can also assist us in reflecting on student behaviour and the meaning we ascribe to it and how we subsequently respond.

Case study 1

Defusing a confrontation

From what you have read in this chapter, develop a plan of action you could use to diffuse this conflict. Try to identify what you would say and the steps in the process from the earliest part of the lesson.

Jasmine Ghodrati was teaching her class when she thought she heard a muffled music sound coming from the corner of the room. She turned around but couldn't see who was playing with their MP3 or mobile phone. At the last staff meeting, the Deputy raised the issue that there had been an increase in mobile use in class and if teachers could keep an eye out for this as it was against school rules to use mobiles in class. Jasmine had not had this issue with phones in her class so she was surprised to hear a noise that sounded like one. She was not sure who was making the noise so she walked around the room and stood at the back of the classroom. She looked at the three students in the corner where she thought the noise came from. Sitting in this corner where Kimon Hyde and Trianda Klopper who were usually pretty engaged students. Next to them was James Dendle who had a history of getting into trouble and the new student Alexander Miles who had only been in the class a few days. James had been exceptional in his behaviour since the last case conference was called with his father, the social worker and school psychologist. Jasmine was beginning to view James in a different light since then and hoped it wasn't him making the noise. Jasmine also had heard that James's father was quick with his fists and often took to James when he got into trouble at school and more so if the father had to come into the school. Jasmine returned to the front of the class to finish off a table she was drawing on the board. As soon as she started to write, she heard the music again and turned around and stared at the students in the corner to see who it was. None of the students seemed bothered by it or were looking around. She decided to finish off the table. As she began to write she heard it again, however, before she could turn around and speak to the class James was standing up and had Alexander by the shirt, shouting, 'I am not going to get into trouble because of you, you little f---wit'. As Jasmine headed for the students the two boys were now wrestling on the floor with some students screaming and others yelling, 'Fight, fight!'

Developing my classroom management plan

In this chapter, we have discussed the need to connect with students as a precursor to building positive relationships. We have also noted that students should be welcome in our classrooms and should be given opportunities for success, even the students who constantly challenge our authority. We also explored the need for whole-school consistency in working positively with students in pain. Working productively with students who challenge us is time consuming, confronting and demands a high level of interpersonal skill.

Often dealing with challenging behaviour exposes our skill level as well as our thinking towards these students. In developing your plan, how you view students who misbehave will influence how you prevent or respond to their misbehaviour. These questions may assist you in your philosophy and practice section of you management plan.

- How do you define misbehaviour? What are some common forms of misbehaviour that you will not tolerate in your classroom?
- How would you describe students who continually misbehave?
- What is your stance on zero tolerance?
- Would you include zero-tolerance policies or approaches in your class or advocate their use in your school? Explain your thinking behind this choice.
- To what degree are students who disconnect and disrupt the class worth the effort involved in re-engaging them?
- How will you be inclusive of Indigenous students?
- What are your views on suspensions and school exclusion?
- How will you prevent student indiscipline in your class?
- Do you agree with using choice as a strategy for misbehaviour and would you use it in your class?
- In your class, will you set up space for 'time-out' and what place does removing a student from the room have in your plan?
- How far do you agree that conflict with a student can be a source of professional learning for you?
- To what degree do you believe it is necessary to negotiate with students about their behaviour? Do you feel comfortable with doing this?
- Is it your role to 'go the extra mile' to engage students who constantly challenge your behaviour? How far do you think you should go?

Summary

In this chapter, we have focussed on working successfully with students whose behaviour constantly interrupts learning and challenges teacher authority. This behaviour is pain based, and caused by unmet needs in one or a combination of the universal needs of belonging, mastery, independence and generosity. Pain-based behaviour in a class setting can be confronting and challenging for the teacher. Despite sensationalist media reports, these behaviours are the minority of those experienced by teachers in school. Most of the indiscipline that teachers experience is low-level and it is these behaviours that are tedious, energy-sapping and annoying. One of the emerging ways to provide a positive environment for students in schools is through a consistent whole-school approach to learning and behaviour. Two different whole-school programs that are used in Australia and around the world were explored.

One of the criticisms of pre-service teacher programs is the lack of preparation in dealing with challenging behaviours. We have attempted to give you a language of discipline in dealing with challenging students. We worked through from preventative approaches to working one on one with a student to problem-solve behaviour issues. The skills and strategies presented are practical and applicable to all ages and developmental levels. Developing a language of discipline takes time and we encourage you to practise these skills so that you feel comfortable with what and how you say the statements. It can be a difficult task in the early years of teaching to use conflict events as a source of professional learning. However, in reflecting on what happened and what could be done differently we will begin to develop a repertoire of skills and strategies that are positive and empowering for students. The skills and strategies in this chapter will assist you in working with challenging students to develop the abilities to act responsibly. Your victories will be, at times, small and there will be times when you say and do things you wish you hadn't. These instances are not failures and are part of the learning journey and the lived reality of working with challenging students. However, we know from experience and the research that the successes are powerful for the students and are achieved in small steps by teachers who are human, caring and respectful.

FURTHER READING

Colvin, G. 2007, *7 Steps for Developing a Proactive School Wide Discipline Plan*, Corwin Press, Thousand Oaks, CA.

Colvin, G. 2004, *Managing the Cycle of Acting out Behaviour in the Classroom*, Behavior Associates, Eugene, OR.

Curwin, R. L., & Mendler, A. N. 1997, *As Tough as Necessary: Countering Violence, Aggression, and Hostility in Our Schools*, Association for Supervision and Curriculum Development, Alexandria, VA.

— 1999, 'Zero Tolerance for Zero Tolerance', *Phi Delta Kappan*, Vol. 81.

Department of Education, Science and Training, 2004, *National Report to Parliament on Indigenous Education and Training*, DEST, Canberra.

Evertson, C.M., & Weinstein, C.S. 2006, *Handbook of Classroom Management: Research, Practice and Contemporary Issues*, Lawrence Erlbaum Associates, London.

Rogers, B. 2004, *Behaviour Management: A Whole School Approach*, Sage Publications, London.

Sailor, W. et al. 2009, *Handbook of Positive Behavior Support*, Springer, New York.

WEBSITES

http://education.qld.gov.au/studentservices/behaviour

The Queensland Education Department Behaviour Management policy.

www.det.nsw.edu.au/proflearn/areas/nt/resources/bm01.htm

Some practical strategies and resources to assist teachers with classroom behaviour from the NSW Education Department.

www.behaviorassociates.org

Effective Professional Development Resources for educators designed to teach and manage students who display the full range of problem behaviour, from Dr G Colvin.

www.whatworks.edu.au

Professional action materials for improving outcomes for Indigenous students

www.aare.edu.au/04pap/fie04560.pdf

Productive pedagogies and discipline; the challenge of aligning teaching and behaviour management.

The Effective Teacher's Learning Journey

Learner outcomes

After reading this chapter, you should be able to:

- identify personal beliefs and assumptions about student learning and behaviour
- state the degree of student autonomy included in your discipline approach
- articulate the work of at least three theorists that support your classroom management philosophy
- explain how you will respond to student misbehaviour
- translate your philosophy into practical and effective management practices in the classroom
- develop your own classroom management plan for effective teaching.

Key terms

Democratic classrooms
Engagement
Inclusion
Student responsibility
Student self-management
Teacher coercion

A Positive Learning Framework approach

As we come to the last chapter of this text, we begin to finalise your approach to classroom management. We believe that the Positive Learning Framework (PLF) offers teachers a structure on which to build a well planned and individual classroom management plan. The PLF provides a framework on which to develop a realistic and workable approach to classroom management that starts before the year begins and caters for the most vulnerable in our classrooms. The approach woven into the PLF allows teachers to create quality learning environments that empower students to be actively engaged in meaningful learning. Quality learning environments provide students with a safe learning community where their academic as well as social and emotional lives are enhanced. This development of quality learning environments has been central to the text and is why we have subtitled the text 'engaging students in learning'.

Numerous texts on the market offer summaries of leading theorists or identify isolated aspects of classroom behaviour or instruction. Many of these texts or professional learning opportunities claim to have 'the answer'. This text does not claim to have the answer but rather provides a research-based collation of current understandings and knowledge in effective classroom management. The philosophy in the PLF allows teachers to cultivate a range of strategies to help work respectfully with students. Some strategies that we have explored in the text may not fit some teachers' personalities or teaching styles. While individual strategies may vary according to personality, the basic beliefs that underpin these strategies, as incorporated into the PLF, serve as a framework from which to build your management plan.

All management plans and approaches to classroom management and learner engagement should be built on sound education and child development principles. This is why in Chapter 1 we outlined the principles that underpin the approach taken in this text. These principles highlight the approach or skill areas involved in developing quality learning environments, where students from all ability levels and socio-economic backgrounds, those with additional needs and students from different ethnic groups will feel nurtured and thrive. These environments meet the needs of students to belong, to have success (mastery), to be independent and know their life has purpose. However, these environments do not just happen; they require careful planning.

In the next section, we will explore what is involved in developing a plan comprising philosophy, theory and practice components. This involves building upon the work you have done in the critical reflections and practical activities from earlier chapters. We will also help you to develop your plan by showing personal management plans that current teachers have developed around the three sections of philosophy, theory and practice. However, we do not provide the answers or give you suggestions that will work one hundred percent of the time with every student. Part of your development as an effective teacher will require you to reflect on current approaches and practices in classroom management, and then synthesise them with your beliefs and convictions.

Your personal management plan

Effective teachers develop their classroom management plans based on their knowledge, experience, professional learning and personal reflection. An effective plan is built upon knowledge of your values, beliefs and educational philosophy and is supportive of your convictions. A thoughtful and comprehensively constructed plan that is built on a personal understanding of our approach to teaching will enable us to respond consistently to student behaviour. From our personal philosophy, we can choose complementary theories to assist us in understanding the complexity of student behaviour, teaching and learning. From this knowledge base, we can then develop practical approaches in the classroom that reflect the philosophy and theory behind our management plan.

Philosophy

How we teach and how we respond to students is a reflection of our personal philosophy. Our philosophy guides us when dealing with the complexities of the classroom. We suggest that the philosophy component of your plan should address your beliefs about the following areas:

- how children learn
- why students behave the way they do
- the outcome and intention of discipline interventions
- the degree of control or coercion that is desirable
- the role of the teacher and the importance of instruction.

We will explore each of these areas. Our exploration will centre on suggesting questions that may be helpful in assisting you in developing a position that is authentic to your convictions.

HOW CHILDREN LEARN

One of the most important factors to look at when developing your plan is your philosophy about how children learn. Traditionally, such philosophies have focused on the nature versus nurture debate and have adopted an either/or position. Children were identified either as having the capacity to self-regulate and having their own will (nature) or as being primarily conditioned by their environment and responding to needs-satisfying stimuli (nurture). How we responded to student indiscipline depended on what we believed about nature vs. nurture. However, this debate is too simplistic and poses a false dichotomy. Nature and nurture are so intertwined that it is difficult to separate them. Our brains develop in the interplay between nature and nurture—we are influenced by our genes and our experiences. Brendtro, Mitchell and McCall, (2009) in their book *Deep Brain Learning*, believe that the dichotomy is not helpful in understanding how students learn and behave. They suggest that the 'brain rules but nature and nurture share the throne', supporting a more ecological view that makes the nature versus nurture debate meaningless:

> Bronfenbrenner saw the nature versus nurture debates as meaningless since both biology and culture affect the brain and behaviour. He called for more detailed studies of children as biological beings living in the natural ecology of childhood—the family, school, peer group, and community. As children's bodies and brains mature, they continually face new challenges, thus the need for a developmental perspective.

To create our management plan, we need to think about how we view student learning. Ask yourself the following questions:

- Do students build upon pre-existing knowledge or is knowledge absorbed through the way the teacher delivers it?
- Are students basically good or do they need to be controlled or conditioned to behave productively?
- Do students have positive potential—even those who challenge my authority?
- Do I need to establish reinforcement programs to manage appropriate behaviour?
- Are students my social equals or subordinates?
- To what degree do I believe that students can be self-managing?

Based on our responses to the questions, we can also ask ourselves:

- What instructional strategies best respond to my view of children and how they learn?

One beginning teacher explains how she views student learning in the philosophy section of her management plan:

> Generally, I believe children are born with the capacity to develop their social and knowledge interests and are inherently motivated to learn new things, and relate to and interact with people – but this must be nurtured and developed. From day one, children will react to situations and treatments depending on their cumulative experiences, thoughts, emotions and behaviour.

Another beginning teacher juxtaposes optimism with the realism of the classroom:

> Traditionally, the words optimistic and realistic evoke opposing views. In my philosophy of behaviour management, I would like to use these polar views to show an ebb and flow in my attitude and thoughts about children as students, and my role as teacher. While my fundamental nature is to be optimistic, working in a teaching environment requires realistic reflection. Optimistically, the nature of children is that they want to learn. There is an inner-self drive toward understanding the world in which they live. Further, children want to be accepted and recognised by the adults around them, including their teachers. They want to achieve and reach goals.

WHY STUDENTS BEHAVE THE WAY THEY DO

How you view and interpret student behaviour will direct your response to the misbehaviour. In your philosophy, you need to address your beliefs on the causes of, and influences on, student behaviour. Do students misbehave because they are inherently naughty or do other factors influence their behaviour? If you view a student's behaviour as solely the problem of that child then you will react differently to someone with a view that the cause may be multilayered and contextual. To illustrate our view that the causes of student misbehaviour are multilayered, we have stated that we believe that in order for students to thrive their universal needs must be met. In our philosophy, we believe that misbehaviour is more than the immediate class interruption. In attempting to engage students in learning, we feel teachers need to look 'inside' the student to find the thinking and emotions that contribute to a student's misbehaviour.

When students' misbehave, we are confronted with yet another decision. Do we perceive the student's actions as misbehaviour given the context, class and student? If we decide the behaviour as inappropriate, we then need to decide what response is necessary. We need to ask ourselves, is the misbehaviour minor? Is it interrupting learning or distracting others? To what extent are my students safe? Should I intervene so that it does not escalate? In the classroom situation, these questions require a split-second response. Part of your plan is to define your idea of what constitutes misbehaviour so that you are prepared with an appropriate response when it occurs. You will then be able to fine-tune your ability to respond appropriately, as you gain more experience. An important element of your preparation is developing your ability to prevent misbehaviour. If we are aware of what situations can prompt misbehaviour then we can be more aware and proactive in our decisions and actions to prevent it.

Our thinking about why students misbehave needs to be cognisant of 'out of school' factors and how much we believe these influence 'in-school' behaviour. To what degree do you believe that a child's family structure, socio-economic level, or ethnic background contributes to them misbehaving in class? How do you incorporate outside factors into your thinking and, ultimately, your response to indiscipline? Do you excuse behaviour based on your beliefs or assumptions about outside influences on your students? For example, do you have a view that students from specific ethnic groups will behave in a particular way? Do you have a belief that well-behaved students come from a particular family structure? Do you have a view that students from low socio-economic levels will behave in particular ways? You need to address these assumptions, as they will influence your understanding of why students misbehave and ultimately how you respond to these students.

One of our beginning teachers saw student misbehaviour as emanating from three major causes:

> Each reason for misbehaviour may be viewed as (1) coming from within a student, irrespective of the teacher and learning environment, (2) being associated with the teacher and the learning environment, or (3) forming from an interaction between a student's innate character and the teacher.

Understanding how you view and respond to student behaviour involves a working knowledge of what classroom management means to you. What do you think is involved in classroom management? What are the parameters or areas that are included in your understanding of classroom management? In creating a definition, you are establishing boundaries of what you mean by classroom management, while also establishing your response to misbehaviour and how you view learning in a classroom context. One beginning teacher acknowledges that misbehaviours will happen and then goes on to start outlining their definition of classroom management with the help of Brophy (1999):

> Classroom misbehaviours are almost certain, but learning how to avoid these misbehaviours and to successfully deal with these are vital in the teaching profession. More defined classroom management refers to the actions taken to create and maintain a learning environment conducive to successful instruction, from establishing rules and policies, maintaining attention and focus to engagement in academic activities that aim to reduce low-level misbehaviours.

OUTCOME AND INTENTION OF DISCIPLINE INTERVENTIONS

When we respond to student misbehaviour, we need to determine what we are trying to achieve. Do we want the student to comply with our instructions in the short term or do we want them to change their behaviour in the long term? (Or a bit of both?) What do we hope will happen with the student's behaviour and how could we help make this happen? There is no doubt that at times we want the student to be compliant immediately: to stop talking and get back to work. We can use a range of strategies to achieve this short-term goal; however, we also need to think about affecting change in the long term. How do we achieve a positive change in a student's behaviour? Woven into this thinking is how we view our role and whether, as the teacher, we feel we should impose discipline *on* students or teach discipline *to* them.

If we take the view that we need to impose discipline, then we take on a lot of responsibility for the students' behaviour. In imposing discipline on students, we take on the responsibility for the behaviour as well as the responsibility for changing it. This responsibility stems from our beliefs about students' lack of capacity for autonomy and independence. This contrasts with teaching discipline, which views students as having the capacity for self-management. If your goal is that you want your students to be responsible for their actions, then you need to tailor your responses to student misbehaviour to try to assist them in becoming more responsible. For example, do you impose discipline for the first term then 'ease off' to help your students become more responsible? Or do you impose discipline for early- to middle-primary classes but then teach discipline more in upper primary and secondary classes? Our response will flow from our belief in students' ability to be autonomous and self-managing.

The broader goal in analysing our intentions and the long-term effects of our responses to student misbehaviour is to address our understanding about the entire purpose of schooling. In terms of their education, what are we trying to achieve when we respond to students' appropriate or inappropriate behaviour? For example, if you have a view that schools exist in a democracy and that our goal as teachers is to prepare students to be active citizens, then your responses to misbehaviour will reflect this. Alternatively, if you view schools as hothouses for academic excellence that require students to have strong discipline to achieve, then you will respond to misbehaviour with a different outcome in mind. We realise that there are complex arguments about the purpose of schooling and many prominent ideologies on which to base an argument. The purpose here is not to trivialise these arguments, but more to highlight that, as beginning teachers, we will have a view of what schools are for and about and these views will influence the way we respond to our students. One of the tasks on our journey to becoming a teacher is to explore what we believe is the purpose of schooling and how this belief is incorporated into our class and our responses. One beginning teacher comments:

> My philosophy concerning classroom management is fundamentally egalitarian and democratic. I strongly believe that we are preparing students for the 'real world'. Therefore, the classroom should emulate, to a certain extent, the society in which they will be living independently in future years.

Another beginning teacher saw the conflict between the theory of a democratic classroom and the reality of his students' experiences of inequality.

He questions his beliefs and his role as the teacher:

> Although I am fundamentally democratic in my beliefs, I am a realist in thinking children of this diverse Australian society have different origins that affect their behaviours. How do I teach democratically when my students have already experienced at least 13 years of undercurrent inequality? Who will my students be and what would be my role as a teacher given this Australian context?

DEGREE OF CONTROL OR COERCION THAT IS DESIRABLE

The level of choice and the degree of control you allow your students will depend on the beliefs you have uncovered by reflecting on your teaching philosophy. If your view is that student behaviour is mostly the responsibility of the teacher, then you will offer students little control over the class. If you believe that students can develop the ability self-regulate and behave responsibly, then you may allow them greater control over the class environment. Finally, if you are at the laissez-faire end of Porter's continuum then you will give students a lot of freedom. Your beliefs about what is age-appropriate for your students will also guide your decisions on class freedoms. Of course, you will give senior school students greater control and responsibility than your Year 1 class. However, the belief behind your actions should be that students need to develop their capacity to be responsible and, therefore, at whatever age, you will structure your class to help develop these capacities for self-management

A follow-on question to ask about the desirable degree of control is: To what extent do I believe that students have the capacity to self-regulate their behaviour and to learn new pro-social behaviours? Do I believe that it is possible to teach students more appropriate behaviours? Can students make conscious decisions to behave in particular ways in different situations? In asking these questions, we have used the term 'capacity' to highlight that students are on a journey or are in a process of developing 'capacity' and as they are only partway through this journey, they may make mistakes or poor choices along the way. These poor choices do not mean that they are not capable of developing self-responsibility but rather highlight the need for extra support, empathy and understanding. As teachers, we should assist the student to develop their abilities to respond in ways that are positive, and that build resilience and responsibility. As teachers, we develop students' abilities to be responsible through what we say when the student misbehaves. We can also teach specific strategies to students to enhance their abilities to become more responsible for their behaviour. However, as a teacher I will only assist students to become more responsible if I believe that students are worth it or have the capacity to be self-managing. One of our beginning teachers believes that as they develop experience and confidence they will be more effective in offering students opportunities and support in self-management. This is a very insightful reflection as it acknowledges that in developing student self-responsibility teachers need to give the students opportunities to grow and make mistakes. As teachers, we need to give some control over to the students to allow for 'space' in which to grow. This approach is less teacher-centred. However, it is just as controlled or planned, as we are aware that students will misbehave and make mistakes and we are prepared with responses that are aimed at developing student responsibility. The beginning teacher asks:

> As time goes on, is it possible for the teacher to become an invisible part of the classroom management? Stated otherwise, is it possible for students to self-manage? In my opinion, the possibility for this grows with the expertise and experience of the teacher. Also, self-management is a learned trait or skill that the students may attain. I see the teacher as a necessary part of a student's successful management. With time and cooperative strategies, the teacher may take on a more catalytic, motivational role in this management.

Case study

A clash of approaches to student autonomy

Mrs Ngo is a new principal at a newly built school in a developing community. She believes that Ms Marino is too strict on her Year 2 students and that she does not allow them to have enough involvement in the rules, routines and expectation in the class. Mrs Ngo also believes that the class-room climate does not give the students opportunities to be spontaneous and creative, and she believes Year 2 students need spontaneity at this age. Mrs Ngo had a conversation with Ms Marino, highlighting that she feels the students spend too much time seated in pairs in silent work. She discussed that she believes they need to be active in their learning, move around the room and have opportunities to develop self-discipline.

Ms Marino does not totally disagree and, in her heart, she wants to make the classroom more active and fun but is terrified about the students getting out of control. She has had problems in the past trying different ways to teach and found that she couldn't get them back on-task. As a pre-service teacher, she also had problems with unruly older students, which why she only wants to teach in the early years. She fears being overrun in middle- and upper-primary classes. Ms Marino is also fearful that other teachers will gossip about her teaching approach and that parents will complain if she gives students more freedom. Therefore, she has settled on a style of teaching that enables the students to be quiet and get on with work. It is a system she feels she can control and she is mostly happy with it.

However, in the yearly performance review Mrs Ngo insists that Ms Marino change her approach and give the students more autonomy. Mrs Ngo feels that allowing students more freedom supports the school's approach to discipline and instruction.

Questions for reflection

1   From your current approach, whom do you support more: Mrs Ngo or Ms Marino? Can you explain your position?
2   Is it possible for Ms Marino to allow her students more autonomy?
3   What strategies could you offer Ms Marino that would support her move to a more active-learning approach?
4   How would you allay Ms Marino's fears about her ability to get the students back to work after they have been moving around the room?
5   As a beginning teacher, how do you view the advice given by Mrs Ngo? To what degree do you think the principal has the power to question your management approach?
6   As a teacher working with other teachers, how do you think staff members can resolve the differences in their approaches to student autonomy?

THE ROLE OF THE TEACHER AND THE IMPORTANCE OF INSTRUCTION

This element of your philosophy urges you to consider the assumptions or beliefs you have about your role as the teacher. What is your role and what importance do you give to instruction? How you view yourself as the teacher is linked to how you view learning and what behaviours you want to promote in your students. If you were in the middle of Porter's continuum, which consists of 'psychoeducational' theorists, then you would view students as rational beings who come with knowledge and have the capacity to co-construct new knowledge in relation with other students and you as the teacher. You believe your role is more to guide or facilitate than to direct learning. It follows then that the learning strategies you would use in your class would be supportive of this approach to learning. The same is true for how you see your role in helping students to develop their capacity to be responsible. We cannot separate how we teach from how we speak or respond to students about their behaviour.

In reflecting on how you see your role as a teacher, you also need to think about how you see that role in relation to students who exhibit pain-based behaviours. How far do you go in assisting these young people to develop their abilities to respond appropriately? Do you believe that your role includes helping students to seek help from appropriate professionals? Do you think it is your job to 'work through' serious issues with your students? At what point do you refer a student to other professionals? When do you seek assistance from colleagues to deal with a student? Where does your role as teacher in the classroom stop? How do you view your role with parents or community organisations? Is it your role to phone or visit parents, or to organise meetings with people who may be able to assist this one student? Students who challenge our authority and are not overtly compliant test our beliefs in what we should be doing. This is the same for students who have difficulty learning. How far do we go in assisting students to learn? Is it our job to work extensively with students who are struggling academically when the rest of the class are ready to move on to a new topic?

Another aspect affecting how you view your role is how you want students to see or remember you when they leave your class. What are the key terms they will use to describe you as a person and as their teacher? What image is dominant in your mind of how you see yourself as a teacher? How will you achieve this image in real life? What actions and behaviours do you need to model to become the teacher you want to be? Is this image or view of you as a teacher compatible with where early childhood, primary or secondary education is heading? One of our beginning teachers saw the teacher's role as a facilitator in both learning and behaviour. This beginning teacher also saw her role as being a mentor who had excellent content and pedagogical knowledge:

> In the improvement process, it is essential for a teacher to understand and acknowledge that his or her students are savvy or wise when interpreting his or her instructional and management abilities. Good, relevant teaching practices are the key elements in setting the tone for a positive classroom. The teacher must be firm yet responsive in their management of the classroom. The teacher is both a facilitator of learning and of classroom management. At an individual student level, the teacher also acts as a mentor or expert of knowledge. In an act of balancing, the teacher is also an arbitrator of behaviour and learning focus.

Theory

After you have determined your teaching philosophy, the next step is to explore existing models or theories of classroom management that are supportive of your preferred approach. We encourage you to explore three or four educational theorists and identify the strategies or elements in their approach that you like or that are supportive of your philosophy. We suggest studying three or four theorists as it is too simplistic to select one theorist or approach and believe that it will address every situation you will face in the classroom. We do not doubt that you will find a model that best fits with your philosophy; however, it is worthwhile viewing other models to have access to a greater range of classroom strategies. This eclectic approach to studying theory is more difficult to develop than just selecting one model and it requires extra effort to explore a range of approaches. However, we believe the result is a management plan that is extremely helpful in assisting you to establish a quality learning environment.

SELECTING THE MOST APPROPRIATE MODEL OF CLASSROOM MANAGEMENT

A number of authors, past and present, have made significant contributions to our understanding of student behaviour and devised techniques that have assisted teachers to prevent and respond to student behaviour in the classroom. It is essential that your selected theorists match your philosophy and that the selected theorists have underlying assumptions and beliefs consistent with each other.

Table 7.1 outlines an overview of the major theorists, their models, the assumptions underpinning their approach and generalised approach to teaching. In gaining an understanding of current approaches to classroom management, it is important to recognise the influence of the early writers. The concepts and particular elements in early influential writers' models are strongly evident in today's current classroom management models. In reading a range of theorists for your plan, you will often be directed back to these writers and it is worthwhile to understand their influence and acknowledge how current theorists build upon these pioneer foundations. Samples of the concepts promoted by these early writers that are further developed in current models include:

- student self-control
- reinforcement
- rewards
- punishment
- engaging lessons
- 'I' messages
- maintaining dignity
- evaluative praise
- self-discipline
- student needs
- mistaken goals
- democratic classroom
- logical consequences
- encouragement
- student rights
- teacher rights
- discipline hierarchy.

The teaching approach ascribed to each model can be linked to Porter's balance of power continuum (2001) that places theorists on a continuum defined by the relative power of teachers and students as outlined in Figure 3.4 on page 93. The balance of power continuum goes from autocratic theories to laissez-faire approaches to student discipline. This overview is intended to support and guide you in your reading of classroom management theorists.

Table 7.1 Early influential writers and contemporary models in classroom management

Pioneers in classroom management			
Theorist	Model	Teaching approach	Main assumptions
Fritz Redl and William Wattenberg	Group behaviour and classroom discipline	Authoritative/ democratic	Students in groups behave differently to individuals; teachers support student self-control & offer 'in the moment' assistance to help change behaviour.
B. F. Skinner	Behaviour modification	Authoritarian	Teachers shape student behaviour through systematic reinforcement including rewards and negative reinforcement.
Jacob Kounin	Instructional management	Authoritative/ democratic	Teachers prevent misbehaviour through awareness in the classroom and by using effective lesson management techniques (student movement, group awareness, smoothness of lesson delivery) to influence student behaviour.
Haim Ginott	Congruent communication	Democratic	Teachers encourage student's autonomy through dignity and awareness of student feelings about situations and themselves. Teachers assist student self discipline by focussing on the situation not the student and view students as capable of making good decisions.
Rudolph Dreikurs	Democratic teaching	Democratic	Teachers promote student self-discipline in a democratic classroom where students and teachers make decisions on how the class will work. Students' behaviour is goal directed and all students want to belong. Students misbehave out of mistaken goals. Teachers use logical consequences and encouragement instead of praise, and should never use punishment.
Thomas Gordon	Teacher effectiveness training	Liberal	Discipline is best achieved through student self-control. Teachers use 'I' messages in influencing student behaviour, preventative strategies and incorporate a no-lose approach to conflict.

Table 7.1 Early influential writers and contemporary models in classroom management (cont.)

Lee and Marlene Canter	Assertive discipline	Authoritarian	The teacher and student have rights in the classroom. Clear rules of behaviour and expectations are written and enforced through a discipline hierarchy of consequences.
William Glasser	Choice theory & quality schools	Democratic	Teachers and schools meet student needs in order for them to flourish. Quality teacher instruction assists in meeting these needs. Teachers encourage student involvement and responsible behaviour.

Contemporary models in classroom management

Theorist	Model	Teaching approach	Main assumptions
Linda Albert	Cooperative discipline	Democratic	Discipline is best achieved through cooperation. Teachers need to establish a classroom that is safe, where students feel connected and belong. Students assist in the development of a code of conduct. Student misbehaviour is viewed as an opportunity for learning.
Barbara Coloroso	Inner discipline	Democratic	Teachers work to instil an inner sense of control in students. The classroom is structured to allow opportunities for responsibility. It is based on a belief that students will make good decisions, are worth the effort and have the capacity to take positive charge of their lives.
Jane Nelson & Lynn Lott	Positive discipline	Authoritative/ democratic	Teachers provide a classroom where students come to view themselves as capable and able to have control in their lives. The classroom climate is built on mutual respect and cooperation. Class meetings are key to class relationship building.

Frederic Jones	Positive classroom discipline	Authoritarian	Teachers maintain student involvement in learning through effective and efficient teacher behaviours such as engaging lessons, setting clear limits, classroom organisation, helping students with work problems and incentives to promote responsibility.
Jerome Freiberg	Consistency management and cooperative discipline	Democratic	As a part of a school-wide approach, teachers provide learning communities that are built on trust, cooperation and consistency of message across the school. Students take on leadership roles and responsibility in developing self-discipline. Effective instruction and increasing student academic achievement are important in taking students from being 'tourists' to citizens.
Harry and Rosemary Wong	Pragmatic classroom management	Authoritarian	Teachers need to have clear classroom procedures that are taught to students in the first weeks of school in order to teach effectively. Teacher planning and organisation are essential and student misbehaviour is the result of poor teacher classroom management.
Spencer Kagan, Patricia Kyle and Sally Scott	Win–win discipline	Authoritative/ democratic	Teachers and students work cooperatively to solve problems in the class. Misbehaviour is seen as a starting point in helping students develop self-responsibility. Teachers work with students, as if on the same side, (win–win) to solve problems and continually reaffirm self-management and proactive life skills.
Richard Curwin and Allen Mendler	Discipline with dignity	Democratic	Teachers maintain a positive learning environment that supports student dignity and gives a sense of hope to those students struggling with school. Teachers consider individual situations rather than relying on a rigid hierarchy of consequences and provide choices for students. Teachers model the values promoted in the classroom.

Table 7.1 Early influential writers and contemporary models in classroom management (cont.)

Alfie Kohn	Beyond discipline	Democratic	Teachers work to develop classrooms as learning communities. In these communities, students and teachers develop respectful relationships and collectively solve problems (class meetings). Teachers respect student interest in instruction and constructing learning that moves students to deeper levels of thinking.
Marvin Marshall	Discipline without stress	Authoritative/ democratic	Teachers focus on student responsibility and empower students to make choices about behaviour. Students are more likely to behave when given responsibility. Students are taught a framework for behaving appropriately. Teachers are positive, offer choices and develop self-reflection as a step towards changing behaviour.
Ronald Morrish	Real discipline	Autocratic	Teachers provide support and guidance for students to behave responsibly. Students need to be taught right from wrong, to comply with adult authority and, when developmentally ready, to begin to make choices about behaviour. Teachers train students so that they can work successfully in society.
Forest Gathercoal	Judicious discipline	Authoritative/ democratic	Schools are set within society and therefore we need to educate students to live in a democratic society. The focus is on student rights and responsibilities and in developing ethical behaviour as reflected in society's laws.
Carolyn Evertson and Alene Harris	Classroom organisation and management program (comp)	Authoritative/ democratic	The teacher organises the classroom for effective instruction and learning opportunities. This organisation includes teaching rules and procedures from day one of the school year and developing student accountability for behaviour and learning. The classroom is viewed as a social and communicative setting suited to learner centred instruction.

MIXING AND MATCHING STRATEGIES FROM A RANGE OF THEORISTS

In order to apply strategies from a range of theorists, we need to be very clear about our assumptions and our approach as articulated in our philosophy. It is easy to get confused or seduced by a particular strategy that, in fact, may contradict our philosophy. Teachers often make this mistake when developing a management plan for the first time. We may read the work of two different theorists and like their strategies, without realising the two theorists are very different in their assumptions and underpinning principles. For example, you may like Marvin Marshall's model (Marvin's 2001 text is titled *Discipline without stress, punishments, or rewards: How teachers and parents promote responsibility and learning*). Marshall's model focuses on student responsibility, stating that this is best achieved through setting clear expectations and empowering students to achieve high levels of self-responsibility. You might also find Canter's idea (1993) of a 'discipline hierarchy' appealing. This idea outlines corrective actions and the order in which they will be imposed on students. The clash with these approaches is that Marshall advocates helping the students to reflect on their behaviour and trying to develop students' intrinsic motivation rather than relying on teacher-led extrinsic motivation and the use of guided choice. These concepts are difficult to defend if you then 'bump' students up Canter's discipline hierarchy in a process that is teacher-led and more coercive. The Canter approach does not help foster responsibility and reflection and therefore may not be appropriate for your management plan. Although these theorists may use similar words, their meanings are very different and their starting assumptions are worlds apart.

One of our beginning teachers provides an example of a plan that incorporates a range of theorists whose assumptions are supportive of each other. This beginning teacher links different elements of these theorists to his philosophy:

> I believe an effective discipline system should first link effectively to cooperative, student-centred democratic classrooms and focus on preventative, rather than corrective strategies (Curwin & Mendler). Second, the discipline system should be non-coercive (Kohn), treat the students with dignity (Curwin & Mendler) and provide choice that restores ownership of learning and behaviour to the student (Glasser). Teachers and students should proactively and collaboratively determine consequences to their actions to create student awareness and foster

a deeper understanding of all effects of their actions on the community and students long-term self image/efficacy (Dreikurs). Finally, effective discipline systems should be fair, responsive and inclusive of the diverse learners within Australian schools (Kohn).

Which models do your peers favour?

Working with a group of students or your class at university, form groups according to the approaches you prefer. Have a representative from each group explain:

- why they are in this group
- what elements of this theory or model supports their philosophy
- how this approach promotes their style of teaching.

Practice

Your classroom will reflect your philosophy and the theory of discipline you have chosen. What you say and do in the classroom will reflect your beliefs about the 'practice of discipline'. This practice section revolves around what you do to establish a quality learning environment and prevent misbehaviour and how you respond effectively to misbehaviour when it occurs. We also think it is important to have an understanding of how your approach fits in with or will support the whole-school approach to student behaviour.

Our starting point for this is the PLF, as it outlines a range of preventative actions and identifies a theoretical approach to teaching. In exploring these elements, we will pose questions to assist you in exploring what might be included in your quality learning environment. You can use the wisdom of our beginning teachers' management plans and see how they aim to prevent and respond to student misbehaviour in the practice sections of their plans. One of these beginning teachers sees her role in preventing misbehaviour as involving six main areas:

My preventative systems to increase academic engagement and prevent student behaviour can be streamed into six main areas: the beginning of the year induction, the ongoing class routines, relationship building with students, communication, instructional effectiveness and the fostering of intrinsic learning and deep modelling. These all will be subject to compatibility to whole-school policies.

Prevention

It is important to have a well thought out preventative strategy in your management plan. A preventative plan enables the teacher not only to reduce initial misbehaviour, but also to stop conflict escalating. In our PLF, we identified a range of strategies that are aimed at assisting teachers to develop a quality learning environment. Let us explore how these strategies may be addressed in your plan. The PLF outlines the following skills and strategies in the first phase of prevention.

Positive Learning Framework

Prevention: self awareness and management plan

- At the start of the year and before each class
- self awareness
- proactive thinking—indiscipline will happen at some stage
- caring and welcoming classroom
- classroom layout and resources
- rules, routines and procedures
- high and specific expectations.

Self-awareness and proactive thinking

In this prevention phase, it is helpful to be aware of how we feel before we work with different groups of students. For example, on our first day we need to be aware of how we may feel anxious or nervous. We need a level of self-awareness to recognise that we are feeling this way and that we usually respond to these feeling through nervous talking, fidgeting or becoming annoyed more easily. This sense of awareness will help us respond to students in a positive manner rather than reacting out of our nervous or anxious states. Self-awareness is helpful in recognising stress levels in the lead up to conflict with students or to acknowledging how we feel after we have had an altercation with a student.

We know that students will misbehave at some stage in our class and around the school. We can be prepared for this misbehaviour. We recognise that when students are moving from one classroom to the next or transitioning from one activity to the next the likelihood of them misbehaving increases. We can be proactive in these situations and lessen the likelihood of them misbehaving. The same goes for yard duty or supervision. We can be prepared for the sorts of common misbehaviour we will encounter while doing yard duty. There is no need to be caught off guard, instead you should have responses ready or strategies discussed with other staff before the duty happens. For example, if, when you are on yard duty, you always seem to meet resistance when asking students not to litter, you could move the bin so it is close by and emphasise how easy it is for them to put their rubbish in the bin. There is no need to continually battle with these students, as this only breeds resentment from both sides.

Caring and welcoming classroom

As mentioned, the PLF is built on the assumption that students have needs. If you state in your philosophy that you believe students have needs, you may ask: How do I create an environment where these needs can be met? What are the teacher actions and words that I need to use to assist me in making my class caring and welcoming? What would a classroom need to give students a sense of importance and a sense that they belong? What would a class environment that develops students' mastery, fosters their independence and helps to build generosity look like? This learning environment will not automatically appear, but rather requires careful consideration and planning. In developing your plan, think about specifics and practical expressions of your approach in posters or visual displays in your room. What will students see on their first day as they enter the room to make them feel welcome? How will students 'know' that this classroom is a safe place of learning?

One of our beginning teachers writes that it is important to incorporate relationships and connecting with students as elements of prevention:

> Several other preventative strategies that I would implement are very important; however, they can sometimes be overlooked. These include being enthusiastic,

friendly, honest, respectful, fun, interesting, and open with students. Using names when calling on students is also an important and powerful tool within the classroom and demonstrates to the student that you are interested and friendly in your approach, rather than pointing or indicating to a student to answer a question without using their name.

In establishing a welcoming and caring learning environment, you will also need to be aware of your student population and to have thought about how you will best include students with additional needs or students from diverse cultural backgrounds. It is worthwhile to have thought about your position on inclusion. To what degree do you support the various arguments around partial inclusion to full inclusion? How does your approach cater for the range of abilities and backgrounds inherent in the student population? A welcoming and caring learning environment that nurtures and supports students is inherently inclusive. In creating a sense of belonging for students with additional needs we will also need to be sensitive to the physical layout of the room, as discussed below.

Classroom layout and resources

There is so much that can be done to set up the physical environment of a classroom. The amount of freedom you will have to arrange the classroom to reflect your approach will depend on the year level you teach, the available resources and the leadership at your school. Regardless of the level of freedom you have, you will need to have an idea of what you want in your room and what purpose it will serve. The thinking and planning can be done well in advance, so that you can adapt your ideas to the situation you find yourself in. In your planning, you might ask: how will my learning environment look? What is the best use of the space and resources to achieve maximum engagement in learning? How will I arrange the desks (groups, horseshoe, single rows or u-shaped)? What are the learning or activity centres I want in my room and where will I place them? How do I store learning resources and to what degree will students have access to them? Where do I put the teacher's desk? What needs to be on the walls, windows and around the room to convey a welcoming feel and learning tone? How does the physical layout of the room facilitate my style of teaching? How do I make the best use of available learning technologies? Have I considered adequate movement space around the room? Irrespective of your exact answers, the focus of how the room is set out should be to increase student engagement in learning and to assist in the establishment of a caring environment.

Rules, routines and procedures, and high expectations

In this section, we have amalgamated the last two points of the 'Prevention: self-awareness and management plan', as we feel that setting your expectations requires similar planning to setting your rules and routines. As highlighted in previous sections, planning your rules, routines and expectations will reflect your views on how best to match student autonomy with teacher control. To what degree will you involve the students in helping you establish rules and expectations in class? How will you establish which behaviours are acceptable and which are unacceptable? How will you respond to student misbehaviour? Will you allow the students to help you enforce the rules? If so, to what degree? Will the students be involved in determining your role as the teacher to some degree? Will the students be able to select one or two rules for you? Will they have input into the procedures and routines in the classroom? The degree of student autonomy in your philosophy or approach to teaching will come into sharp focus when thinking of rules. The extent to which you let the students have a say in setting class rules is a central issue for your philosophy and will need addressing in your plan before day one of teaching. You also need to think about your position on the level of parent involvement you would like and plan how you will communicate your expectations of your students to their parents. In addition, you need to think about the role parents might play in helping develop rules and expectations.

One of our beginning teachers sees the importance of clear rules and routines, as they are an important part of maintaining safety in his Design and Technology learning area.

> The essential class rules (Curwin and Mendler) are social contracts that make sense and the resulting collaboratively chosen logical consequences are aimed at understanding and empathy to all affected rather than punishments for broken rules and misbehaviour (Kohn). Additionally, they promote safety and accountability. Finally, there would be need for ongoing class routines. Routines promote safe environments. Class routines include lining up before class, bag storage on entry, roll call, outline of objectives of the lesson (students can add an

item to every lesson), the beginning- and end-of-class equipment stocktake, the handing out of portfolios and the end-of-class workshop cleanup.

Rules, routines and expectations in the classroom will need reviewing throughout the term. What process will you follow to review them? Will it be teacher-led with the need for review depending on the frequency of student misbehaviour? Or will it be an in-built process that includes student input? Will you conduct class meetings? Will students have positions of responsibility in these meetings? How far will you go in allowing your class to set their own rules, routines, expectations and consequences?

Responding to student misbehaviour

An effective management plan will not only have a clear direction for preventing misbehaviour but will also address how you respond to misbehaviour and promote positive behaviour. The PLF outlines a range of positive strategies in which to respond or correct student misbehaviour. These are outlined in the PLF on page 247.

The PLF provides a good example of corrective actions you can use in your management plan, as the strategies listed are consistent with each other and reflect a unified approach to misbehaviour. The strategies are supportive of a dignified and respectful approach to students. When developing a range of responses to student misbehaviour, it is important to maintain an internal consistency and coherence in your approach. If your approach is democratic and focuses on the strengths of students then it would be inconsistent to suddenly include blanket punishments as a response to student misbehaviour. Punishments and teacher coercion are not compatible with a dignified, respectfully oriented management plan.

In planning your strategies to correct student indiscipline, you will need to identify how you will respond to student misbehaviour. What will your strategies be to change behaviour and re-engage the student in learning? Will you have consequences and, if so, who will help construct these? To what degree will you explore the motivations and intentions behind behaviour? How will you use this information in working with student misbehaviour?

It is worthwhile planning how you will respond to more challenging behaviours. How will you respond (what will you say and do) when a student is noncompliant and will not follow instructions? What about the student who continues a behaviour despite previous interventions? How do you deal with explosive behaviours, where a student shouts, screams, throws objects, knocks over chairs or runs out of the class? How will you handle the aggressive student or verbally abusive student? How do your responses support the development of student responsibility? In responding to these escalating behaviours it is important to know your philosophy and own ability to deal with challenging behaviours. It is crucial that in times of conflict, your response is consistent with your overall approach to students and learning and that students see you model behaviours that are consistent with what they are hearing and seeing when the class is working well.

School-wide application

Your classroom management plan will be set within a school environment that has clearly defined policies and expectations on student behaviour and learning. You will need to be aware of these school-wide policies and understand how the school promotes positive behaviour in the classrooms and playground. Does the school have values or particular messages that they actively promote? For example, this could be a school motto, such as 'Strive for Excellence', around which the school weaves their rationale for rules or expectations. Maybe the school has identified a set of values that it will promote and incorporate into the life of the school. Your management plan will need to incorporate awareness of these values and be supportive of them in practice.

In a whole-school setting, your plan will have to account for the range of situations that will provide you with the opportunity to relate to students and promote positive behaviour. These opportunities may include yard duty, sport supervision, lunch supervision, teaching someone else's class when they are away, assemblies, gymnasiums, bus duty and excursions.

Part of the school-wide application of your plan will involve how you understand and use the discipline structure in the school. Often teachers can be frustrated when a student they have sent to the principal or assistant principal returns and the teacher does not know what happened or what actions, if any, have been taken. Some teachers interpret the perceived lack of action as tacit support for the student and, therefore, a lack of support for them as teachers. It is important to have an understanding of what the principal or deputy are trying to accomplish and how this supports the school's approach, so that you are not disappointed if the student does not return contrite. Effective school-wide discipline needs to be supportive of the principles on which classroom discipline is based. If the classroom approach to student behaviour is at odds with the school or administrator's approach then conflict will occur and the opportunity to develop positive behaviour in the students will be diminished through delivering mixed messages. In the lead up to school starting or as part of the school induction program for new staff, it is helpful to have these conversations with the school administration, and clarify and coordinate approaches to managing student behaviour.

Critical reflection

School-wide approaches to student behaviour

All schools will have similarities and differences in the way they approach student discipline. It would be naïve to think that the school you are starting with will have policies and expectations as yours or that they will be written in the same style or language. Therefore, it is a useful activity to research several school policies on behaviour. When you have policies from a few different schools, ask yourself the following questions:

1   What is the approach to learning for each school?
2   What counts as misbehaviour? How has each school spelt out how they will respond to misbehaviour?
3   Do they describe consequences for student misbehaviour?
4   Is instruction a key feature?
5   Is there clarity around student behaviour outside of the classroom—during lunchtimes, assemblies and going to and coming home from school?
6   To what degree does your approach support these schools' policies or management plans?

It is also worthwhile to look at system-level (public, independent or Catholic) policies and how they frame their approach in published documents. You can access this information on system level websites.

Developing my classroom management plan— bringing it all together

Now that you have had the opportunity to think about your philosophy and beliefs about student learning and behaviour, have read and reviewed supportive models or theories and have explored how your approach will look in the classroom, it is time to put everything together into your own classroom management plan. We have asked numerous questions in this chapter and throughout the text to assist you in developing your plan. However, you may also have questions that are relevant to your teaching level or subject. These are important and need to be addressed in your plan. When writing your plan, incorporate the responses you have created to the questions in the *Developing my management plan* section at the end of each chapter. You will also have identified some insights in your responses to the *Critical reflection* activities and the *Case studies* as well as practising your classroom management skills in the *Practice activities*. If you have been adding to and developing your mind map from Chapter 1 you will have mountains of insightful thoughts and responses on which to build your plan.

Below is a suggested structure for your classroom management plan that includes some areas that we believe is crucial for you to address. This structure provides you with a framework for a dynamic plan to implement on day one of your new career, which can be reviewed and updated frequently as you gain more experience, knowledge and insight into working with students in schools.

My management plan	
Philosophy	What are my beliefs and assumptions about: • how children learn • why students behave the way they do • the outcome and intention of discipline interventions • the degree of control or coercion that is desirable • the role of the teacher • the importance of instruction and • the potential of students to be self-managing?
Theory	In relation to your philosophy, what are the key elements of at least three existing classroom management theories or models that support your philosophy or approach to classroom management?

Practice	What does your philosophy look like in the classroom? List the practical steps you will use in class that reflect your philosophy. Include elements such as rules, expectations, a code of conduct, responsibility rosters, a class motto, seating plans, student work, procedures and routines, classroom layout and so on.

Summary

Effective teachers develop their plans based on reflecting on their personal beliefs, professional knowledge and their experience. Quality learning environments are developed through careful construction by the teacher, and are based on a plan that includes their philosophy of education, supported by current theories or evidence on effective classroom management and brought to life in the classroom through purposeful teacher strategies. A management plan is a working document that will be altered and changed as you gain experience and knowledge of students, schools and yourself as a teacher.

Classroom management is a challenge; however, it should not be a source of fear or concern. Your plan sets out your vision of how you want your class to operate and how you intend to have a positive impact on students' academic, social and emotional development. The purpose of the vision embedded in your plan is exemplified in the concluding comments from one of our beginning teachers. She states very clearly her intention to develop positive relationships with students through the process of engaging them in learning:

> In concluding this management plan, I would like to state that I feel effective classroom management is all about maintaining a positive and productive learning environment. This can be achieved through creating a fair and harmonious classroom, engaging students in class activities and encouraging their cooperation.
>
> I have created my own classroom management plan based on my philosophy, the three theorists I have researched, and on how I would apply these ideas practically in a classroom. I feel that as I gain experience in the classroom and acquire further knowledge in the teaching domain, my management plan will change and my beliefs and practical skills will alter. However, I will always consider the learning environment to be one where students enjoy learning and achieving and where teachers provide the best possible care and respect for their students.

FURTHER READING

Borich, G. D. 2006, *Effective Teaching Methods*, Prentice Hall, New Jersey.

Charles, C. M. 2007, *Building Classroom Discipline*, Longman Publishing Company, White Plains, NY.

Emmer, E. T. & Evertson, C. M. 2008, *Classroom Management for Middle and High School Teachers*, Allyn & Bacon, Boston.

Jones, V. & Jones, L. 2009, *Comprehensive Classroom Management*, Prentice Hall, New Jersey.

Manning, M. L. & Bucher, K. T. 2006, *Classroom Management: Models, Applications and Cases*, Prentice Hall, New Jersey.

WEBSITES

www.suite101.com/reference/classroom_management_plan

This site features a collection of articles related to creating a classroom management plan.

www.prodait.org/teaching/critical_teaching

This site looks at reflective teaching—what it is, and how we reflect on our teaching, starting with our beliefs and assumptions.

www.brains.org/classroom_management.htm

Gene Van Tassell takes a general look at brain research and classroom management.

www.humboldt.edu/~tha1/discip-options.html

This site by Thomas H. Allen gives instruction on developing a discipline plan.

www.nwrel.org/archive/sirs/5/cu9.html

An article 'Schoolwide and Classroom Discipline' by Kathleen Cotton, part of the School Improvement Research Series.

www.plsweb.com/resources/newsletters/enews_archives/40/2005/01/06

This site provides information on how to implement a proactive approach to classroom management and prevent discipline problems.

www.nasponline.org/educators/HCHSII_PreventiveStrategies.pdf

This document deals with preventive strategies in comprehensive classroom management.

Theorists' websites

www.kidsareworthit.com

Barbara Coloroso's site

www.tlc-sems.com

    Richard Curwin and Allen Mendler's site

www.fredjones.com

    Frederic Jones's site

www.MarvinMarshall.com

www.disciplinewithoutstress.com

    Marvin Marshall's sites

www.realdiscipline.com

    Ronald Morrish's site

www.effectiveteaching.com

    Harry and Rosemary Wong's site

Bibliography

Adler, A. 1930, *The Problem Child*, Putnam's, New York.

Advancement Project and Civil Rights Project 2000, *Opportunities Suspended: The Devastating Consequences of Zero Tolerance and School Discipline Policies*, Harvard Civil Rights Project, Boston.

Albert, L. 1989, *A Teacher's Guide To Cooperative Discipline: How To Manage Your Classroom and Promote Self-Esteem*, American Guidance Services, Circle Pines, MN.

Anderson, L., Evertson, C. & Emmer, E. T. 1980, 'Dimensions in Classroom Management Derived from Recent Research', *Journal of Curriculum Studies*, vol. 12, pp. 343–356.

Angus M., McDonald T., Ormond. C., Rybarczyk. R., Taylor, A. & Winterton, A. 2009, *Trajectories of Classroom Behaviour and Academic Progress: A Study of Engagement with Learning*, Edith Cowan University, Western Australia.

Arrends, R. I. 1998, *Learning to Teach*, McGraw Hill, New York.

Audas, R. & Willms, J. D. 2001, *Engagement and Dropping out of School: A Life-course Perspective*, Applied Research Branch, Human Resources Development, Canada, Ontario.

Baer, D., Wolf, M. & Risley, T. 1968, 'Some Current Dimensions of Applied Behaviour Analysis', *Journal of Applied Behaviour Analysis*, vol. 1, pp. 91–97.

Bagley, W. 1907, *Classroom Management*, Macmillan, New York.

Baumrind, D. 1991, 'Parenting Styles and Adolescent Development', in R. M. Lerner, A. C. Peterson, & J. Brooks-Gunn (eds), *Encyclopedia of Adolescence* vol. 2, Garland, New York, pp. 746–758.

Benard, B. 2004, *Resilience: What we have Learned*, WestEd, San Francisco.

Bennett, B. & Rolheiser, C. 2001, *Beyond Monet: The Artful Science of Instructional Integration*, Bookation Inc., Toronto.

Bennett, B. & Smilanich, P. 1994, *Classroom Management: A Thinking and Caring Approach*, Bookation Inc., Toronto.

Bohn, C. M., Roehrig, A. D. & Pressley, M. 2004, *The First Days of School in the Classrooms of Two More Effective and Four Less Effective Primary-Grades Teachers*, The University of Chicago Press, Chicago.

Borich, G. D. 2006, *Effective Teaching Methods*, Prentice Hall, New Jersey.

Bowes, J. & Grace, R. (eds) 2009, *Children, Families and Communities: Contexts and Consequences*, 3rd edn, Oxford University Press, Melbourne.

Breed, F. 1933, *Classroom Organisation and Management*, World Book Company, Yonkers-on-Hudson, NY.

Brendtro, L., Brokenleg, M. & Van Bockern, S. 1990, *Reclaiming Youth at Risk*, National Education Service, United States.

Brendtro, L., Brokenleg, M., & Van Bockern, S. (2002). *Reclaiming Youth at Risk: Our Hope for the Future*, rev. edn. National Education Service, Bloomington, IN.

Brendtro, L. & du Toit, L. 2005, *Response Ability Pathways: Restoring Bonds of Respect*, Pre-Text, Cape Town.

Brendtro, L., Mitchell, M. & McCall, H. 2009, *Deep Brain Learning: Pathways to Potential with Challenging Youth*, Circle of Courage Institute and Starr Commonwealth, Albion, Michigan.

Brendtro, L., Ness, A. & Mitchell, M. 2001, *No Disposable Kids*, Sopris West, Longmont, CO.

Brendtro, L. & Shahbazian, M. 2004, *Troubled Children and Youth: Turning Problems into Opportunities*, Research Press, Illinois.

Bronfenbrenner, U. 1994, 'Ecological Models of Human Development', *International Encyclopedia of Education*, 2nd edn, vol. 3, Elsevier, Oxford.

Bronfenbrenner, U. 2005, *Making Human Beings Human: Bioecological Perspectives on Human Development*, Sage Publications, Thousand Oaks, CA.

Brophy, J. E. 1979, 'Teacher Behaviour and its Effects', *Journal of Educational Psychology*, vol. 71, pp. 733–750.

Brophy, J. E. 1982, 'Classroom Management and Learning', *American Education*, vol. 18 (2), pp. 20–23.

Brophy, J. E. 1983, 'Classroom Organisation and Management', *Elementary School Journal*, vol. 83, pp. 265–285.

Burden, R. 2000, *Powerful Classroom Management Strategies: Motivating Students to Learn*, Corwin Press, Thousand Oaks, CA.

Burgoon, J., Buller, D. & Woodall, W. 1996, *Non Verbal Communication: The Unspoken Dialogue*, McGraw-Hill, New York.

Burns R. B. 1984, 'How Time is used in Elementary Schools: The Activity Structure of Classrooms', in L. W. Anderson (ed.), *Time and School Learning: Theory, Research and Practice*, Croom Helm, London, pp. 52–71.

Casella, R. 2003, 'Zero Tolerance Policy in Schools: Rationale, Consequences, and Alternatives', *Teachers College Record*, vol. 105 no. 5, pp. 872–892

Chao, R. K. 1994, 'Beyond Parental Control and Authoritarian Parenting Style: Understanding Chinese Parenting Through the Cultural Notion of Training', *Child Development*, vol. 65, 1111–1119.

Charles, C. M. 2007, *Building Classroom Discipline*, Longman Publishing Company, White Plains, New York.

Cohen, E. 1992, *Restructuring the Classroom: Conditions for Productive Small Groups*, Center on Organization and Restructuring of Schools, Wisconsin Center for Education Research, Madison.

Colvin, G. 2004, *Managing the Cycle of Acting out Behaviour in the Classroom*, Behavior Associates, Eugene, OR.

Colvin, G. 2007, *7 Steps for Developing a Proactive School Wide Discipline Plan*, Corwin Press, Thousand Oaks, CA.

Corno, L. & Mandinach, E. B. 2004, 'What we have Learned About Student Engagement in the Past Twenty Years', in D. M. McInerney & S. Van Etten (eds), *Big Theories Revisited*, Information Age Publishing Inc., Charlotte, NC, pp. 299–328.

Csikszentmihalyi, M. 1996, *Flow: The Psychology of Optimal Experience*, Harper Collins, New York.

Curwin, R. & Mendler, A. 1988, *Discipline with Dignity*, Association for Supervision and Curriculum Development, Alexandria, VA.

Curwin, R. & Mendler, A. 1997, *As Tough as Necessary: Countering Violence, Aggression, and Hostility in our Schools*, Association for Supervision and Curriculum Development, Alexandria, VA.

Curwin, R. & Mendler, A. 1999, 'Zero Tolerance for Zero Tolerance', *Phi Delta Kappan*, vol. 81.

Curwin, R. & Mendler, A. 1999, *Discipline with Dignity with Challenging Youth*, National Educational Service, Bloomington, IN.

Davidson, A. L. 1999, 'Negotiating Social Differences: Youth's Assessments of Educators' Strategies', *Urban Education*, vol. 34 (3), pp. 338–369.

Department of Education and Science 1989, *Discipline in Schools: Report of the Committee of Enquiry Chaired by Lord Elton*, HMSO, London.

Dewey, J. 1933, *How we Think*, D. C. Heath, Boston.

Dodge, K. A. 1993, 'Social-Cognitive Mechanisms in the Development of Conduct Disorder and Depression', *Annual Review of Psychology*, vol. 44, pp. 559–584.

Doyle, W. 1984, 'How Order is Achieved in Classrooms: An Interim Report', *Journal of Curriculum Studies*, vol. 16, pp. 259–277.

Doyle, W. 1986, 'Classroom Organisation and Management', in M. C. Wittrock (ed.), *Handbook of Research on Teaching*, 3rd edn, John Wiley, New York, pp. 392–431.

Dreikurs, R. 1968, *Psychology in the Classroom*, 2nd edn, Harper & Row, New York.

Dreikurs, R. & Cassel, P. 1972, *Discipline without Tears: What to do when Children Misbehave*, Hawthorn, New York.

Dreikurs, R., Grunmald, B. & Pepper, F. 1982, *Maintaining Sanity in the Classroom: Classroom Management Techniques*, 2nd edn, Harper & Row, New York.

Dunbar, C. & Villarruel, F. A. 2002, 'Urban School Leaders and the Implementation of Zero-Tolerance Policies: An Examination of Its Implications', *Peabody Journal of Education*, 1532–7930, vol. 77, no. 1, pp. 82–104.

Edwards, C. 2008, *Classroom Discipline and Management*, 5th edn, John Wiley & Sons, New York.

Edwards, C. & Watts, V. 2004, *Classroom Discipline and Management: An Australasian Perspective*, John Wiley & Sons, Australia.

Eggen, P. D. & Kauchak, D. P. 2006, *Strategies and Models for Teachers: Teaching Content and Thinking Skills*, 5th edn, Pearson, New York.

Emmer, E. T., Evertson, C. M. & Anderson, L. M. 1980, *Effective Classroom Management at the Beginning of the School Year*, The University of Chicago Press, Chicago.

Emmer, E. T. & Evertson, C. M. 2008, *Classroom Management for Middle and High School Teachers*, Allyn & Bacon, Boston.

Evertson, C., Anderson, C., Anderson, L. & Brophy, J. 1980, 'Relationships between Classroom Behaviours and Student Outcomes in Junior High Mathematics and English Classes', *American Educational Research Journal*, vol. 17, pp. 43–60.

Evertson, C. & Emmer, E. T. 1982, 'Effective Management at the Beginning of the Year in Junior High Classes', *Journal of Educational Psychology*, vol. 74, pp. 485–498.

Evertson, C. & Harris, A. H., 1992, 'What we Know about Managing Classrooms', *Educational Leadership*, vol. 49 (7), pp. 74–78.

Evertson, C. & Weinstein, C. S. 2006, *Handbook of Classroom Management: Research, Practice, and Contemporary Issues*, Lawrence Erlbaum Associates, New Jersey.

Fredricks, J. A., Blumenfeld, P. C. & Paris A. H. 2004, *School Engagement: Potential of the Concept, State of Evidence,* Review of Educational research, vol. 74 (1), pp. 59–109.

Fredricks, J. A. & Eccles, J. S. 2006, 'Is Extracurricular Participation Associated with Beneficial Outcomes? Concurrent and Longitudinal Relations', *Developmental Psychology*, vol. 42 (4), pp. 698–713.

Freiberg, H. J. 1999, *Beyond Behaviourism: Changing the Classroom Management Paradigm*, Allyn & Bacon, Boston.

Frieberg, H. J. 1999, *School Climate: Measuring, Improving and Sustaining Healthy Learning Environments*, Falmer Press, New York.

Freiberg, H. J. & Driscoll, A. 2005, *Universal Teaching Strategies*, 4th edn, Pearson, New York.

Gable, S. L. & Haidt, J. 2005, 'What (and) Why is Positive Psychology', *Review of General Psychology*, vol. 9, no. 2, pp. 103–110.

Gagne, R. (1985). *The Conditions of Learning*, 4th edn. Holt, Rinehart & Winston, New York.

Gardner, H. 1993, *Multiple Intelligences: The Theory into Practice*, Basic Books, New York.

Gibbs, J. 2006, *Reaching All by Creating Tribes: Learning Communities*, CenterSource Systems, Santa Rosa.

Gibbs, J., Potter, G. & Goldstein, A. P. 1995, *The EQUIP Program: Teaching Youth to Think and Act Responsibly Through a Peer-helping Approach*, Research Press, Champaign, IL.

Ginott, H. 1971, *Teacher and Child*, Macmillan, New York.

Glasser, W. 1969, *Schools Without Failure*, Harper & Row, New York.

Glasser, W. 1986, *Control Theory in the Classroom*, Harper & Row, New York.

Glasser, W. 1992, *The Quality School: Managing Students without Coercion,* 2nd edn, Harper & Row, New York.

Glantz, K. & Pearce, J. K. 1989, *Exiles from Eden: Psychotherapy from an Evolutionary Perspective*, Norton, New York.

Good, T. L. & Brophy, J. E. 1994, *Looking in Classrooms*, Harper Collins, New York.

Gordon, T. 1974, *T.E.T. Teacher Effectiveness Training*, Wyden, New York.

Gump, P.V. 1982, 'School Settings and Their Keeping', in D. L. Duke (ed.) *Helping Teachers Manage Classrooms*, Association for Supervision and Curriculum Development, Alexandria, VA, pp. 98–114.

Hallowell, E. M. 1999, *Connect*, Simon & Schuster, New York.

Heider, F. 1958, *The Psychology Of Interpersonal Relations*, Wiley, New York.

Hobbs, N. 1978, *The Futures of Children*, Jossey-Bass, San Francisco.

Hubble, M., Duncan, B. & Miller, S. 1999, *The Heart and Soul of Change: What Works in Therapy*, American Psychological Association. Washington, DC.

Hunter, J. M. & Csikszentmihalyi, M. 2003, 'The Positive Psychology of Interested Adolescents', *Journal of Youth and Adolescents,* vol. 32, pp. 27–35.

Hunter, R. 2004, *Madeline Hunter's Mastery Teaching: Increasing Instructional Effectiveness in Elementary and Secondary Schools*, Corwin Press, California.

Jimerson, S., Campos, E. & Greif, J. 2003, 'Towards an Understanding of Definitions and Measures of School Engagement and Related Terms', *The California School Psychologist*, vol. 8, pp. 7–27.

Johnson, D. & Johnson, R., 1992, 'Positive Interdependence: The Heart of Cooperative Learning', *15-minute VHS Videotape Presenting the Nature of Positive Interdependence and How to Structure It within Cooperative Learning Lessons.*

Johnson, D. & Johnson, R. 1999, 'Making Cooperative Learning Work', *Theory into Practice*, vol. 38, no. 2, Building Community through Cooperative Learning, pp. 67–73, <www.jstor.org/pss/1477225>.

Johnson, D. & Johnson, R. 2000, *Joining Together: Group Theory and Group Skills*, 7th edn, Pearson, New York.

Jones, V. & Jones, L. 2009, *Comprehensive Classroom Management*, Prentice Hall, New Jersey.

Joyce, B. & Weil, M. 2000, *Models of Teaching*, Allyn & Bacon, Boston.

Kadzin, A. E. 1978, *History of Behaviour Modification: Experimental Foundations of Contemporary Research*, University Press, Baltimore.

Kagan, S. 1994, *Cooperative Learning*, Kagan Publishing, San Juan Capistrano

Kohn, A. 1993, *Punished by Rewards*, Houghton Mifflin, Boston.

Kohn, A. 2001, *Beyond Discipline: From Compliance to Community*, Merrill/Prentice Hall, Upper Saddle River, NJ.

Kroll, L., Cossey, R., Donahue, D., Galguera, T., LaBoskey, V. K., Richert., A. E. & Tucher, P. 2005, *Teaching as Principled Practice: Managing Complexity for Social Justice*, Sage Publications, Thousand Oaks.

Lang, H. R., McBeath, A. & Hebert, J. 1995, *Teaching: Strategies and Methods for Student-centered Instruction*, Harcourt Brace, New York.

Larivee, B. 2005, *Authentic Classroom Management: Creating a Learning Community and Building Reflective Practice*, Pearson Education Inc., New York.

Lazarus, R. & Folkman, S. 1984, *Stress, Appraisal and Coping*, Springer, New York.

Levin, J. & Nolan, J. 2007, *Principles of Classroom Management: A Professional Decision-Making Model*, 5th edn, Allyn & Bacon, Boston.

Lewin, K. 1943/1999, 'The Process of Group Living', in M. Gold (ed.) *The Complete Social Scientist: A Kurt Lewin Reader*, American Psychological Association, Washington DC, pp. 383–384.

Libbey, H. 2004, 'Measuring Student Relationships to School: Attachment, Bonding, Connectedness, and Engagement', *Journal of School Health*, vol. 74, no. 7.

Long, N. Wood, M. & Fecser, F. 2001, *Life Space Crisis Intervention*, Pro-Ed, Austin, TX.

Manning, M. L. & Bucher, K. T. 2006, *Classroom Management, Models, Applications and Cases*, Prentice Hall, New Jersey.

Marzano, R. J. 2007, *The Art And Science Of Teaching: A Comprehensive Framework For Effective Instruction*, Association for Supervision and Curriculum Development, Virginia.

Maslow, A. H. 1970, *Motivation and Personality*, 2nd edn, Harper & Row, New York.

McDonald, T. 2001, 'What is of Value in a Pupil Referral Unit? Lessons from the Discourse', unpublished ed.

McDonald, T. & Thomas, G. 2003, 'Parents' Reflections on Their Children Being Excluded', *Emotional Behavioural Difficulties*, Vol. 8, No. 2, May, Sage Publications, London.

Mendler, A. 2001, *Connecting with Students*, Association for Supervision and Curriculum Development, Virginia.

Mendler, A. 2007, *What do I do when …? How to Achieve Discipline with Dignity in the Classroom*, Solution Tree, Indiana.

Morgan, N. & Saxton, J. 1994, *Asking Better Questions*, Pembroke Publishers, Markham, ON.

Moskowitz, G. & Herman, J. 1976, 'Success Strategies of Inner City Teachers: A Year Long Study', *Journal of Educational Research*, vol. 69, 283–289.

Munn, P. & Johnstone, M. 1990, 'Pupils' Perception of "Effective Disciplinarians"', *British Educational Research Journal,* vol. 16 (2), pp. 191–198.

Nelson, J., Lott, L. & Glenn, H. S. 1997, *Positive Discipline in the Classroom*, Prima. Rocklin, CA.

Newmann, F., Wehlage, G. & Lamborn, S. 1992, 'The Significance and Sources of Student Engagement', in F. Newmann (ed.), *Student Engagement and Achievement in American Secondary Schools*, Teachers College Press, New York, pp. 11–39.

Noddings, N. 2002, *Educating Moral People: A Caring Alternative to Character Education*, Teacher's College Press, New York.

Osterman, K. F. 2000, 'Students' Need for Belonging in the School Community', *Review of Educational Research*, vol. 70, pp. 323–367.

Pomeroy, E. 2000, *Experiencing Exclusion*, Trentham Books, Stoke on Trent.

Porter L. 2000, *Behaviour in Schools; Theory and Practice for Teachers*, Open University Press, Buckingham.

Porter, L. 2003, *Young Children's Behaviour: Practical Approaches for Caregivers and Teachers*, 2nd edn, Elsevier Australia, Sydney.

Pratt, M. W., Green. D., MacVicar, J. & Bountrogianni, M. 1992, 'The Mathematical Parent: Parental Scaffolding, Parent Style and Learning Outcomes in Long-division mathematics Homework', *Journal of Applied Developmental Psychology*, vol. 13, pp. 17–34.

Pryor, D. B. & Tollerud, T. R. 1999, 'Applications in Adlerian Principles in School Settings', *Professional School Counselling*, vol. 2 (4), 299–304.

Redl, F. & Wineman, D. 1951, *Children Who Hate*, Free Press, Glencoe, IL.

Redl, F. & Wineman, D. 1957, *The Aggressive Child*, Free Press, Glencoe, IL.

Reeve, J. 2004, *Understanding Motivation and Emotion*, 4th edn, John Wiley, Hoboken, NJ.

Rogers, B. 2004, *Behaviour Management: A Whole School Approach*, Sage Publications, London.

Rogers, C. 1951, *Client-centered Therapy*, Constable, London.

Rogers, C. 1980, *A Way of Being*, Houghton-Mifflin, Boston.

Rogers, C. & Freiberg, J. 1994, *Freedom to Learn*, Merrill, Columbus, OH.

Rosenshine, B. 1980, 'How Time is Spent In Elementary Classrooms', in C. Denham & A. Lieberman (eds), *Time to Learn*, National Institute of Education, Washington, DC, pp. 4–18.

Sackett D. L., Rosenberg M. C., Gray J. A., Haynes R. B. & Richardson W. S. 1996, 'Evidence Based Medicine: What it is and what it isn't', *British Medical Journal*, vol. 312, pp. 71–72.

Sailor, W., Dunlap, G., Sugai, G. & Horner, R. 2009, *Handbook of Positive Behavior Support*, Springer, New York.

Seligman, M. 1998, *Learned Optimism*, Simon and Schuster, New York.

Seligman, M. 2007, *The Optimistic Child*, Mariner Books, New York.

Seligman, M. & Csikszentmihalyi, M. 2000, 'Positive Psychology: An Introduction', *American Psychologist*, vol. 55 (1), pp. 5–14.

Sharan, S. 1980, 'Cooperative Learning in Small Groups: Recent Methods and Effects on Achievement, Attitudes, and Ethnic Relations', *Review of Educational Research*, vol. 50, no. 2, pp. 241–271, <www.jstor.org/pss/1170146>.

Shernoff, D., Csikszentmihalyi, M., Schneider, B. & Shernoff, E. 2003, 'Student Engagement in High School Classes from the Perspective of Flow Theory', *School Psychology Quarterly*, vol. 18, pp. 158–176.

Slavin, R. E. 1987, 'Cooperative Learning: Where Behavioral and Humanistic Approaches to Classroom Motivation Meet', *The Elementary School Journal*, vol. 88, no. 1, pp. 29–37, <www.jstor.org/pss/1002001>.

Slavin, R. E. 1999, 'Comprehensive Approaches to Cooperative Learning', *Theory into Practice*, vol. 38, no. 2, pp. 74–79, <www.jstor.org/pss/1477226>.

Stanley, F., Richardson, S. & Prior, M. 2005, *Children of the Lucky Country? How Australian Society has Turned its Back on Children and Why Children Matter*, Pan Macmillan, Sydney.

Stevens, R. J. & Slavin, R. E. 1995, 'The Cooperative Elementary School: Effects on Students' Achievement, Attitudes, and Social Relations', *American Educational Research Journal*, vol. 32, no. 2, pp. 321–351, <www.jstor.org/pss/1163434>.

Stinchcomb J., Reistenberg N. & Bazemore, G. 2006, 'Beyond Zero Tolerance: Restoring Justice in Secondary Schools', *Youth Violence and Juvenile Justice*, vol. 4, pp. 123–147.

Sugai, G. & Horner, R. 2002, 'The Evolution of Discipline Practices: School-wide Positive Behavior Supports', *Child & Family Behavior Therapy*, 1545–228X, vol. 24, iss. 1, 2002, pp. 23–50.

Tremblay, R., Hartup, W. & Archer, J. 2005, *Developmental Origins of Aggression*, Guilford Press, New York.

Valenzuela, A. 1999, *Subtractive Schooling: US–Mexican Youth and the Politics of Caring*, SUNY Press, Albany.

Ward, C. & Craigen, J. 2004, *What's This Got to Do with Anything*, Kagan Cooperative Learning, San Clemente.

Weiss, I. R. & Pasley, J. D. 2004, February, 'What is High-quality Instruction?', *Educational Leadership*, vol. 61(5), pp. 24–28.

Whewell, W. 1847, *The Philosophy Of The Inductive Sciences*, Parker, London.

Widaman, K. & Kagan, S. 1987, 'Cooperativeness and Achievement: Interaction of Student Cooperativeness with Cooperative versus Competitive Classroom Organization', *Journal of School Psychology*, vol. 25, no. 4, pp. 355–65.

Wilson, E. O. 1998, *Consilience: The Unity of Knowledge*, Alfred A. Knopf, New York.

Wong, H. K. & Wong R. T. 1998, *The First Days of School: How to Be an Effective Teacher*, Harry K. Wong Publications, California.

Index